A Place to Stand

Place to Stand

Essays for Educators in Troubled Times

Mark A. Clarke

University of Colorado at Denver

Foreword by Mary Catherine Bateson

Surviving Innovation Volume 1

The University of Michigan Press

Ann Arbor

Published in the United States of America by
The University of Michigan Press
Manufactured in the United States of America
∞ Printed on acid-free paper

2006   2005   2004   2003   4 3 2 1

A CIP catalog record for this book is available from the British Library.

Library of Congress Cataloging-in-Publication Data

Clarke, Mark A.
    A place to stand : essays for educators in troubled times / Mark A. Clarke ; foreword by Mary Catherine Bateson.
        p.   cm. – (Surviving innovation ; v. 1)
    Includes bibliographical references and index.
    ISBN 0-472-08879-3 (paper : alk. paper)
    1. Education–United States–Philosophy.   2. Educational change–United States.
    3. Effective teaching–United States.   4. Education–Social aspects–United States.
    I. Title.   II. Series.
    LB885.C5235 P53   2003
    370′.1–dc21   2002015816

Cover: *Apple,* bead embroidery by Amy C. Clarke. Apples represent life–they are symbols of corporal sustenance, passion, and desire, as well as earthly connection. They appear throughout mythology and folklore in such stories as Snow White, the Juniper Tree, and the myths of Eve, Persephone, Atalanta, Hesperides, and Helen of Troy. In this piece the apple contains a soul–it is both offered and protected. Clarke is the editor of *Spin-Off* magazine published by Interweave Press in Loveland, Colorado. She bead embroiders images from everyday life in which she alludes to the myths and fairy tales of her childhood.

For Patricia, siendo como eres.

Contents

Foreword

by Mary Catherine Bateson

Mark Clarke is committed for the long haul, proposing a sustainable approach to change. He reminds teachers that they are, willy-nilly, *change agents,* because this is part of the basic nature of teaching. But he invites them to go further and become *agitators;* by this he refers to discovering the leeway in the system and shaking it up, ever so gently. He speaks of reasonable success and sanity, of working quietly and patiently, of listening rather than preaching. But unlike the great majority of those working to improve schools and the experience of young people, he has set out to describe an approach that will not lead to the kind of burnout that has driven many reformers to despair and their colleagues to bewilderment and cynicism.

This sustainable approach to change is presented from two points of view, systems theory and uncommon common sense. Clarke introduces systems theory in direct, accessible language that makes it clear why institutions are so resistant to the unilateral imposition of change and so ready to revert to previous patterns. Schools involve many persons and parts, their common behavior linked by multiple factors and constraints; as such they function like living systems, with capacities for self-correction and self-healing to maintain familiar patterns and settings, so a bright new idea may sink like a stone in a pond or be rapidly reinterpreted to conform to older models. It should be some comfort to realize that resistance to change is a sign of health and resilience, however infuriating. But living systems also have the capacity to adapt and learn, to adopt new patterns that will then be maintained, and it is this capacity Clarke would have teachers address, just as they do in the classroom. To do this, he invites his readers to examine their own efforts to change themselves and to learn from their successes and failures.

Systems theory developed as a way to think about organization at very different levels that have significant similarities: either a tree or a forest, a nation or a family, a classroom of children and their teacher learning along with them. Because there are similarities between these different levels of systemic organization, Clarke puts great emphasis on *coherence:* acting in ways congruent with (and therefore respectful of) other systems, including persons, ways that build trust. These essays suggest a way of thinking about a wide variety of issues, considering education as one of many related processes. One can ask of each chapter how it applies to environmental issues, to urban violence, to world peace? In every case, there have been efforts to solve problems that have made them worse.

In addition to exploring systems theory, Clarke seeks ways to present this material that will resonate with familiar experience. All too frequently, systems theory is presented as a form of engineering, with off-putting diagrams and technical terminology that give it a sort of modernistic glamour. However, it is best presented in ways that connect with the sense of what it is to be alive and with intuitions about how living beings can meet and learn from each other. Diagrams are useful and important, but they encourage mechanistic thinking. As our society has moved more deeply into its romance with change combined with an insistence on speed, we have begun to apply ever simpler epistemologies to bring it about—we want to find a button to push for each desired change, the social equivalent of a silver bullet. It is simpler to scapegoat teachers than to ask whether the society, as a whole, presses children into adaptations that work against learning. Punishment is easier than persuasion. Regulations are easy to promulgate but difficult to adjust to a living system, which may have an extraordinary capacity to circumvent them. Above all, it is easier to tell others that they need to change than to begin by changing oneself. Much of Clarke's presentation is deceptively simple, sounding like good old-fashioned common sense, which of course it is, good old-fashioned common sense that needs to be reconsidered.

The homespun quality of some of this wisdom should not be surprising. Indeed, it might be an interesting exercise to match each chapter of this book with a familiar proverb—and to notice how routinely such folk wisdom is ignored, for proverbs encapsulate a wide range of human experience, tested over many generations. The modern tendency is to pursue a goal through a simple lineal sequence of cause and effect rather than a complex and recursive unfolding, full of paradoxical reverses and unexpected side effects, that can sometimes gradually spiral into a healthier state. For some chapters you might find a pair of contradictory proverbs ("Look before you leap," but "He who hesitates is lost") that reflect two equally important aspects of the process, both to be respected. Unfortunately, when some desired change is not adopted, we interpret that as failure rather than as an invitation to reflect more deeply. "If a theory can't help you deal with life and death, what good is it?"

This book offers a subtle tool kit for moving toward viable strategies for educational renewal, ways of reflecting rather than answers. There is a need in our time for theory to guide reflection and action, and while some aspects of that theory have been around for a long time, others run against routine instrumental assumptions and the desire for the quick fix. There is much in the world today that is threatening, crying out for remedial action that often makes things worse. My own belief is that teachers have a critical role to play in creating a sustainable future for the next generation and for the world, for the way we move ahead in renewing education will implicitly transmit a way of thinking about change. Thus this book can be taken narrowly as an application of ecological ideas, based on systems thinking, to teaching; but it is also a modest reminder of the many examples of paradoxical effects produced by human efforts to modify the natural world, and a model for rethinking common errors in politics and economics.

Make no mistake, Mark Clarke is calling for revolution, but this is "a quiet revolution with shots not heard."

Introduction

This book was written for pragmatic idealists. People who can imagine a better world and are committed to working toward it. Individuals who are dissatisfied with the status quo and discouraged at the pace of change. People who are passionate about making the world a better place but realistic about what it takes to accomplish it.

The tone I want to strike is one of grim hopefulness—a reasoned balance between faith in people, particularly teachers, and awareness that we are living in dangerous times. We cannot escape the maelstrom of change that surrounds us, but we can position ourselves to respond thoughtfully.

Recently, in the midst of a class discussion, a young teacher declared passionately that she did not want to change her students but that she did want them to learn. A friend who is a counselor made a similar statement in response to a comment I made about his efforts to change his clients; he said that he preferred to think about his work as helping people grow. Parents want their children to be happy and well adjusted, but not at the expense of their creativity and originality. These comments reveal our ambivalence about change; we would prefer to think of people as autonomous and inner-directed, and we dislike the authoritarian implications that come from thinking we are working to change others. However, individuals cannot learn, or grow, or be well adjusted, without changing.

Most individuals whose work deals directly with other people must live with the fact that change is an important outcome of their efforts. We may prefer to use different terms when we discuss our work—coaching, counseling, learning, growth, development, curriculum reform, instructional innovation—but basically, if there has been no change at the end of a designated period of time, we count our efforts as a failure.

We also must learn to see the changes that we undergo as a result of our work. We are accustomed to thinking back on our youth as a time when we made lots of mistakes and learned (or not) from them, but only rarely do we look upon our daily work as an opportunity to change. The position taken in these essays is that the only person over whom we have any real control is ourselves—and even that is limited—so that the most productive approach to change efforts is to assume that we are the ones who are going to do the most changing.

These essays proceed from a single theoretical perspective—that provided by *systems theory*. Taken together, they provide a coherent approach to identifying problems and formulating strategies for solving them. But they do not provide a sequential, logical approach to effecting change. That is to say, the approach is not "logical" as this term is commonly employed in discussions of social and educational problem solving. Any attempt at setting in motion a "sequential" course of events is usually doomed to failure by the very nature of things. Indeed, I will argue that the customary way of viewing problems and approaching solutions is, in fact, part of the problem.

Bookstores are brimming with volumes of advice on how to make the world a better place or, at least, how to improve that part of the world where we live and work. Some provide guidelines for becoming more efficient, for using time better, and for improving productivity. Others offer advice on managing money more effectively, giving tips on investing, getting out of debt, and turning junk into treasures. A growing number will give you a hard body (or a marathon trophy or clean arteries or slimmer thighs) if you follow a set regimen of diet and exercise. Spiritual guides aim a bit higher; if you have lost your sense of oneness with the universe, they will help you reclaim it through a program of inspirational reading, contemplative rituals, and activities designed to improve your sensitivity. Moving beyond the improvement of self, other books provide a foundation for living that encompasses all aspects of life–family, work, worship, recreation. Several best-sellers offer frameworks and procedures for improving company productivity through a heightened awareness of chaos theory–the nonlinear, recursive nature of change.

The numbers of such books, and the extent to which self-improvement (perhaps the most pervasive synonym for *change*) is featured in the popular press (recently, while waiting in line at the grocery store, I counted 15 articles in five magazines that dealt in one way or another with the topic), are an indication of the importance of change in people's lives today–or, at least, of the perceived need for a sense of control over the changes that are occurring. Indeed, an observant visitor from another planet could be forgiven for thinking that we are obsessed with change.

What is interesting, however, is the fact that I have found no appreciable intersection of books on personal change and those on organizational or educational change in spite of the fact that lasting change in society or its institutions will require corresponding changes in individuals, including the individuals instigating the change. Throughout these essays I treat individuals and groups as examples of the same phenomenon–open systems. What is true for individuals is true for groups, although one may have to adjust one's perspective in order to accommodate the number and complexity of interacting variables. Most important, throughout the book I emphasize the need for personal change. The essays are intended as resources for individuals who are trying to change things, and my assumption is that people who are working for change are willing to change themselves as part of the process.

An important result of this approach to changing things is that I do not take the view that organized change–what is called "innovation" by most scholars–is necessarily healthy. This is not a handbook for administrators so much as a mental-health guide for conscientious professionals. This book is intended for individuals who are motivated by ideals, who are working from a framework of personal values and commitment. I assume that your formal training and practical experience provide leavening for your zeal but that you are in the teaching profession because you feel strongly about issues of right and wrong. I take it for granted that you conscientiously examine the merits of proposed innovations and that you will not fall in line behind an "innovator" merely because she or he has the formal title of professor, principal, or assistant superintendent. Indeed, history teaches us that it is often necessary to resist the commands of a leader. These essays are offered both as a guide for effecting change and as a source of strategies for *principled resistance*.

This book contains no prescriptions, other than the paradoxical admonition that there are no prescriptions. However, the essays were written to provide individuals with resources for change. The one piece of advice that I have found helpful comes from my grandfather, who said that the only good advice is the advice you take. I think what he was trying to say is that it is easy to give advice but that the person who has to live with the consequences should be given the courtesy of deciding what constitutes good advice.

Teaching is portrayed here as a higher calling, a vocation in the original sense of the word. I do not believe that teaching is a role we play in front of students or that to be a good teacher we must develop a special persona. I do not think we should strive to be someone different in the classroom or faculty meeting from the person we are "in real life." The same values and strategies should guide us in all spheres of our lives. Our students and colleagues should not be surprised when they encounter us in an unfamiliar setting—the behavior they observe there should be consistent with their impression of us. In fact, I believe that the most important teaching we do is that which is often called "modeling"—the unconscious messages we send merely by acting the way we act. You have heard the admonition, "Do as I say, not as I do." This reveals our culture's ambivalence about the disparity between the ideal and the real. I think we should be working to make them one thing. This alignment between our values and our behavior is referred to as *coherence* in these essays, and it figures prominently in all the arguments I make.

The book is an example of this approach. All of the essays examine the same issues from the same point of view, but at differing levels of complexity and with differing focuses. Each essay was written to be read independently of the others, and for this reason there is some redundancy. The argument I am making requires a recursive reading, a cycling back to themes and topics from different angles, and for this reason each essay needs to be complete in itself. You can read them in any order, but to the extent that there is a linear progression of topics, it is represented in the order in which they appear. Here are brief summaries of the essays.

1–The Way Things Are: The Rationale for This Book

This essay presents a brief summary of systems thinking and an introduction to its key concepts. All living organisms and groups of organisms are systems and behave according to the same general principles. For this reason, whether we are talking about personal, organizational, or societal change, we should be using the same frame of reference and the same strategies for action. I identify six principles that help me keep the complexity of systems in mind without becoming overwhelmed. They are: (1) Systems have no purpose, in the conventional sense of a universally agreed-upon goal for their existence. (2) Systems cannot be controlled directly and unilaterally. (3) Systems function in cycles, which means, among other things, that if we can identify the cycle, we can improve on our attempts to change things. (4) Systems function on the basis of internal and external information. This requires us to appreciate the nature of information and to acknowledge that an individual's history and perceptions are just as important as external pressures as we attempt to understand events. (5) Systems cannot be understood independently of their contexts. And finally, (6) systems require a budget of flexibility; in our change efforts we need to create environments for change and give ourselves and others room to operate.

2–A Systems Perspective of Changing, Teaching, and Learning

Presented here are implications of systems thinking for the daily grind. I work from three assumptions: that teachers are change agents, that they are guided in their efforts by a dedication to the greater good, and that it's all one thing–the rules for teaching are the same as the rules for living. Because systems theory can get a bit abstract, I develop a number of assertions about the nature of change, teaching, and learning that can serve as guidelines for daily activity, touchstones for decision making. The list is an effort to connect the grand sweep of the cosmos with the mundane details of my waking hours. I remind myself that I have limited influence over the big issues but that what control I do have is not insignificant for the individuals involved. I recognize that I am the individual who has to do most of the learning and changing and that patience is required and pain is expected if the cause is just. In particular, it is important to create environments in which people can make good decisions, and this requires getting a lot of good people involved in the effort.

3–Elements of the Change Process

Change is the natural result of living, and all change can be seen as a variation on life. That is the central theme of this essay. If we can find a way of understanding all aspects of our lives–work and play, teaching and learning, partnering and parenting–as essentially the same process, then we increase the probability of success in all of our endeavors. I identify seven elements of the change process and explain how using these elements as lenses or touchstones can provide a sense of coherence in otherwise chaotic times. The seven elements are: (1) the problem; (2) the issue; (3) the solution, or innovation; (4) the players; (5) evidence of change; (6) activity cycles; and (7) constraints and strategies. The tendency is to focus in on one aspect of a change project and to become frustrated when it does not yield results. I argue that we need to remain flexible in our efforts and that having seven ways of approaching a project provides us with a structure that encourages flexibility.

4—Changing Things: The Rhythms of Reform and Resistance

Considered from a systems perspective, "reform" and "resistance" are expectable tensions in life, and from your position as a change agent, change and persistence occur as a rhythmic pattern, one that you need to understand if you are to be successful. I anchor my analysis in two brief vignettes about systemic change efforts, one in a school and the other in a church. I then explore aspects of systems theory using the vignettes as sources of examples. I extract a number of guidelines for you to keep in mind as you work: Change yourself. Learn the players. Don't preach. Don't lay blame for problems, and don't take credit for solutions. Form support groups without becoming isolated. Create disturbances and force wobbles in the system. Work for effects. Work for policy reform. Be content with small changes; be patient. Work quietly. Another guideline that emerges from the discussion is: Leave the system if you discover that your efforts are being wasted. Life is too short and the opportunities for doing good elsewhere too abundant to continue where hope for change in your lifetime is slim.

5—Coherence: Aligning Thought and Action in Teaching

I was part of a research team that studied three elementary teachers over a period of three years. We were amazed at the similarities of their success despite dramatic differences in their methods and materials. We concluded that what mattered was the relationships they established with their students and their ability to work from a set of core values as they responded to different situations and events. We dubbed this alignment between thought and action "coherence," and the concept has shaped every aspect of my work since then. I have taken the idea beyond the boundaries we originally set for it, and in this essay I attempt to show how efforts at aligning behavior and beliefs cut across all human endeavor. The ways that we organize our teaching are just one indication of this relationship; we must also consider the organization of the school day, the relationships we have with our colleagues and the parents of students, school-community interaction, and the nature of assessment. The key point is that this is not a matter of working out your philosophy in detail and then enacting it in your teaching. It is far more complicated than that, because what you believe is just as much a function of your experiences as it is of your reading, research, and contemplation. In other words, you need to work for balance between the facts of experience and the facts of theory.

6–Empowerment: Issues, Constraints, and Cautionary Comments

Reform advocates call for "empowerment" of linguistic minorities and educational minorities, as if power, self-confidence, and efficacy were some*thing* we could give to others. When we look at empowerment from a systems perspective, however, we see that individual "power" is a complex phenomenon that is inextricably intertwined with societal and organizational constraints. In this essay I argue that we need to decide what the issue is—societal inequity, organizational or bureaucratic inertia, individual incompetence, for example—as we develop an action agenda. Then, we need to understand that empowerment is not a causal phenomenon; rather, given the fact that human beings and organizations are open systems, we need an approach that relies on communication and influence rather than carrot-and-stick strategies. I present an adaptation of Gregory Bateson's "cybernetic explanation" and give an example from my own decision making in a graduate course. This is an approach that requires an understanding of constraints, rather than causes, in change efforts. I conclude the essay with an examination of cautionary comments: "Empower" and "liberate" are not transitive verbs. Empowerment will not come quickly or easily. Empowered individuals cause trouble. Attempts at liberation education must be individually and culturally appropriate. Skill development is not, by itself, empowering.

7—Finding a Place to Stand: Teaching in Dangerous Times

In this essay I attempt to understand what the massacre at Columbine High School and the attacks on the World Trade Center and the Pentagon have to do with my values and behaviors as a teacher. At the time of the events, I wrote letters to teachers who were using early drafts of this book in an attempt to put the two tragedies in perspective, and I include those letters as an appendix. The letters, written in the vortex of confusion and apprehension, provided me with a sense of comfort in the moment. Now, in retrospect, and in an attempt to develop a more stable perspective on teaching in troubled times, I explore ways that we might position ourselves in relation to the violence that is too much a part of the world today. I argue that violence is natural—literally, a phenomenon of nature—and that global violence and local violence are merely different in terms of scale and perspective. We cannot ignore violence, and we cannot isolate ourselves from it. At the same time, we need to be realistic about what we can do about it. The essay constitutes my own effort at finding a place to stand in troubled times. I use the elements of change developed in chapter 3 as the framework for describing my own efforts at organizing in- and after-school activities for urban youth in the context of university/school/community collaboration.

1 The Way Things Are:
The Rationale for This Book

This book constitutes an effort to make sense of two profoundly puzzling facts.

- Most of the people I know are working to solve problems, change things, make the world a better place.
- In spite of this effort, things pretty much seem to continue on in the same way, to settle back into familiar patterns—if not precisely the same problem, at least a recognizable variation on a familiar theme.

Take the mundane example of weeds in the garden or trash in the alley. It seems to require superhuman effort and constant vigilance to maintain the garden or the alley at an acceptable level of "tidiness."

Or New Year's resolutions. They never seem to change. Last January I heard a commentator on the radio read a humorous poem about losing weight. The gist of it was that the writer was gearing up for her personal, annual "battle of the bulge" and that she knew she would be successful–after all, she had lost those same 10 pounds every year since her first child was born 15 years ago, so why shouldn't she be successful this year?

The same thing is true at larger levels of scale. Here in Colorado, coalitions of activists seemed to have won a long-fought battle for the preservation of open space and the protection of endangered species through allocation of state lottery funds. However, suddenly we discovered that a shortfall in state or federal funds has led legislators to propose using these monies for highway repair and the construction of prisons. The long-term goal of preserving the planet seems to have lost out to short-term solutions to more compelling problems.

Similarly, the struggle to achieve reasonable class size in public schools is a perennial battle that everyone wants to win but that never quite seems to work out. Parents and teachers are the most vocal supporters of small classes, but most administrators and policymakers agree that the number of children in a classroom is an important determiner of the quality of learning. So if everyone agrees, why doesn't it happen? Why is it that every year elementary teachers face 25 to 30 students or more in their classes and secondary teachers are expected to provide a quality educational experience for 100 to 150 students a day?

My answer to these questions, which I develop here and which runs through all of the essays in this book, provides cold comfort for the weary pilgrim. Weeds in the garden, flabby waistlines, deterioration of the environment, unwieldy class size–these all represent variations on one fundamental reality: life. They are all examples of the inexorable cycle of the natural pattern of living systems. Things are the way they are because living systems tend to function toward stability; they resist change.

"Not very encouraging," you say. I agree, if what you seek is the quick fix. Because, as these examples and–I argue–all of history demonstrate, there are no quick fixes.

But if you are committed to these struggles for the long haul, if you are willing to adjust your perspective and modify your behavior, then this approach is strangely energizing. It gives you a worldview that helps you deal with the agonizing slowness of change while providing a reasonable approach for developing strategies for action. It also helps you cope with the apparently incessant onslaught of innovation that confronts you every day.

The argument I put forward here is that things are the way they are *not* by accident, that the problems we encounter at home and work are the result of the natural functioning of the world. If we want to change things, or even if we just want to understand what is going on, we need a way of thinking and talking that permits us to understand self, family, community, and work. This perspective is *systems theory*. Systems thinking helps with the following kinds of questions.

- What's the meaning of life? Who am I, and where do I fit in the grand scheme of things? *Is* there a grand scheme?
- What's going on here? How do I make sense of the overwhelming number of new things I am expected to understand and use? What about all the seemingly nonsensical edicts, memos, and policies that bombard me from all sides?
- How do I cope with others' attempts to change me? It seems that everyone, from my mother and significant other to my boss and close colleagues, has a plan for how I should improve. How do I manage to stay true to myself yet deal sensitively and effectively with their demands?
- How do I change myself? How to get rid of debt, pounds, unappealing habits, etc., and make the change stick?
- How can I change others—my students, employees, friends, lovers, brothers, and sisters—to make life better, or at least easier?

My guess is that those questions pretty much summarize all of the issues you are dealing with in your life today. Change is the one thing that is constant.

Of course, this is not a novel assertion. From the French aphorism *Plus ça change, plus c'est la même chose,* to the street wisdom of *What goes around comes around,* there seems to be universal agreement that change is one thing that doesn't change. Change is on everyone's mind, and the bookstore and grocery-store turnstiles are full of information about change and advice on how to change yourself and others and how to cope with change—an amazing variety of strategies for a bewildering array of problems. But we don't need a variety of strategies because we are dealing with just one thing—life. *Problems* are merely those details of life and living that have captured our attention at the moment. Gregory Bateson and Robert Frost, scientist and poet, respectively, arrived at the same conclusion.

> I picked up a vague mystical feeling that we must look for the same sort of processes in all fields of natural phenomena—that we might expect to find the same sort of laws at work in the structure of a crystal as in the structure of society, or that the segmentation of an earthworm might really be comparable to the process by which basalt pillars are formed. (G. Bateson 1999, 74)

> Only where love and need are one,
> And the work is play for mortal stakes,
> Is the deed ever really done
> For Heaven and the future's sakes.
>
> (Frost 1969, 275)

Theory and practice, in a nutshell—Bateson's conviction that all natural processes are essentially the same and Frost's belief that our exertions should all proceed from the same motivation. In our daily lives we increase our chances for success, or at least satisfaction, if we adopt a holistic view of who we are and what we are trying to do, if we assume that every activity we engage in is essentially contributing to the same end. And if we assume that the "end" is not an end at all, but merely a continuing process of life.

This book addresses a wide range of topics, from focused explorations of personal change and classroom techniques to broad examinations of theoretical, professional, and political aspects of living, teaching, and learning. I use systems theory as the lens for examining ideas, policies, and everyday situations, and I attempt to blur the line between theory and practice, philosophy and action, attitude and behavior, in ways that permit a coherent view of living, teaching, and learning. For the most part, I will not rely on the scholarly practice of footnotes or citations to support my arguments; I hope to convince you by using examples from everyday life. But it seems reasonable to establish the academic credentials of the approach I am using, so the following section provides a brief overview of systems theory.

What Is Systems Theory?

Systems theory has a respectable intellectual tradition in the social sciences, one that began early in the twentieth century when scholars began to recognize the limitations of a mechanistic view of the world. Fritjof Capra provides an engaging summary of systems thinking in his books *The Web of Life* (1996, 17–71) and *The Hidden Connections* (2002, 3–94). The computer revolution and the environmental movement grew out of systems theory, as have recent explorations of chaos, complexity, and emergence (Wiener 1950; Lovelock 1979; Gleick 1987; Waldrop 1992; Kelly 1994; Johnson 2001).

However, the seeds of the arguments I develop here and in the following essays were sown primarily by Gregory Bateson and scholars directly influenced by him (G. Bateson 1979, 1999).

Bateson represents the quintessential example of the individual who sees the world as all one thing. He explored the communicational patterns of octopuses, the play of otters, and the family contexts of schizophrenics. He was interested in the arms race and the contributions of propaganda that lead to war and genocide. For Bateson, these were all variations on the natural order. It's all one thing–life–but it comes in different sizes, shapes, and temporal expanses.

His thinking has had a profound influence on scholars in a wide range of disciplines–education, psychology, counseling, ecology– and upon policymakers, environmentalists, and politicians. Mary Catherine Bateson (1972, 1989, 1994, 2000) examines teaching and learning in a variety of contexts and ties together societal, institutional, and interpersonal dynamics as she argues for a holistic approach to life, work, and play. Anthropologist Peter Harries-Jones (1995) and physicist Fritjof Capra (1996) explore systems applications to the interactions of human institutions and larger environmental forces. Paul Watzlawick and his colleagues have used systems concepts in exploring individual and organizational change (Watzlawick, Beavin, and Jackson 1967; Watzlawick, Weakland, and Fisch 1974). Peter Senge and Margaret Wheatley, gurus of the corporate world and advocates of learning organizations, use systems principles to explore ways of creating responsive business strategies (Senge 1990, 1999; Wheatley 1999; Senge et al. 2000). Educational reformers Michael Fullan (1999) and Robert Evans (1996) have developed strategies for innovation using systems concepts. And a few writers, notably C. A. Bowers and David J. Flinders (1990), have attempted to use Bateson's insights as the basis for teaching. The Principia Cybernetica Web site provides an instant connection to hundreds of individuals and organizations working with systems theory in a wide variety of contexts (<http://pespmc1.vub.ac.be/INTRO.html>).

First, a brief definition of *systems*. Systems are all living organisms and stable groups of living organisms, from single cell organisms to plants and animals. The individual human being is the system we are most interested in, along with families, classrooms, schools, and communities, which are also systems. Systems are assemblages of parts that function as a whole. They can be characterized as goal seeking, or self-organizing; that is, they seem to function with an identifiable purpose. At the same time, they are open to information from their environments. In part because of this tension between internal and external control, their behavior is not strictly predictable. It is patterned, however, and if we observe systems over a period of time we will notice that they exhibit behaviors that permit us to guess with a high probability of success what is going to happen next.

If this sounds unnecessarily abstract, then consider an individual whose behavior you are in a position to observe over time—your partner, parent, or child. The individual is composed of many parts—

bones, muscles, organs, etc.–all of which operate together to form a unique human being. On the most fundamental level, the body temperature of 98.6 degrees provides evidence of self-organizing behavior, just as a change in that temperature indicates a response to outside elements–infection or illness, for example. But no matter how intimately you know this individual, you cannot predict precisely what she or he will do in the next 24 hours, although you can probably speculate with some success on more general behavior.

Similarly, every classroom of students exhibits what might be called a "personality"–a range of expectable but not strictly predictable behaviors–that permits teachers to plan their instruction.

Recognition of this fundamental unifying characteristic of individuals and organizations provides us with a powerful lens for viewing our work. At the same time, it can be mind numbing to try to keep all of the connections in focus all of the time. I have found it helpful to consolidate the complexity by remembering six organizing principles of systems thinking.

1. Systems have no purpose.
2. We cannot control systems.
3. Systems function in cycles.
4. Systems function in response to internal and external information.
5. Systems cannot be understood independently of their contexts.
6. Systems require a budget of flexibility.

In the next few pages I will elaborate on each of these points briefly.

PRINCIPLE 1
Systems have no purpose.

"Purpose" is an artifact of our human desire to make sense of the world. We are accustomed to thinking of our own behavior as being rational, goal directed, and purposeful, and we generalize that habit of mind to societal institutions–schools, hospitals, courts. But these are just our perceptions of what their purposes are. Systems function to survive; they have no purpose, in the usual sense of the term. They are alive, and if it were correct to speak of purposes, we would say that their purpose is to continue living. But it is not correct to say even this, because this would imply that they have decided to live, that there is some source of conscious control exercised in this business of living, and this is inaccurate.

This is a difficult fact to accept, I know, but it is essential if you are to take advantage of the power of systems thinking. Most activists assume a common or shared purpose as they embark on a change effort, and they become frustrated when people behave in ways that do not support that assumption. We can save a lot of time and energy if we remember that our view of the purpose of a particular endeavor is merely our view and if we work to understand others' positions. This is a relentlessly empirical approach; it is important to pay attention to what people say and do, rather than proceed as if everyone shared our understanding of the situation.

Ours is a culture that glorifies individual initiative and takes control for granted, but a moment's reflection reveals that our own behavior and the functioning of our most cherished institutions cannot be unambiguously attributed to simple purposes.

Let's get personal for a moment. What is your purpose in life? What is the primary reason you are here on earth? You are, or soon will be, a teacher. What is the purpose of teachers? Is it to create independent thinkers, future revolutionaries, or is it to mold docile citizens, meek and mild law-abiding individuals who contribute to the gross national product? Are you able to articulate a single purpose for your existence? And can you state with confidence that all of your actions unambiguously reveal that purpose?

Or take schools, the system with which we all have extensive experience. It is common to hear people complaining about schools. Parents become frustrated with bureaucratic rules and regulations. Administrators and policymakers fume over the sluggish implementation of mandated reforms. Teachers wonder why they have to waste so much time giving tests when they could be teaching the skills and knowledge that the tests are designed to measure. At one time or another, everyone concerned with schools can be heard complaining that the purpose of schools has been thwarted by the myopic behaviors of special-interest groups. This merely reveals that people have different expectations of schools and that they are complaining about the fact that *their* purpose is not being efficiently pursued.

Observation of people's priorities as revealed by their behaviors on a day-to-day basis demonstrates that everyone involved in schools–children, janitors, teachers, bus drivers, parents, administrators, etc.–has different perceptions of the purpose of schools: to give an education, supply a paycheck, provide babysitting, prepare workers for the needs of business. Different purposes, same institution, and the system continues to function in spite of differing perceptions of its purpose.

Perhaps it is easier to see this point if we talk of other systems. What, for example, would you say is the purpose of a butterfly? Or of a mountain pond? These are systems, in exactly the same sense that schools or families or human beings are systems, but somehow the question seems irrelevant when applied to a "natural" system. If you find the question out of focus for butterflies, it is probably because you perceive that butterflies play a particular role in nature but that they really can't be said to have a purpose in the way that an automobile or computer does. The reason for this is that cars and computers are tools created by humans to make certain jobs easier–they do have purposes. Butterflies, on the other hand, are natural phenomena, not entities created for the convenience of humans.

But, you say, schools (or hospitals or courts) *were* created by humans, and for a particular purpose. Yes, schools were established by humans, and originally, it can be assumed, there were official reasons for their founding. But a number of interpretations can be offered for the unofficial reasons. Were they established to provide basic knowledge and skills so that children might learn to participate more effectively in the democracy, or were they established to provide a means for inculcating particular values in the nation's children, to make them more governable? Your answers to these questions will depend on your ideological bias. However, even the original purpose of such institutions becomes irrelevant, because once a system is up and running, it functions effectively on its own with only indirect reference to the original goals of those who established it.

The key point here is this: *As we work for changes in society's institutions we need to keep reminding ourselves that everyone participates according to their own understanding of relevant purposes and that changes will not be accomplished merely because we declare that our purposes should be taken as primary.*

PRINCIPLE 2
We cannot control systems.

The meaning of *control* becomes an important issue in systems theory. For our purposes, I will define *control* as the demonstrated ability to influence the functioning of others. We are accustomed to thinking of control in terms of vertical hierarchies—the boss is at the top, and the degree of control others exercise diminishes as you move down the hierarchy. And, at least since René Descartes, this perspective also applies to the individual. The brain controls the body—"I think, therefore I am." But this is a flawed perception. A moment's reflection will convince you that all control is relative and that power is always negotiated. Even at the level of the individual this is true—witness the struggles people have with New Year's resolutions. In organizations, the situation is even more complex. The mayor may be the titular head of city government, but she or he has to tiptoe through political minefields every day in order to get anything done, and any first-year teacher will tell you that nothing can be more terrifying than a room full of rebellious kindergartners.

Gregory Bateson used the phrase "immanent mind" to refer to the complex nature of control in systems (1999, 319–20, 467–68, 472–73), and it is worth the effort to work through his thinking on this issue. Systems display immanent mind—immanent, as opposed to transcendent—spread throughout the system, rather than coming from the top. "Mind" is used here to refer to knowledge that the system can be shown to have by virtue of the responses it makes to variations in events. It is the patterns of behaviors exhibited as events unfold. If a factory manages to turn out automobiles at a certain rate, we surmise that there is some level of organization—roles and relationships, procedures and rules—that accounts for the accomplishment. Much of this organization is explicit, conforming to the company's flowchart; but we also know that there are probably two or three people, line workers and assistants, perhaps, who respond to events so as to keep production high. They are the ones you go to if you want to know something about the company or if you want to get something done. They are also the ones whom the company can least afford to lose on a day-to-day basis. In other words, we discover how the company *really* works by observing the daily functioning and the actual decision-making processes used by participants to get things done.

The same is true of schools and classrooms. There are rules that everyone follows, and then there are rules that no one appears to follow. You have to participate in the culture of the school before you discover which ones you are expected to take seriously.

We are accustomed to thinking that the brain controls the body, that our minds rule our behaviors. We believe we are in control, that we are rational beings who set goals, devise plans, and discipline ourselves to accomplish what we have set out to accomplish. This is an illusion. We must always negotiate with others, and even when others are not involved we often find it difficult to accomplish important tasks.

If our bodies were controlled by our brains, if parents were the undisputed authority in the family, if the principal were in charge of the school—we would not need New Year's resolutions, children would not ignore parents' advice, and test scores would improve in response to the principal's mandates. But it just isn't so.

The lion gets a thorn in his paw. It festers, he develops a fever, the paw rejects the thorn, he recovers—all without his conscious attention to the matter.

You resolve to lose 10 pounds after the holidays, and you put yourself on a strict diet. But in a couple of weeks you're back to your same old habits—cake and ice cream after dinner, a snack with the 10 o'clock news, Saturday-morning brunch with friends, etc.—and you find it impossible to lose weight. This happens in spite of your best intentions and your focused effort; it is almost as if your body and your life circumstances conspire to keep the thin you inside where no one can see it.

The principal of a school has a good plan for integrating literacy work throughout the grades, and her enthusiasm for the project snares most of the teachers for a few weeks. But it isn't long before the paperwork, the regular class requirements, and other responsibilities begin to erode people's commitment to the new program. Everyone started off with good intentions and high energy, but the weight of everyday life began to wear them down, and soon they discovered they had slipped back into familiar routines. In other words, it's back to "business as usual."

These examples show that systems operate according to established but nonexplicit norms, what we might call thermostatic settings for behavior. Perhaps our greatest failing as a society is our faith in rationality—our unquestioning confidence in the ability of reason and authority to solve the problems of the human race. All of the earlier examples reveal the nature of systems to function according to their thermostatic setting in spite of our best efforts to control them. This is not to say that we cannot influence events, but it is important to remember that we do not have unilateral control over ourselves, our families, colleagues, subordinates, or students.

PRINCIPLE 3
Systems function in cycles.

We do not exercise unilateral control over systems, but we can influence their functioning if we keep in mind their cyclical nature and if we learn to adjust factors that affect those cycles. In our efforts at seeing the patterns of life, whether we are talking about big ones such as *birth-growth-death* or smaller ones like *breakfast-lunch-dinner* or *spring-*

summer-fall-winter, we need to remember that what we are discussing is not static but dynamic—whatever we are interested in will be coming around again. If we don't like how something turned out, we will always get a second (and third and fourth) chance to influence it.

We have basically two choices regarding influence—to amplify the change in the cycle or to dampen the change; these choices are referred to as positive and negative feedback, respectively. Let's take the example of the meal cycle—breakfast-lunch-dinner—and let's assume that you are launched on a New Year's resolution to lose weight. If you eat more you gain weight, and your body adapts to the higher caloric intake and as a result requires more food, which prompts your appetite and makes you want to eat more. And so on. The actual relationship among caloric intake and appetite and exercise is more complicated than I have portrayed it here, but you get the idea.

The point is that as we develop strategies for change we need to remember that people's habits are actually cycles of familiar behavior—activity cycles—and that our efforts are best understood as attempts to influence how the cycles function. All activity cycles reveal some variation; after all, even the most organized individual does not do everything the same way every day. This variation is referred to as "wobble" by systems thinkers (Kauffman 1980, 13–19), and one way of characterizing change efforts is to say that you want to increase or decrease the wobble of a system in a particular direction. So, for example, you might be interested in developing classroom activities that reduce the noise level or that increase individual initiative.

PRINCIPLE 4

**Systems function in response to
internal and external information.**

We are conditioned by experience and cultural assumptions to believe in smooth linear trajectories of cause and effect, but unlike the bowling ball curving gracefully toward the 12–11 pin gap, humans are not so easily propelled toward a goal. There are always distractions, and people respond differently to different situations. It seems clear that in order to understand how systems work, we need more a sophisticated conceptualization than the one that permits us to understand bowling balls.

Bowling balls are subject to the laws of physics; they respond to physical impact and gravity and the rules of cause and effect. People and organizations, however, respond to the information conveyed by events.

The ball hits the pin.
The pin falls.

The man kicks the dog.
The dog . . . what?
Turns and attacks its attacker?
Runs away, tail tucked between its legs?
Snarls and circles the man, waiting for a chance to move in?

The girl slaps the guy.
The guy . . . what?
Slaps her back?
Apologizes for his crass remark?
Moves on to the next girl at the bar?

The teacher demands silence from the rowdy class.
The class . . . what?
Quiets down?
Continues talking?
Behaves disrespectfully without talking?

With dogs and guys, as with classes of children, it is impossible to know exactly what the response will be to a particular event. There is no way to say what happens next because human beings are not bowling balls.

The example of a man kicking a dog is taken from Gregory Bateson, who used the story to illustrate the difference between the world of physics and the informational world of systems theory

(1999, 409). If you kick a pebble, simple physics provides the information you need to know how far it will travel and where it will land. Kicking a dog, however, is another matter, because the dog is a living system, internally energized and operating on its own. It may hit the ground and keep running, or it may turn and attack you. If the dog turns and attacks, the obvious explanation is to say that it attacked because you kicked it. However, perhaps a number of other factors could be shown to explain the attack—the breeding of the dog, the history of interaction between you and the dog, whether you appeared frightened after kicking it, the size of the dog, whether the dog had eaten recently, whose turf the attack occurred on, and so on.

A girl slapping a guy is a familiar cultural theme that evokes a whole universe of potential stories; indeed, sitcoms and stand-up comics depend on the audience recognizing the range of possible meanings that the scene might have. But to understand the event, we have to know who the two people are, what their relationship is, and what they mean to each other. Even with all this information, however, we cannot know for certain what will happen next, because humans are complex beings whose responses to situations are only partially shaped by external stimuli.

It is similar with a classroom full of children. The authority of a teacher is derived only partially from the formal role that she or he fills in the school. If she or he has not earned the respect of the students, it will be impossible to maintain order.

In attempting to solve problems or create conditions for learning, it is important to understand that there are proximal causes for events, but if we overlook the complexity of motives and the history of interactions, we run the risk of oversimplification and of making matters worse.

People act on the basis of their understanding of situations, a complex interaction of attention and previous experience. This is why police have such difficulty with witnesses—same event, but multiple perspectives of it. Everyone sees something different. This also explains common misunderstandings and disputes, because what matters is not events or things but the meaning that people attribute to them. Take tattoos and body piercing, for example. Both practices are common throughout the world, but in some cultures they represent symbols of maturity and community prestige, while in other cultures they represent youthful rejection of adult mores. It is clear that the practices themselves have no inherent meaning apart from that given by the people who experience them.

Understanding this principle is essential if you are to have success as a teacher, or in any role where "success" is defined as getting people to change. *Your job is to create the conditions that increase the probability of a particular kind and direction of change.* To do this you need to understand the internal as well as the external signals that individuals are attending to. That is, you need to get to know the people you are attempting to influence, and you need to create conditions that will capture their attention and engage their energy. Teaching is learning; you are changing as much as the students because you are constantly adjusting your understanding of the students and their world and constantly searching for ways of adjusting your efforts to bring them into your world.

> ## PRINCIPLE 5
>
> ### Systems cannot be understood independently of their contexts.

Context is "a collective term for all those events which tell the organism among what *set* of alternatives he must make his next choice" (G. Bateson 1999, 289). That is, context is a mental map, a vision of the world in the head of the individual, and it influences behavior, attitudes, and thinking. It includes the more conventional definition of physical and social setting that most people think of when the word is used, but it emphasizes the subjective experience of those settings more than the objective description. That is, it may be factually correct to say that the context is a "normal" classroom full of middle-school students, but if you are attempting to understand the teacher's decision making or the students' response to an assignment, you would need to know whether they experience the classroom as, say, a haven of intellectual stimulation or a prison.

As we attempt to understand people and organizations, and as we engage in change efforts, we need to remember that the unit of analysis is *system + context*. In fact, we cannot separate systems from their contexts. Systems are imbedded within systems. All of the systems we are interested in as teachers are composed of people, and the guidelines we use for understanding individuals are the same as those used to understand groups. And, of course, the same is true when we are attempting to understand smaller groups within larger groups or classrooms within schools, schools within communities, etc.

Identifying the system you want to understand can be a challenge. The individual, as a biological entity, is easy enough to identify, and in fact the family in most cases can also be readily agreed upon. But schools, hospitals, courts, and businesses, while having physical plants and temporal existence (daily schedules, people coming and going, etc.), are complex manifestations of the communities they serve. That is, each of these organizations is a distinct entity in the community, but each also consists of individuals who are also members of the community. They are at one and the same time both distinct and indistinguishable from their contexts.

Anthony Wilden observes that the boundary between an open system and its environment is a locus of communication and exchange (1987, 75), similar to the semipermeable membranes of cells. The same is true of humans and their organizations. Take, for example, adolescents' struggle to distinguish themselves from the family, a natural part of growing up. While the physical self is easy to identify (a visible and tangible organism with a skin holding everything together) the social self is invisible and intangible, and definitions of "self" in the social sense become a complex, changing interaction of messages sent and received. It is, in fact, the role of information and communication that makes context so important and so difficult to understand. Remember, "things" themselves are less important than their *meaning* for people in particular situations. This requires us to acknowledge that context is, in fact, whatever information the individual pays attention to as he or she makes decisions and modifies his or her behavior accordingly.

A brief example might help to illustrate the point. Let us consider the contexts of teaching. The most obvious sources of information that teachers must consider in making decisions and attempting to change the behavior, attitude, and skills of students are the classroom and the school. That is, as you plan activities and gather materials, you take into account the size and shape of the classroom, the number of students in the class, the available furniture and instructional paraphernalia. In addition, you have to consider the rules and regulations of the school, coordination of schedules with colleagues, the schedule of special classes such as gym and music, and the general layout of the building. As the school year gets under way, however, the levels of context that you must take into account expand. You get to know the students better, and their home situations become part of the picture. It may turn out that, in addition to the family, you must also weigh neighborhood or peer considerations, such as gangs, drugs, violence, etc. In other words, as you examine the options available for instruction you find that the range and complexity of information required become much larger. At some point, of course, you have to act, even though you are aware of the fact that you do not have all the information required to understand a situation.

It is impossible to exaggerate the importance of understanding context in the conduct of human affairs. Seeing the world through the eyes of our students and colleagues and attempting to understand how they experience the events of the day provide us with a framework and foundation for our professional and interpersonal conduct.

PRINCIPLE 6

**Open systems require
a budget of flexibility.**

Flexibility is defined as the uncommitted resources available for change. In environmental terms, this refers to the earth's ability to correct itself after massive oil spills, for example, or to adjust to a thinning atmosphere. In human terms, responses of societies to war, famine, and overpopulation reveal the amount of flexibility in the system. For example, the human race has always had wars, and people have been displaced as a result of these conflicts. The effects of these displacements have always been localized, but now, because of technology, we have less slack in the system. We now have Palestinian children who have no fear of soldiers or of dying. They face Israeli troops fearlessly, throwing rocks and taking their casualties. In terms of the larger social system, what is significant is that technology permits everyone to follow events in the Middle East on a day-by-day basis, so that the conflict has become a global affair, rather than a local affair. Technology permits marginalized individuals to take heart from the struggles of others, and it puts privileged individuals in a position to see the potential threat of distant wars to their lifestyle. In addition, technology makes global destruction possible. In this sense, the system has less flexibility, fewer uncommitted resources available for change.

In more personal terms, we have the example of employee "burnout"—people who are working under stress and with so little sense of purpose or accomplishment that they quit their jobs or suffer breakdowns rather than continue. In schools, the pressures on teachers have resulted in a near-crisis situation. Teachers have always worked under a certain amount of pressure, and individuals have always chosen to quit rather than continue (quitting represents a "resource"—a way of responding to a bad situation to restore equilibrium and health to the individual), but when large numbers of teachers begin to drop out of the schools and competent individuals cannot be found to replace them, the entry into the profession of less qualified, less competent people contributes to more classroom problems and stronger efforts by central administrations to control teachers. And these two trends, among many, further exacerbate the conditions that caused the burnout in the first place. Meanwhile, the increase in the numbers of young, low-income, culturally diverse children in inner-city poverty swells the numbers of non-school-oriented schoolchildren whose low achievement frustrates teachers and contributes to disciplinary problems. So we witness a downward spiral in the situation—in spite of all the rhetoric, the campaign promises, the money, things just seem to get worse. School systems appear to be losing their budget of flexibility.

Understanding this principle is key, both in maintaining your mental health and sense of perspective and in guiding your decision making in school. Your colleagues and your students are under tremendous pressure from a variety of sources, and your ability to orchestrate events and activities that encourage change will depend on the extent to which you can create pockets of flexibility for yourself and others.

Conclusion: It's all one thing.
No purpose. No control. Cycles. Information.
Context. Flexibility.

Keep this list in mind as you think about your work. These six assertions about the nature of life constitute guidelines to keep in mind as you plan your New Year's resolutions or develop materials for your next class; principles to use as touchstones as you attempt to understand global warming or the political maneuvering around protection of the rain forests and toxic emissions; reminders about human nature and cultural difference as you read about conflict in your own country, the Middle East, Northern Ireland, or India.

The theory and practice of teaching is merely a variation on the more encompassing enterprise of living and working and getting along in the world. Teaching is a process of nurturing, of creating environments for healthy growth and development. Teaching is building relationships with learners and helping them move toward goals that are engaging for them and acceptable to school and society—the same process we engage in with friends, family, and colleagues.

Teaching results in change, in yourself and others, most notably your students, but also in organizations and, ultimately, in society. In fact, it is often the case that you cannot do a good job of teaching your students without first getting support from colleagues, administrators, and the parents/guardians of the students–promoting change in the immediate environment. In a very important sense, all of this kind of work is a variation on the activity of teaching–it's all one thing.

Any focused interaction between people that results in change ought to be thought of as teaching. There is very little difference between preparing and conducting a lesson with students, on the one hand, and collaborating with colleagues or administrators on new curricula, or working with parents and sponsors on supporting learners' efforts, on the other. We tend to think only of the first as teaching, to reserve the label "teaching" for those occasions when individuals are *in role,* in classrooms doing instructional sorts of things, but it is important to expand our understanding of the word to include all attempts to change the thinking and behavior of others.

Another aspect of "all one thing" is a bit more abstract. This involves differences in scale. Classrooms, schools, and communities–in fact, all human organizations–are best understood in the same way we think of individuals. All principles of learning, growth, and development that we use to plan our interaction with learners apply with equal validity to other groups and organizations. The rationale for this requires an understanding of systems theory. In order to think of individual people and groups of people as the same sort of entity, a word is needed that conveys the qualities we wish to discuss. In these essays the word will be *system.* An open system is any living organism or aggregate of organisms that functions according to internal criteria and that uses information from the environment to maintain stable functioning. Examples include mountain ponds and ocean tide pools, the human body, cormorants, classrooms, and Congress.

This essay has been a very brief summary of key concepts in systems theory as they apply to personal and organizational change. I have attempted to account for a fact of life of which you are well aware: Life is complex, and people cannot easily be changed. My hope is that the points made in this essay will provide a general conceptual framework to which you will return regularly as you proceed through the essays that follow.

2 A Systems Perspective of Changing, Teaching, and Learning

These are strange times for educators. Never before has there been so much riding on the shoulders of teachers. At the same time there exists a general air of suspicion and mistrust about the competence of teachers and the ability of schools to meet the demands of the public. It is baffling; you would expect the heightened sense of need to lead the public and politicians to rally around people working in education—"What can we do to help?" strikes me as the appropriate stance. Yet I don't think it is an exaggeration to say that instead what we have is, "What have you done today to mess things up?"

Education has become the center of attention in national and local politics—which you would think to be a good thing. But as the sage said, "Be careful what you wish for—you might get it." With an unprecedented flow of funding and public attention has also come an intense scrutiny founded on suspicions about the intentions and skills of teachers and the value of schools. "Accountability" has become the key word and mandatory testing the primary mechanism of control. At a time when you might reasonably look for collegial rapport and selfless dedication to the common good there exists instead an underlying hostility in the discourse, as if policymakers recognize the need for supporting teachers but suspect that they are essentially lazy and untrustworthy rogues whose every move must be carefully monitored.

It is not uncommon to encounter people who see teaching as easy money. A good career: "You work short hours and have the summers free." This sentiment exists side by side with a genuine sense of awe of teachers, as newspapers report metal detectors being installed in high schools and elementary kids bringing weapons to school.

There seems to be general agreement that schools represent the litmus test of the nation's health and the single best leverage point for sustaining the democracy. At the same time it is difficult to escape the impression that education represents a hopeless morass of petty politics and entrenched bureaucracy.

There are several valid analyses that would explain this situation, but I believe they would all have to account for a number of key factors, among which the following would seem to me to be central.

- The diversity of students entering schools today in terms of race and ethnicity, socioeconomic status, cultural values, and academic preparedness
- The explosion of knowledge and skills that students must master and that teachers must be prepared to teach
- The pressures of modern life that leave parents searching for support in schools that traditionally came from family
- The social and economic pressures on communities that surface in demographic data: single-parent homes, welfare support, drug and alcohol abuse, gangs and street violence
- The pattern that emerges when economic factors are mapped onto racial data: the privileged public who must pay the bills tending to be white and the recipients to be brown or black

However the analysis is conducted, the conclusion will be the same: schools represent a complex tangle of issues and problems at the same time that they hold the key to the future of the world. There is no other institution where so much is at stake.

Now, let's bring the discussion down to the personal level. What about you? Why are you in education? Take the following quiz and compare your answers with a colleague.

1. The primary reason I got into teaching was . . .
   a. because the money is good, and I wanted the summers off.
   b. because of the influence of a teacher in my life.
   c. because of the fame and prestige.
   d. because I wanted to make a difference in kids' lives and in society.
   e. because a friend was applying to the School of Education and I filled out an application on a lark.
   f. because I had done other work and didn't find it satisfying.

2. The most persistent problem I encounter in my teaching is . . .
   a. too many students.
   b. not enough time to really engage learners.
   c. the lack of compelling, relevant materials.
   d. too many interruptions.
   e. the pressure of a politicized environment, punctuated by standardized tests and the ranting of ignorant politicians.
   f. too many students who have severe problems that are beyond my control and whose parents seem to have abdicated their responsibilities to me.

3. At the end of a typical school day I . . .
   a. feel energized by the stimulating engagement with students and colleagues.
   b. am totally exhausted and feel overwhelmed by all that I have to get done by tomorrow.
   c. look forward to reading the assignments the students just submitted.
   d. find myself scrambling from one task to another, unable to satisfactorily complete any one of them because of the distracting pressures from the others.
   e. dawdle over my journal, writing reflections on the students and assessing the progress we are all making toward important learning.
   f. rush to a committee meeting or coaching job or other assignment that I have been given and feel unable to refuse.

Your answers will vary, of course, depending on where you are in your career and what sort of experiences you have had. The following represents a summary of impressions I have gathered from teachers in recent conversations.

Question 1: If you answered a, c, or e to this question you may be in for a rude awakening. It has not been my experience that teachers make a lot of money or enjoy much fame and prestige. And teaching certainly is not a profession that one should go into without serious consideration of the work and dedication required. Answers b, d, and f are the ones I hear most as I talk to teachers. Most of us have memories of teachers who excited us with their commitment to their fields, whose enthusiasm for teaching and learning shone through in everything they did, and whose confidence in us fired our imaginations and fueled our desire to succeed. Most of the teachers I talk to are driven by a desire to be that sort of teacher for their students, to contribute to the greater good. And many report that they put in enough hours in office work or laboratories to know that they needed something more out of life.

Question 2: The choices listed here represent a list of the most common complaints I hear about the nature of teaching and the environment in schools today.

Question 3: Answers a, c, and e reflect the way the world should be if you are a teacher. Answers b, d, and f, unfortunately, reflect the experience of most teachers today.

The analysis of schooling with which I began this essay connects directly to the scenario portrayed in the quiz; the only difference is one of scale. In the former, the issues are stated in terms of broad societal factors, while in the latter they are portrayed as the grit of everyday life. In a systems perspective of the world, the two views cannot be separated. Your efforts as an individual to meet the call of your conscience and deal with the problems of your life need to be approached with an understanding of the converging trajectories of cultural, economic, political, and institutional forces that shape the world.

The problems that face teachers today are many, and they are complex, and they will not all yield to technical solutions—that is, solutions that involve merely improving the techniques we are using. In general, the significant problems we face will require fundamental re-alignments in how we view the world and how we position ourselves to act in it. If you are interested in learning more about this distinction between technical and adaptive work, read Ronald Heifetz's book *Leadership without Easy Answers* (1994). He argues that most problems we encounter can be sorted into two types—those that require us merely to be more efficient and skilled in our problem-solving techniques and those that require us to develop a different attitude toward the problem and a new set of techniques. The former are easier to deal with; they merely require us to bear down a bit harder and do what we were doing but do it better. The second sort of problem is more challenging because it requires us to change. The distinction is important to the central argument in this book, that coping with change at different levels of scale is the unifying feature of life. I operate from three assumptions that need to be made explicit if the argument is to make sense.

The first assumption is that teachers are change agents—agitators and instigators, individuals who see how the world is and are determined to change it.

The second is that teachers are essentially altruistic and driven by moral values. It is not sufficient to produce students who can read and write and do their sums. We want our students to leave our classrooms as better human beings, as solid citizens who will make the world a better place.

The third assumption is that teaching is a variation on the business of living, that how we choose to live our lives and how we choose to teach constitute essentially the same work. Teaching is not a role we assume, a stage persona that we adopt when we enter the classroom; it is an extension of who we are, and our success as teachers is very much entwined in our success as human beings. "Success," in this instance, is determined by the extent to which we have been able to achieve alignment between what we believe and how we behave.

Perhaps you have no difficulty agreeing with the first assumption, but a significant portion of the population does. In fact, many people would argue that it is the teacher's job to teach math, or science, or history, and that values are the concern of the family. Many critics of education believe that teaching should be value free, that the convictions of teachers should not be apparent to students, should not influence what is taught or how it is taught.

Similarly, a significant portion of the public believes that teachers should be servants of the status quo, and they would have you toe an ideological line. They believe that teachers should teach the curriculum and that the curriculum should promote and protect the values of home and community. Teachers, they say, should not teach their own values, but the values of the state.

I won't examine the details or the merits of this debate, because it is too complex and tangled an issue and because I believe that this is an area where debate—that is, argumentation based on careful assessment of facts and issues—is impossible. It is a heated emotional issue, and you are not likely to change anyone's mind by exploring either the historical or the socio-cognitive issues that underlie it.

I will merely assert that the values we convey are as important as the subjects we teach. We need to understand our subject matter, and we need to improve our technical skills in teaching it—no argument there. But it is impossible to spend significant amounts of time with learners without conveying our values—merely by the way we conduct class, answer questions, model learning, and go about our business throughout the day. Even if we do not actively seek to teach our values, we cannot avoid revealing them, and our students will acquire them if we are effective teachers. So, if this is the case, we need to give serious thought to how we are going to conduct ourselves if we discover that the school or the community demands political or intellectual compliance. What I am arguing is that we need to participate in this debate in a meaningful way, rather than merely toeing the line, and this requires us to become agents for change.

The third assumption, that teaching is life, is a bit more philosophical, and it cuts to the core of what it means to be a good teacher. It means, among other things, that there is no single best way of teaching. You have to find the approach that suits you. By extension of that point, it means that you have to be comfortable with who you are, and you have to find ways of dealing with students that permit you to be relaxed and confident with them. Teaching, viewed in this light, is a function of communication within relationship, not merely the formulaic completion of procedure. Teaching is not primarily a function of presenting facts or of improving test scores; it is a calling that requires us to become public intellectuals. This view of teaching requires us to look beyond the classroom, to engage in change efforts in the school, the community, and the larger political arenas that shape the issues we deal with.

On Change

It may be helpful to explore the various meanings of *change*. On the one hand, it is a common, everyday phenomenon, one that needs no elaboration. Change is change. Things change, people change, the weather changes. Surely this is all that need be said. On the other hand, change is a highly abstract phenomenon. It is not some*thing*. It is not contained in an event or an object or a person. It can only be noticed, and this requires an observer who can remember how something was and then compare it to how it is now. In other words, change is a difference noticed over time: person or situation at point A, compared to person or situation at point B. That is the first piece of complexity we have to deal with—change is largely in the eyes of the beholder.

A second source of difficulty is that not all change is the same, as a sampling of the verbs that imply change reveals—*learn, develop, die, rot, grow, evolve, shift, bloom, start, accelerate, slow down, decline, increase, deteriorate, mature,* to name just a few. All of these words indicate differences noted over time, but each one implies particular conditions and entails different assumptions.

Let us examine a simple example. Change is obvious when you get in your car and pull away from the curb—a change from stationary to moving. As you speed up, you notice a different kind of change—acceleration. When you shift from first to second to third and then fourth, you make even more dramatic kinds of changes. Acceleration is change within determined limits, while shifting gears involves changing the limits—a change of a change, so to speak.

This can serve as a loose metaphor for personal and organizational change. Let's say you are working on getting your teenage son through school. Rousting him out of bed in the morning is a first step, analogous to pulling away from the curb in a car. Creating rules and rewards that encourage him to get up and out the door, books in hand, homework done, represents additional progress. The rules can be seen as analogous to the limits within which the car operates in each gear. You begin to breathe easier, however, only when he takes charge—sets the alarm an hour early, organizes his study time, shows up for special tutoring, turns down a ski trip to study for an exam. The type of change represented by his response to the slightly coercive rules and regulations is positive, but significantly different from the change that has occurred when he is directing himself.

Some scholars distinguish between "first-order change" and "second-order change" in this regard (Watzlawick, Weakland, and Fisch 1974). *First-order change* refers to change within established norms; *second-order change* refers to changes in the norms themselves. Acceleration in first gear would be first-order change, and shifting to second gear would be seen as second-order change. Another mechanical example: all of the changes that occur in the heating system of a house to keep the temperature at 65 degrees (first order), versus changing the thermostat to 70 degrees (second order). With regard to your son and school, all of his compliance to your rules and incentives would be first-order changes, and his adopting the identity of a scholar would be an example of second-order change.

As you become involved in serious attempts at promoting change, it is important to be clear on what kind of change you are working for. Is compliance enough, or do you require conversion? Will you be content with merely adjusting the behavior of people within the rules and regulations currently operating, or do you want to change the rules and regulations themselves? And, regarding your own personal change efforts, do you merely want to lose 10 pounds, or do you want to completely change your attitude toward life so that food becomes a nonissue in your efforts to live healthily? The answers to these questions will vary depending on the change effort you are involved in, and depending on the circumstances, but until you are aware of the differences between the perspectives implied by the questions, you will not operate effectively as a change agent.

On Learning and Teaching

A few words on learning and teaching are also in order. The most concise way to define *learning* is "change over time." Of course, we teachers are interested in promoting change in particular directions, so we do not value all change equally. Specifically, we need to pay attention to changes that can be seen as "progress" in terms of the curriculum and the exams. Also, we hope to see changes in attitudes and behavior that indicate a love of learning. So perhaps the definition should be something like, "Learning is change that indicates the learners are realizing their potential and achieving knowledge, skills, and attitudes that are valued by society."

There are a few significant points here, however, that need to be emphasized. First, humans cannot *not* learn. Every event, situation, and activity provides opportunities for learning, and the people involved *will* learn something. Second, teaching becomes not a didactic event, a unilateral transfer of information, but rather a matter of creating environments that encourage learning. And third, this perspective reveals the tensions that exist between commitment to the integrity and interests of the learner, on the one hand, and the requirements of society and the schools, on the other.

Given the complexity of the issues we are dealing with as teachers, and the fact that all of the issues in education seem to be inextricably intertwined with broad social, economic, and political forces, it seems important to arrive at an understanding of change, teaching, and learning that can serve as a framework for decision making. In the remainder of this essay, I will examine a number of assertions that grow out of the arguments I have made here. I hope that they will become a touchstone for you as you continue to work with these ideas. I list them below, in summary.

1. To change society, you have to change institutions.
2. To change institutions, individuals have to change.
3. I am the individual who has to change. The only individual over whom I have any control is myself (and even that control is limited). I can only change things over which I have control.
4. I can't change myself without affecting others. And, because I cannot change others unilaterally, I will need to engage them in some principled interactions. This may precipitate crises of various magnitude, as I discover where people stand and the relative importance (to me) of my change efforts versus the good opinions of my friends and colleagues.
5. I cannot predict the course of change, so I will need to adopt a flexible approach to my efforts: Ready, fire, aim! Some planning is necessary, but usually setting some preliminary goals and jumping in is the approach most likely to produce results.
6. I cannot change any important aspect of my life without changing all other aspects of my life.
7. I must come to grips with the real forces of my life (no lies). I will need to learn to see more clearly, to pay attention to what is going on, and to describe things as they are. What I see happening over time reveals what really matters. What gets done is important, and things are the way they are _**not**_ by accident.
8. I cannot change other people (only individuals can change themselves). However, in some cases, I can change the conditions within which others work and interact, and in these cases I can increase the probability of some changes occurring rather than others.

9. I need to have a vision of how things will look when they have improved. What will I see happening when things are better? I need to focus on how far I have come, in addition to how far I have to go.

10. I must pay attention to what is happening while it is happening. I can't change yesterday, and tomorrow isn't here yet.

11. Patience! I must trust processes as well as people.

12. Pain! It is rare for important change to occur without conflict and pain.

13. Learning is change over time through engagement in activity. Human beings cannot not learn.

14. As teachers we create environments in which learners can become authentically engaged in meaningful activity.

15. The most powerful learning is that which occurs *apperceptively,* at the edges of consciousness.

16. Teaching is a particular form of learning.

17. Good teaching is an institutional accomplishment as much as an individual *tour de force.*

Everyone is in favor of change—as long as it is someone else who has to do the changing. We all prefer to avoid changes ourselves, and we would be very happy if we could go about our business without having to consider the needs and demands of others. In general, we are very good about making lists of things that other people should do. It is human nature to prefer change in the abstract. Mark Twain's observation about the weather ("Everyone talks about it, but no one does anything about it") is also true of change efforts. Have you ever noticed how much people talk about their new diets or workout regimens? How much time do you suppose is spent in selecting new jogging togs or shopping for exotic foods by people beginning the new year determined to lose weight? And how many goal-setting meetings have you participated in where everyone leaves exhausted after several hours of discussing the advisability of change and the relative value of particular goals without having actually taken any action that would lead to change? Why, I have been known to celebrate the decision to lose weight by going out to dinner(!)

When we talk about change, what we are talking about is people changing. In every change effort, it is essential to focus clearly on who has to change and how. And the changes will be in the minute particulars of daily life. We always begin with ourselves. These points will be reiterated in virtually every item that follows.

1. To change society, you have to change institutions.

"Whoa!" you say. "I am not interested in changing society. I just want to make my little corner of the world a better place." I understand that, and I agree that we need to focus our energies on things we are able to change. Draper L. Kauffman (1980) refers to this as "leverage points"—knowing exactly where our influence will have the greatest effect. Society is too large and too amorphous, so we will typically find ourselves working for change within institutions—schools, companies, organizations of various sorts, churches, families. However, given the interconnectedness and dynamic interaction of systems, changes at one level will have consequences at other levels, and it is important to remember this as we work on our own change efforts. If society does not improve, we will all be in danger of extinction. The unit of survival is *individual* + *context,* and while you may not immediately see the connection between this ambitious claim and your own daily comings and goings, it remains as the underlying truth that will not go away. We can remain appropriately humble about our efforts at local improvements, but it is important to labor with an awareness of how our efforts affect the greater good. This is the essence behind the bumper sticker, "Think globally, act locally."

2. To change institutions, individuals have to change.

Institutions are, of course, composed of individuals, so this would seem to be patently obvious, but in fact it is not uncommon to hear people talking about changing the schools or courts or health-care delivery systems as if this could be done without affecting how people spend their time in a typical day.

On a local level, this is what happens when the principal at the faculty meeting or parent at the dinner table says something like, "We need to cut down on expenses," without organizing a discussion about what, specifically, "we" are going to do without, and how. If people have become used to unrestricted long-distance telephone calls, the decision to limit them will have dramatic consequences for their daily schedules, whether we are talking about a school or a family. People will have to plan ahead in order to communicate by conventional mail or gear up to use email. This will cause disruptions as individuals change their preferred modes of communication. Technology will need to be adopted, or advanced planning will be required so that letters get mailed in time to meet deadlines. In other words, it is one thing to say that expenses need to be reduced; it is quite another to change habits and routines in order to accomplish it.

The focus here extends beyond changes in roles and responsibilities normally associated with change efforts to the minutiae of daily life. In fact, the latter may be more important than the former. We all develop comfortable rhythms that get us through the day, and because these are often beneath awareness, we fail to realize how important they have become. As we proceed with change efforts, it is often such daily-life changes that are the most difficult to accomplish.

3. **I am the individual who has to change. The only individual over whom I have any control is myself (and even that control is limited). I can only change things over which I have control.**

Let us take each of these assertions in order. First, the assertion that I am the individual who has to change. This is obvious if the change project is my personal effort to lose weight or become better organized, but it may be less obvious when we focus on organizational change efforts in which others are also required to change. However, if we accept the point that humans are not billiard balls, and that direct physical action is almost never appropriate in changing others, then we arrive at the conclusion that communication, not control, is the essential feature of change projects.

But effective communication depends on my understanding what kinds of arguments will appeal to the people I am attempting to influence. In other words, I have to study the situation and adapt my behavior to increase the likelihood that others will change. I cannot merely voice my desires and expect others to fall in line. This requires accommodation on my part. I have to consider the most effective means of communication—phone, memo, email, meeting, etc.—and adapt according to what I learn. When the desired change involves effort or discomfort, I expend time and energy studying the most effective ways to present and encourage change strategies.

What about the assertion that I am the only person over whom I have any control and that that control is limited? This is difficult to accept. Ours is a goal-oriented society; we take for granted that control is possible. The annual New Year's resolution frenzy and the continuing explosion of self-help books provide evidence of our conviction that control is possible while simultaneously demonstrating the apparent futility of our efforts—after all, if we could achieve self-control, we would not need self-help books. The assertion that open systems cannot be unilaterally controlled applies to ourselves as well as to others. The familiar internal struggle to stay on a diet, or to exercise regularly, is evidence of the need to see ourselves as systems requiring negotiation in essentially the same way that we recognize that leadership is negotiated in our roles as heads of families, classrooms, and businesses.

With this in mind, we need to take a close look at the last sentence in assertion 3: "I can only change things over which I have control." The language betrays us here, because *change* and *control* connote direct, unilateral action, and what we are discussing is, in fact, merely influence. The important point to keep in mind is that we cannot control others and that change always requires negotiation. I will need to assess the situation I am in and the individuals I have to deal with and come to a realistic understanding of just how much influence I can expect to wield. This admonition applies equally to the boss as well as to the most recently hired employee.

Let me register a caution with regard to items 1–3. Stated forthrightly as they are, they seem to imply a purposefulness that is unintended. That is, I do not mean to imply that all individual change is consciously aimed at changing society or that the reason for working for change within an institution is to improve the world at large. Further, I do not want to be understood as advocating a linear approach to change—first change oneself, then one's organizations, then society. Nor am I arguing that change must always begin with individual action. Change is a fact of life. So whether we like it or not, we have to learn to deal with change. What I *am* saying is that change is constantly occurring at different levels of scale all the time. We cannot know exactly what effects we are having or what the reverberations of our efforts will be. Conversely, we are usually only dimly aware of societal and institutional events that impinge on us and cause us to change. We can only hope that the values we hold and the direction in which we want to move can somehow be translated into meaningful action that reverberates throughout the system and results in noticeable changes.

4. **I can't change myself without affecting others. And, because I cannot change others unilaterally, I will need to engage them in some principled interactions. This may precipitate crises of various magnitude, as I discover where people stand and the relative importance (to me) of my change efforts versus the good opinions of my friends and colleagues.**

Even the most personal of change efforts requires collaboration. You cannot lose weight if your family and friends continue to press you to eat, and the alcoholic who is trying to stay sober requires a lot of encouragement and support, not invitations to parties. The need for collaboration increases, of course, as the change effort broadens to include others. It is obvious that you will need the cooperation of colleagues and staff members if you hope to reorganize your department, and if you are PTA president you know that even the simplest of projects requires the support of the principal, teachers, and other parents.

These considerations are usually not factored in immediately, however, when we vow "to turn over a new leaf" or to "whip that group into shape." It is down the road, as the first blush of confidence begins to fade, that we discover how much work is involved in getting people to adjust their schedules and priorities to accommodate our plans. I may be surprised to learn that my grandmother considers refusal of her sweet-potato pie as betrayal of family tradition or that colleagues consider me a compulsive maniac because I actually intend to implement a new accounting procedure (rather than, for example, passively resisting pressures to learn the new spreadsheet software). What started out as an impulse to improve things suddenly looms as a major family or professional crisis. It is at this point that I may discover that I have to choose between tranquility and change. Remain grandmother's favorite or lose weight? Maintain collegial relations with coworkers or insist on reforming accounting procedures? Of course, I hope that somehow both are possible, and sometimes this is the case, but at some point in a serious change effort I will be forced to draw the line.

It is usually at this point that I discover that my change effort will need to be expanded if I am going to be successful. Not only must I focus on counting calories, but I must also spend more time with grandmother to convince her that there are good reasons for my behavior, not mere willfulness and ingratitude. Similar efforts are required with my colleagues. I may resent the time and energy required for this, because I am trying to stay focused, but then I remind myself that I am inextricably interconnected with others and that I have to expect change efforts of all sizes to involve others.

In fact, a good case can be made for asserting that attention to the psychological and emotional aspects of change is as important as attention to the technical details required by change. All change entails some sense of loss; implicit in any change effort is a critique of past ways of doing things, and we need to deal with this critique without losing confidence or enthusiasm (Evans 1996).

> **5. I cannot predict the course of change, so I will need to adopt a flexible approach to my efforts: Ready, fire, aim! Some planning is necessary, but usually setting some preliminary goals and jumping in is the approach most likely to produce results.**

We need to learn to ride the course of events with an eye cocked for opportunities to influence the direction of change. Too much planning delays action and often counts as change itself, especially among individuals who would rather talk about change than actually do something (and that includes all of us at times). Because life is so complex and unpredictable, detailed planning is often a waste of time. We need to have a general idea of where we are going and then just jump in.

Take curriculum development, for example. It seems as if we teachers are constantly caught up in long-range planning of instruction, and it is not uncommon for a group of teachers to be called downtown to develop new units for the year. These curricula are notorious, however, for gathering dust in closets once the school year begins. There are good reasons for this. One is that often only a fraction of the teachers who are supposed to implement the new curriculum were involved in producing it, a point that also falls under assertion 4, that we cannot change others. Another reason for the failure of curriculum reform revolves around the fact that half of the equation in schooling—the students—is often left out of consideration as curricula are developed. This is somewhat of an exaggeration, because images of students are undoubtedly very much present as teachers work on new curricula, but when the school year gets under way, the very messy and dynamic reality of teaching and learning with particular students under specific situations takes precedence. The tidily arranged lessons suddenly become less relevant than the realities that have to be negotiated in the heat of the moment.

The same analysis applies to all organizational change efforts. In general, what is required is agreement on the essential values and the direction of change desired, some preliminary strategies, and a timetable with mechanisms for checking on progress.

6. I cannot change any important aspect of my life without changing all other aspects of my life.

Any change that does not require adjustments in other parts of my life should probably not be counted as significant change. We may think that we can compartmentalize our lives so that changes can be made in specific areas without affecting others, but we soon discover this is not so. Attempts to reduce credit-card debt run up against social commitments and the need to dress professionally. Becoming more efficient in our use of time causes difficulties with the schedules of other family members or colleagues at school. The reason for this is simple. We are individuals with many interconnected commitments, living in continuous time—there are no gaps in time or space or relationships; changes in one aspect of life will cause reverberations in other aspects of life.

The caution here is to avoid believing that you can tinker, that you can keep everything else the same except this one little aspect of life that needs perfecting. We believe that life would just be perfect if there weren't so many bills coming in every month. But lo! We discover that the joys of our getaway weekend are, in fact, reflected in the Visa bills that appear a few weeks later. When a couple attempts to engage in less expensive forms of recreation—for example, spending more time with the kids hiking and picnicking, rather than sending the kids to the movies while they play a round of golf and have dinner out—they discover that both they and the kids have become accustomed to the more affluent lifestyle. Not only that, but the more time they spend with the children in conversation the more alarmed they become about their language, dress, interests, friends. Suddenly they discover that the New Year's resolution to reduce credit-card bills has turned into an exercise in family-values clarification that promises to be far more important and time consuming than they had planned on.

7. I must come to grips with the real forces of my life (no lies). I will need to learn to see more clearly, to pay attention to what is going on, and to describe things as they are. What I see happening over time reveals what really matters. What gets done is important, and things are the way they are _not_ by accident.

This is a relentlessly empirical approach. If I make a New Year's resolution and adopt a regimen to accomplish it, but then look back on the past week and discern no evidence of change, then I must conclude that I am not serious about changing. If I didn't find time to write a close friend, I have to conclude the friend is not close. If I have spent more time on the job than with the family, I am forced to conclude that the job is more important than the family.

"Get real!" you exclaim. "I am required by my contract to spend 40 hours a week at my job; there is no slack there." Yes, but a week contains 168 hours, and if you allow yourself eight hours of sleep a night, that still leaves 72 hours of potential quality time with family. If you examine those 72 hours and still find that the job outscored the family, then you must conclude that this reveals your priorities.

Admittedly, this is a simplistic accounting of priorities, and you could argue that the job (and its income) are a major indicator of commitment to the family. How else are you supposed to pay for food, shelter, and clothing, not to mention braces and art classes? There is no grand scorecard of family commitment on which your efforts and intents are registered. This is where the "no lies" admonition comes in. Only you can decide whether your commitments to family and work are balanced and healthy.

"Lies" may be too strong a word, but what should we call systematic distortion of the facts? We all come up against this from time to time. The familiar phrase is, "I have been kidding myself." The situation in which these words are uttered is usually one in which you have had to face an unpleasant fact, and you realize that you were not unaware of the impending crisis but for a period of time preferred to focus on other things rather than "face the music." The same approach applies to institutions and society at large. If, over time, inner-city minority children drop out in greater numbers than majority children, then we must conclude that the system functions to maintain that steady drop-out rate. It may not be intentional, and it may not be anyone's fault, but it is not an accident.

This approach to change requires that we work to understand the patterns and interactions of elements of the system that maintain the status quo or that provide the resistance to changes we are trying to implement. In the process we will discover that convenient labels such as "liberal" or "conservative" have less meaning than we were accustomed to giving them. When we pay close attention to how people behave, and when we assess the important outcomes, we see that everyone, including ourselves, contributes to the problems we are trying to solve.

8. I cannot change other people (only individuals can change themselves). However, in some cases, I can change the conditions within which others work and interact, and in these cases I can increase the probability of some changes occurring rather than others.

One of the most important strategies available for change efforts involves changing environments so as to make certain behaviors and attitudes more likely to occur than others. Dieters know that they must avoid going in the bakery, and alcoholics avoid bars—a simple rationale based on keeping away from temptation. However, if they are going to be successful in this effort they need to go beyond the negative sanctions and create environments that are enjoyable alternatives to the familiar but dangerous contexts that got them into difficulty in the first place. So, for example, they join health clubs or church groups so as to be actively engaged with other people doing things that make resisting temptation irrelevant.

The teacher who wants children to read fills her room with books and comfortable chairs, provides free time for reading, encourages students to seek answers to questions in books, and regularly spends time presenting books that she has recently acquired. All of these changes are indirect efforts at influencing the children that go beyond the more expectable assignments that are directly aimed at getting students to read, although these may also be part of the approach. The goal is to create opportunities for people to exercise their freedoms, to make the right behavior easier, rather than merely making the wrong behavior more difficult.

9. **I need to have a vision of how things will look when they have improved. What will I see happening when things are better? I need to focus on how far I have come, in addition to how far I have to go.**

It has been said that the greatest imperfection is to require perfection. When we set out on a change project, we often set lofty and abstract goals when what is actually needed are realistic, concrete, and particular images of improvements over the current situation. Rather than focusing on losing 20 pounds by the time of my high-school reunion, I need to learn to pay attention to the daily behaviors that will need to change if such change is going to occur. Initially, I need to give myself credit for getting through the day without excessive caloric intake; perhaps what I notice is that I had carrots rather than Twinkies for a midmorning snack or that I turned down a lunch with colleagues and went to the gym instead. As the days roll by, I may not be able to discern much slack in my waistband, but I need to be able to recognize changes in my routines that will ultimately lead to the goals I have set.

Parents who want their children to get straight As on their report cards will have more success if they focus on immediate and attainable short-term goals that will lead to school success: recognizing the progress represented by children remembering to bring home their books or starting in on a long-range project instead of waiting until the last moment. These might appear insignificant when measured against graduation or academic honors, but they represent the first steps in the change process.

These examples represent strategies for change efforts, but they also indicate an important shift in perspective that can have a significant impact on people involved in change efforts. Often we become so consumed by the problems we are trying to solve that we forget to envision how we want things to be when they have improved. Or we focus so exclusively on the goal that we fail to see how much progress we have made. We need to develop a perspective on problems that permits us to keep the big picture in mind at the same time that we give ourselves (and others) credit for gains that have been made.

10. I must pay attention to what is happening while it is happening. I can't change yesterday, and tomorrow isn't here yet.

It is easy to become obsessed with things we should have done or to waste time daydreaming about how things will be in the future. The outcomes of an activity are contained in the minute particulars of the activity itself, and we need to focus on how we are behaving at the moment. This is merely a philosophical way of acknowledging the wisdom of the farmer's refrain, "Make hay while the sun shines." Or the inevitability of the present: *Now* is the only thing that is happening. And there is an old saying that admonishes the procrastinator: "You may not be able to make up your mind, but you make up your life as each day passes." As trite and obvious as all this sounds, it is surprisingly difficult to act upon. When I was a teenager my mother used to say, "Don't fret and fuss about some problem. If you can do something about it, do it. If not, forget about it and do something useful." This is advice that is easy to give and hard to follow. I may believe in my mother's admonition and still have difficulty focusing on a committee meeting because of a more important commitment that is coming up. The young mother knows that she has to attend to the baby when it is crying, however important other tasks may be to the smooth functioning of the household.

Change efforts require us to work from within relationships to construct environments conducive to the change we are trying to accomplish. The quality of relationships depends on the attention and effort we expend, and this means attending to the moment while it is happening.

11. Patience! I must trust processes as well as people.

Because we cannot mandate change, and because we cannot directly change people, we are forced to become philosophical in our approach to change. We can create the conditions for change, and we can set things in motion, but then we have to let things take their course. This is familiar advice for parents, but it applies as well to bosses, spouses, and friends. There is no substitute for experience, and so there will be setbacks along the way, but it is safe to say that most of us tend to micromanage, so the major lesson to be learned is how to let well enough alone. There is nothing profound about this stance; it is, in fact, merely recognizing the obvious, that people are going to take their own sweet time in adjusting to mandates and guidelines, so we might as well relax.

Of course, the same advice applies to self-improvement projects. We tend to be too hard on ourselves, demanding perfection early and becoming frustrated with the amount of time that it takes us to accomplish our goals. As anyone knows who has read self-help magazines in the grocery-store line, setting overly ambitious goals at the outset is a frequent culprit in failed New Year's resolutions. This is especially true for aging jocks, who are accustomed to jumping in and getting back in shape in short order, following their old coaches' truism, "No pain, no gain." It does not take long to discover that getting in shape at 50 is a much different process than it was at 20 (or even 30 or 40, which accounts in part for the slowness with which the lesson is learned).

12. Pain! It is rare for important change to occur without conflict and pain.

Whether we are considering losing 10 pounds or reorganizing the company, the fact is that change involves adjustments that we would just as soon not make. If changing were easy, we would not have a booming self-help industry, or massive enrollments in counseling and psychotherapy, or nationwide fitness campaigns. There is something comforting and comfortable about our routines of thinking and behaving, and serious change efforts threaten both. We cannot do anything about the fact that change involves discomfort, but perhaps recognizing this to be true is the first step toward the mental adjustments required to accomplish change.

13. Learning is change over time through engagement in activity. Human beings cannot not learn.

To learn is to gain insight, knowledge, understanding, or skill, and this is happening all the time from the moment of birth. Each learner changes in ways that vary according to where she or he started and which aspects of the learning we focus on. This view also implies that learning will extend beyond the mere acquisition of facts. It goes to "identity"; one comes to see oneself as a reader and writer, for example, or as a legitimate member of the academic community. The visible evidence of this kind of change will not be of the sort that is easily demonstrated by conventional measures.

Learning occurs at different levels of awareness and skill, in bits and pieces, fits and starts over time; it is an indeterminate, trial and error process, a significant portion of which occurs at the periphery of conscious attention. Good teachers know this, and they will repeat facts or review material before proceeding, asking students to rephrase ideas and insights in their own words. They are also patient, because they know that skills and concepts will gradually take hold as students continue to work.

14. As teachers we create environments in which learners can become authentically engaged in meaningful activity

"Authenticity" is a difficult concept to define, but it is easy to recognize. When learners seem totally absorbed in an activity, lose track of time, and develop their own standards for completion, we can call the activity "authentic." Creating opportunities for such activities requires hard work on the part of teachers, because it requires our knowing the learners and adjusting aspects of the curriculum to fit their interests. "Meaningfulness," in fact, becomes a criterion that is stretched on a continuum between what the learner is interested in and what the school requires. The trick is to balance the tension between what we are supposed to be teaching and what learners want to be learning.

15. The most powerful learning is that which occurs *apperceptively,* at the edges of consciousness.

In general, we—the teaching profession and the public—are far too focused on the content of the curriculum, on the facts that students are supposed to learn and that can be tested. In fact, we should balance this focus with attention to the environments of learning where subtle but enduring lessons are learned that shape not only the content of learning but the students' attitude toward that content and toward the whole experience of school. The lessons learned in the lap of the family and in the comfort of culture are enduring precisely because of the power of this aspect of learning. An awareness of this fact puts a great burden on teachers, because there is so much about the environment that we do not control—schedules, the pressure of tests, the availability of materials, etc. But, on the other hand, one element in the learners' experience is available to our influence, and this is the extent to which we model the attitudes and behaviors we want students to acquire.

16. Teaching is a particular form of learning.

We study the learners. They study the lessons. We create environments for learning. The students do the learning. The curriculum is a framework for organizing these environments, but the most important learning comes from the implicit *messages* we send by the ways we organize time, space, tools, and activity. We may tell students that we value curiosity and creativity, but they will learn just how serious we are about this by the amount of time we allocate to projects and our tolerance for questions and conversation. If we cut them off just as they are getting interested in a topic, or if we have little patience for free-ranging discussion of ideas, they will learn the extent of the value we place on new ideas. In general, this assertion means that we need to focus less on our role as authority in the classroom and more on how we model curiosity and risk taking. It also frees us from having to have the right answers in every situation.

17. Good teaching is an institutional accomplishment as much as an individual *tour de force*.

The best teacher in the world can be rendered less effective if the school where she or he works does not provide adequate support through allocation of resources, sensible scheduling, judicious distribution of students, and a framework for professional collaboration and development. On the other hand, the most inexperienced or unskilled teacher can achieve better results if the school in which she or he works provides those features.

Elaborations and Applications

The abstractions of systems theory require grounding to make them real, so what I would like to do now is tell a story of my own involvement in school/neighborhood change so that you have one example of how I have used the 17 assertions listed to guide my understanding of change efforts. I have used numbers in parentheses to indicate connections between the narrative and the assertions.

But where to begin the story? Should I start with my decision to accept the position at the School of Education, Colorado University, Denver, rather than the one offered by the English department at Colorado State University? The latter was more of a conventional ESL position and would have required less adjustment on my part, so choosing to come to Denver definitely represented a personal change decision with the concomitant repercussions (3, 5, 6). The position required me to work with public school teachers and to teach courses on literacy as well as ESL, both of which were a stretch, given my prior experience and my formal training. I had to adjust my perspective to that of the prospective teachers who entered my classroom. I had to learn the details of their daily lives so that I could make connections between what I knew about second-language learning and literacy and the sorts of challenges they faced (16).

I could begin the story with our decision to settle in Park Hill, an urban neighborhood located in east Denver, rather than returning to the suburban Littleton where I had grown up. Park Hill is an integrated neighborhood with a tradition of civil-rights activism balanced by its share of racial tension, gang violence, and school difficulties (Woods 1998). We knew that moving to Park Hill would involve us in school and community struggles that we could avoid if we lived in the suburbs, and there was a certain amount of anxiety associated with our decision (5, 6, 12).

Another logical starting point for the story might be our decision to establish the Park Hill Bike Club in the summer of 1995. This was definitely a commitment with risks (5), made in response to the rising tide of gang violence in the neighborhood. It was a conscious effort to create an alternative environment for kids, one that would put them in contact with caring adults who modeled the kind of discipline and focused effort required for success in today's achievement-oriented world (8, 13, 14, 15).

 JUNIOR

But you can begin a story anywhere you want—this is the storyteller's prerogative. So I'll begin mine with Junior, the waif who

grew up across the street from us. He is a few years younger than my son, Ben, but he was big for his age, so he got into a fair share of the ball games that surged up and down our front lawn during the 10 years or so that the kids were growing up. Several images float in front of my mind's eye when I think of Junior.

An early one: I came out of our front door to get the newspaper on a chilly winter morning to see Junior on the sidewalk in his pajamas bawling his eyes out. I went across the street to see how I could help, but he was inconsolable; the best I could understand between the sobs was that his mom had left without him. I knocked at the door, but no one answered, so I took him home and wiped his nose, gave him some hot chocolate, and loaned him some of Ben's sweats. I was wondering what my next move should be when I noticed his grandmother on their front stoop calling his name. It turned out that she had been in the basement doing laundry and had not heard my knock and that, yes, his mother had left him home this morning; she did that every day when she went to work.

Junior seemed to always be on the sidewalk in front of his house. He would hail me whenever I was outside, asking if Ben was home and if he could come over. As he got older and was allowed to cross the street he would show up to ask the same question, and when Ben and his friends did start a game, he was right there pestering them to be included. One hot summer day the boys swarmed around a football all day long, a frenzied mass of sweaty kids churning up and down the long stretch of lawn on the side of the house. They would take breaks for lemonade from time to time on the back porch and play Trivial Pursuit as they cooled down in the shade of the birch tree. I would overhear them as I worked around the house, and it was a hoot listening to them read the cards, stumbling over unfamiliar words and adult concepts, posturing after missing a question, begging for the sports category as they rolled the dice. They played in the same teams as on the field, taking turns reading and responding to questions, gyrating in Michael Jacksonesque contortions, interspersing rap and jive as they hazarded answers. Junior was the youngest of the group, and academic contests were not his strength, but he was game. He struggled when it was his turn to read the card, and he threw out desperate guesses when answering, taking a greater share of kidding during Trivial Pursuit than he did during football. I remember thinking that he probably endured a lot less kinder cuts at school than he did among his friends on the block.

As the kids grew up, Junior was not around our house as much, but I would see him coming and going, and we exchanged pleasantries whenever we crossed paths. In the early 1990s, the neighborhood went through some rough times with gang and drug activity, and we attended a number of block meetings organized to reduce tensions between the teenagers and the adults. Junior attended some of these, and I have a vivid memory of him at one meeting, absentmindedly sucking his middle two fingers as he listened to the talk—an unconscious gesture of comfort left over from childhood. On another occasion we spoke briefly in the street after a misunderstanding between police and some guys working on a car erupted into a confrontation between him and one of the neighbors. It was a polite exchange, but he was still simmering from the encounter, and I could see why our neighbor would feel threatened. He was in his late teens or early twenties by this time, and bigger than most of us on the block. I think he had dropped out of school, and I don't know what sort of job he had, but he always seemed to have money. He drove a new little SUV that was firebombed one evening in front of his house. He had a girlfriend, and they had a baby girl, and from time to time a domestic drama would play out in front of the house.

There was a period when we didn't see much of him or the girlfriend and baby, and there were rumors that he had moved to a nearby suburb or even California and that he was involved in gang activity. Then, suddenly, we learned that he was a suspect in a robbery. The victims were neighbors, people we knew from community work, and the details as they came out were chilling. Junior was convicted and is now serving hard time.

What does all this have to do with systems theory and change agency? Nothing, perhaps. Or everything.

On the one hand, Junior's story is one of countless episodes of urban violence, a confluence of circumstances and bad choices. It involves absent fathers, older siblings tutoring youngsters in bad decision making, working mothers who struggle to make ends meet and watch helplessly as their children drift away from them. It includes alienation from teachers and rejection of education as a way of getting ahead. It represents a variation on the excess materialism of our national identity. It is profoundly depressing in its apparent inevitability.

On the other hand, it is an intense episode in my life, much more than an urban statistic for me. I am engulfed in melancholy and frustration whenever I think about Junior today. And I think about him often as I work with this year's crop of sixth graders at the neighborhood middle school. I wonder how many of the little boys I see every day will head down the same path as Junior. "He was such a sweet kid," my daughter Julia said when she learned what had happened. Yes. Yes. They are all sweet and innocent as kids. What happens between sixth grade and eighth grade to transform them from innocence and hope to cynicism and anger? What role can we reasonably expect to play in kids' lives? How do we create the possibility for different endings to these sorts of stories?

Well, for one thing, we have to recognize that our influence is limited. As neighbors and teachers, we do not have the time or the prerogative for extensive, direct intervention in kids' lives. We cannot make people change, but we can create opportunities for better choices (8).

So while the decisions to accept the position at CU Denver and to move to Park Hill do not represent conscious choices of change agency and community activism, they did lead inexorably, if not inevitably, to a series of decisions that does reveal the accuracy of the 17 assertions developed earlier.

When I decided to put significant energy and time into the Park Hill Bike Club I knew that I would have to make adjustments in how

I spent my time, that summer weekends would become more tightly scheduled, and that I would be drawn into kids' lives in ways that would not permit me the luxury of merely observing from the sidelines. The Bike Club grew. We attracted community attention and support. A bike expert joined the group, and together we wrote grants and opened a small business—Recycles Bike Shop—organized as a learning environment for kids. It is a place where they can repair bikes or rebuild bikes that have been donated. We applied for and were granted IRS status as a 501(c)(3), a nonprofit entity. We developed a business plan. The club was beginning to take over my life. What had begun as a well-intentioned effort at community involvement had become a full-time concern.

And it is not as if running a bike club will pay the rent. You know the expression, "Don't give up your day job"? That was the position I found myself in. I knew that something would have to give because there just were not enough hours in the day to accommodate all the demands on my time.

So I began to formalize the decision I had made somewhat unconsciously some 20 years earlier. I began to shift my attention as a teacher and researcher from English as a second language and language education toward action research in school and community. I requested changes in my teaching load so that I could deal directly with urban education and teacher preparation, and I began declining requests from doctoral students to serve as an advisor on dissertations that were narrowly focused on academic issues. I shifted my reading from familiar fields to new disciplines. I worked with my closest colleagues to get grants that would permit us to do research in the neighborhood, and I used my friendships with teachers in the local schools as the basis for involvement in their classes.

As I look back on this story, I realize how seemingly insignificant decisions contributed to the general trajectory and that these forced me to make more momentous decisions to either continue in the direction of activism or pull back. The details are not important, but the analysis is. Significant change—that is, change that endures and that contributes to the greater good—does not come easily or quickly. The decisions I have made over the past 20 years—personal and professional—cannot all be lined up according to how they have contributed to the school and community issues described here, but they do support a systems perspective of changing, teaching, and learning.

However, the analysis requires a caveat, one faced by all historians. We need to resist the beguiling illusion of inevitability that personal narratives carry with them, and as the storyteller I need to balance the inclination to view my decisions with a gratifying sense of personal accomplishment. All stories have a point, and the point of the story I have told here is to convince you of the value of a systems perspective of life. The same story could be told just as convincingly by a historian who believes in manifest destiny, or a narrator who believes that Junior got what he deserves and that I am a bumbling bike rider who should stick to his books.

My response has two angles. The first provides a slant on the past, on our attempts to make sense of our decisions and to learn from our mistakes. I think it is important to reflect on our personal histories and to attempt to discover the values that have guided our decisions. These will be emergent values, ones that *emerge* from the actions we have taken, not necessarily the intentions that guided us going in or the explicit reasons we might have given for our actions at the time. That is, I believe we need to pay attention to the effects of our efforts and to the investments of time and energy we have made over time in order to discover what we might want to call "the meaning of life."

The second angle provides a lens for the future. If a systems perspective makes sense for understanding the past, then it can also give us a framework for decision making in the future. We all face countless decision points every day, and it is only in retrospect that the choices we made seem to be the obvious ones. That is because we often do not see the options available to us, or we are under such pressure that we do not have time to examine all the possibilities. However, it is important to remember that we have considerable discretion in the construction of our realities and that all decisions, small and large, contribute to the landscape of our lives in ways that we can only begin to imagine at the time. We cannot predict the outcome of particular decisions, but we can examine the apparent direction that they take us in, and we can ask ourselves as we go, "How will this decision look 10 or 20 years from now?"

③ Elements of the Change Process

Ah, bumper stickers! Grains of truth glimpsed through highway grit. Here's a recent sampling.

Life—it just keeps coming at you.
And now, war. It's always something.
I love you. You're perfect. Now change.
Life is what happened while you were making plans.
For every complex problem, there is a simple solution—
and it is always wrong.
When you're up to your eyeballs in alligators, it is difficult
to remember that your goal was to drain the swamp.

When I saw these particular automotive footnotes they prompted a rueful smile, reminding me that, whatever details I am in control of, life is not one of them. But they also promised the possibility of facing confusion with an attitude of cheerful defiance. The goal of this essay is similar. I explore an approach to living that, while not a panacea, has the potential for helping you cope with the barrage of events and circumstances that you face each day.

There is no denying the cliché that the world is a complex place and there are no easy answers, but what does one do with that information, apart from using it for consolation? If recognition of life's complexity is to be useful, it needs to contribute to a theory for living. I am looking for a way to get through the day that

- promises some measure of control over the immediate future
- addresses the immediate problem without creating bigger ones
- permits me to deal effectively with troublesome people, especially those I have to live and work with
- helps me organize my teaching so that I satisfy not only students and administrators but also myself
- aligns my everyday behavior with my life goals

What is needed is an orientation to the world and all its complexity, a way of seeing, a way of organizing my thinking and my activity. I want to resist the urge to oversimplify, to avoid complexity, but at the same time I need to be able to move forward with the day confident that what I am doing is at least not making things worse. Here is a sampling of the sorts of problems I have in mind.

- Tests, report cards, school evaluations—everywhere you turn someone is passing judgment on someone else. The heat seems to come from all sides, and it exists at all levels of society. Everyone takes the pressure from above and passes it on to the person below.
- Home, school, community—just about the time you get one area of your life organized, another area falls apart. You need a system for keeping track of details and organizing your time so that important tasks get taken care of first and little problems get resolved before they become big problems.

- You find that you have one or two colleagues who make it difficult to get things done. Whether it is malice or mere incompetence, they can't seem to get with the program, and you end up spending as much time coaching them and repairing the damage they have caused as you do on any other aspect of your work.
- Your school or district has adopted an instructional or disciplinary plan that has caused more trouble than the problem it was intended to solve. You find yourself swamped with paperwork and procedure when you could actually be doing something important.
- Your students seem to be suffering from recurring amnesia. It seems as if you continue to teach some things over and over, and just when you think they get it, they act as if they have never seen it before.
- You can see what needs to be done, and you think it is important, but you just cannot find the time to organize the effort to make it happen—and this seems to apply to every aspect of your life.

As you would expect, the topic resists organization; it is big and clumsy and complex, and this essay provides an example of the problem it was written to address. After a few preliminaries, I'll just jump in with examples and commentary. Take what you can use, and leave the rest for later. Remember, "The only good advice is the advice you take."

Systems Thinking

Individuals, classrooms, schools, communities—systems within systems within systems. All are open systems operating according to internal thermostatic settings and reacting in patterned ways to stimuli from the environment (Watzlawick, Weakland, and Fisch 1974; G. Bateson 1979, 1999; M. C. Bateson 1994, 1999, 2000; Wilden 1987; Bowers and Flinders 1990; Harries-Jones 1995; Capra 1996).

And all systems change. Change at all levels involves the same processes, but we use different words to describe it so we tend to think they are different. Learning is change, and so is development—maturing, aging, dying. Adjusting to a new neighborhood, job, or culture and acquiring a new language are other common examples of change. Sometimes we are the agents of change, and sometimes we are the objects of someone else's change effort. Very often these days, especially in education, we are both at the same time; we are attempting to cope with increased demands for accountability, with ever more intrusive measures of student learning, even as we implement new classroom methods that require our students to modify their behavior.

And it is important to understand that organizations behave the same way as people, because they are both systems. Some organizational analysts and scholars of leadership have begun to use the phrase *learning organizations* to capture this fact (Senge 1990, 1999; Fullan 1999, 2001; Senge et al. 2000), but most people have difficulty seeing the similarities between the process of, say, an individual becoming more skilled at dealing with anger and interpersonal disputes and the process of a community developing ways of resolving political tensions. They are, however, essentially the same, and if we can see the patterns we can become more adept at dealing with and instigating change.

On the one hand, it's very elegant; on the other, it's so complex as to be mind numbing. If we are to think of all change as involving the same factors, but merely at different levels of scale, and if the one thing that is constant in life is change, how do we sort it all out so that we are able to act meaningfully? How can we participate in organizational change when our own behavior is subject the same principles as organizations are? These are the questions that I attempt to answer here.

The environmentalists' slogan, "Think globally, act locally," captures the approach. We need a perspective of events and situations that provides an awareness of how details fit with the overall picture. There are seven details we should pay attention to.

❧ **The problem.** What *is* the problem? What, exactly, is bothering me? Naming the problem is an important step toward making progress on developing a solution. It is also very often an impediment to change, because it limits my ability to see all the ways that the situation might be conceptualized. Just being aware of the fact that problems are constructions of my own making can be helpful.

❧ **The issue.** How is this problem a variation on life's natural functioning? All problems are local examples of larger issues. I need to understand the larger issues so that I am prepared for the variety of ways that they surface in my life. Identifying the larger issue also helps me think about how I will respond to the problem I am dealing with.

❧ **The solution, or innovation.** What is the response to the problem? Of the limitless options available, which one has been selected? Solutions tend to become problems when commitment to a particular procedure or approach takes precedence over attempts to see the problem clearly and to attend to progress being made. Sustained change efforts often take on a life of their own. Remembering that naming the innovation shapes the approach to change helps me keep from getting mired in routines and forgetting what my original goals were.

❧ **The players.** Who is involved, and how? All change requires individuals to change. Who are the primary players, and what are their attitudes toward change? The principal player is always me, and I have to do most of the changing, but I assume that others will have to change as well, and I need to approach them differently depending on their attitude toward the problem, toward the solution, and toward me.

❧ **Evidence of change.** How do I know if I am making progress? How do I keep myself psyched up in the face of frus-

trations? Having a list of visible indicators of progress is help-ful. It is as important to see how far I have come as it is to see how far I have to go.

      Activity cycles. Where am I in the process? Is this the begin-ning, middle, or end of a cycle of change? All problems are part of a larger pattern, points in a cycle that will come around again. Seeing the cycle is essential to organizing change strate-gies or coping with someone else's attempts to change me.

      Constraints and strategies. What are the factors that con-tribute to the way things are? What are the approaches that make sense, given the pressures of resistance? I always have choices as I face change efforts, and it is important to under-stand what those choices are and what factors contribute to the probability of their success.

The Routine

This approach does not constitute a solution, because there are no solutions to life's persistent problems, at least not in the sense of com-fortable, uncomplicated resolutions that permit you to forget about them. But we can adopt a routine as we work on problems, one that permits us to work for accommodations and adjustments, hoping to achieve some mental relief for ourselves and to nudge people and processes toward our goals. Most of us have been socialized to be-lieve in our own agency and in the value of direct action, and so this more conservative, time-consuming approach may be frustrating. But it can also be liberating to realize that there is a limit to our responsi-bility and to the amount of time and energy we can reasonably de-vote to important causes—we remain engaged but realistic in our ef-forts. This approach gives you a place to stand, a perspective on life and strife that promises some improvement and some peace of mind. Here is how it works.

You become aware of something that is bothering you, and you focus on it long enough to decide that it is, indeed, worthy of your attention and sustained effort. You step back and examine it from a variety of angles in a spirit of playful scrutiny—the idea is to resist the natural tendency to become prematurely committed to a particular solution. Instead, imagine a string of worry beads or an ophthalmologist's collection of lenses. Your approach is to shift from one bead or lens to another as you think the situation through. You recognize that your own perceptions and actions contribute in some way to the problem, and you want to proceed in such a way as to avoid making things worse.

Part of the "solution" is realizing that there are no solutions. Things are the way they are not by accident, and problems continue to recur because of patterns and cycles in the culture and institutions. In other words, we can expect certain kinds of problems to occur in a variety of guises, given the way the world works. Realizing this at least gives us a principled basis for planning and action.

Take recurring New Year's resolutions, for example. This is a boom industry in America, and I don't think it's because people are successfully solving one set of problems and then pushing on to new ones. I suspect that the resolutions sector of the economy is profitable precisely because people do not succeed and so find themselves back at the bookstore each December searching for the latest approach to their personal problems.

It is possible that this cycle could be explained as the result of the personal weakness of all those resolvers; they just can't get it together. It is far more likely, however, that the individual effort is too much to sustain in the face of converging social pressures, which is just another way of saying that the patterns of systems functioning make it unlikely that most of us will be able to sustain a personal change effort. If this is the case, then the area of New Year's resolutions is prime territory for examining systems approaches to change because it permits us to examine the phenomenon at different levels of scale and because every year we can renew our study of the phenomenon.

One common recurring problem is weight; every winter I lose and gain about 10 pounds. Just when I think maybe this year I have succeeded in making the resolution stick, I pass a store window in an unguarded moment and I get a glimpse of those extra 10 pounds, settled comfortably and not so attractively around my midriff. So I make my annual resolution to trim down. My strategy varies from year to year, but I approach it with total confidence, and on one level I do succeed. Within a couple of months I notice a difference. I feel better, slacks hang gratifyingly loose on the hips, I have more energy and enthusiasm. In addition, I enjoy a sense of accomplishment and control. Then, inevitably it seems, things return to normal–I slip back into my familiar pudgy profile–and the cycle continues.

This phenomenon of intransigent problems and recurring solutions is a feature of school and community as well. Take student achievement, especially among minority students. Or drop-out rates, teen pregnancy, drug and alcohol abuse. Or parental participation in school.

School-board campaigns are built on these issues, and increasingly state and national politicians have become involved in the debate, even though the statutory basis for their involvement is suspect. You would think that if everyone agrees that a problem is, in fact, a problem, we should be able to solve it. But that isn't the case. It seems clear that an approach is required in which we work not only on the solutions to problems but on the whole process of refining our understanding of issues, formulating definitions and parameters of problems, and examining factors that contribute to problems. It may be that in fashioning an approach to change, we need to spend more time understanding persistence.

The important problems have a way of sneaking up on you. Take the typical scuffle in the hallway during a passing period at a middle school. Two boys flailing at each other and shouting ugly epithets while kids gather around egging them on. You separate them before too much damage is done, but you are alarmed at the intensity of the anger and racial slurs that the boys sling at each other, and you take them into your classroom for a cool-down period. After a brief talk you let them go without the mandatory referral to the assistant principal's office, thinking to yourself that they seem to have calmed down. Later, you learn that this is not the first time these two have been at each other, and a colleague expresses her suspicion that the disputes go beyond school-yard rivalry. She thinks this might be the beginning of gang affiliation. You are troubled by this statement and think to yourself that the parents probably ought to be called, but then the week picks up pace, and you let the incident slip to the back burner. However, the next week one of the boys is involved in a scuffle with another student, and you feel yourself being sucked into a complicated situation. The student clams up when you try to find out the source of the dispute, and you decide you cannot let the matter slide. You call the parents, but without much success; both work outside the home, and you leave a message, which is not returned. You feel the familiar frustration as you begin going through the motions of phone tag that seldom result in a parent conference. You resolve to push the process this time to see if you can actually do something to make a difference. It is clear, however, that the boys' fighting is just the tip of an iceberg that includes a wide range of school and community issues.

The one thing that these examples have in common is this: Persistent problems are recurring points in larger patterns of individual and social phenomena. They will not yield to simple solutions or formulaic approaches. If, however, we can develop a patient approach of reflective decision making, we will begin to see enough progress to help us maintain the faith as we work. I will elaborate on the seven elements listed earlier and then explore examples of decision making that permit me to illustrate the approach.

The Issue

All significant problems are local manifestations of larger issues. Recognizing this gives you a broader perspective from which to work, and it helps you keep things in perspective. You keep your eyes open for programs that others have developed, and you recognize that there is a limit to what you can hope to accomplish. The important thing to remember is that there are as many ways to describe issues as there are observers, so the key is to not become prematurely or stubbornly committed to a particular perspective. How you think about an issue shapes the choices you make as you attempt to understand the problem and search for solutions.

Take my New Year's resolution to lose 10 pounds. What is the issue? Is it appearance or health? If I am doing a crash diet before the high-school reunion, it is probably the former, whether I have recognized it or not. If the doctor has declared that I won't make it to the next reunion unless I pay attention to my weight, then my approach will be much more deliberate and long-term. And how does this aspect of my life relate to other areas? I have a niggling suspicion that the issue has more to do with procrastination and a tendency to spend time doing things I enjoy rather than things that need my attention. If I were to look closely at my approach to the family budget, or house and garden projects, I might see a similar pattern.

And what is the issue behind the boys fighting in the hall? Do the tensions revolve around sexual awakening, race, identity crises, etc.? Of course, it may be that all of these issues are relevant, but it is important to avoid getting blindsided by issues you have not been paying attention to. And there are times when a scuffle is merely a scuffle— the boys just bumped into each other—and the best approach is to cool the kids down and send them along without making a big deal out of it. In the post-Columbine era, however, you can't be too careful, and you do not want to ignore a serious problem in the making. Depending on your assessment of the roots of the conflict, you will choose different approaches to the situation.

The Problem

What did Shakespeare say? "There is no problem but thinking makes it so"? Issues can be represented abstractly, but problems are problems precisely because they are not abstract. They are in your face. You cannot ignore them. Conversely, if I do not notice the extra 10 pounds, then I haven't got a weight problem. If I think that boys will be boys, then two kids fighting in the hall is not a big deal.

We all have our personal antennae, our own sensitivities to the way things should be, and until a problem makes it to our radar screen, we do not notice it. The same is true of everyone else, which explains why we can be passionately consumed with a problem of which the next person is blissfully ignorant. You are laboring to save the planet by marching in a nuclear-disarmament demonstration, and your neighbor is passing out fliers about homelessness. You pass each other as you leave your houses, shaking your heads at the apathy of the neighborhood.

This fact indicates that we have to attempt a somewhat objective approach to understanding what is bugging us. What is the problem? List two or three ways you might refer to it. How do you know it is a problem? What do you see happening that you don't like, that provides evidence that a problem exists? Do this at the global level as well as at the local level. The more connections you can make between the global and the local, the better you will be able to see how systems function to maintain the problem. How is the problem viewed by others? What role do people play in the problem? What is the history of the problem? How long has it been recognized as a problem, and what other attempts have been made to solve it? How do definitions of the problem affect the attempted solutions?

In terms of my New Year's resolution, is my problem weight or inattention? Portion size or choice of food? Genetic endowment, upbringing, sloth? Are the extra 10 pounds the problem or the symptom of the problem? Am I merely a local example of affluent gluttony and fast-food fixation? Are we all headed toward a plump senility? Or are all of these things in different proportions at different times? The fact is that I tend to frame the problem initially in a sort of knee-jerk reaction, attending to the aspect that is most comfortable for me to contemplate and easiest for me to deal with. As an aging jock and former wrestler, I favor exercise and strict regimens, so I am more likely to call my problem "weight gain" than, say, "procrastination coupled with a propensity toward self-indulgence." But both descriptions capture elements of truth about the situation.

Is the fight in the hall a problem that should be located in the personalities and home lives of the boys or in the decision making that led the school leaders to put several hundred squirming adolescents into a building and then move them from classroom to classroom every 50 minutes? Is it a curricular issue, one that can be handled by working on academic programs, or does it require collaboration of community and city agencies and perhaps involvement of parents? There are strong arguments for each characterization, but each decision about what to call the problem sends you down a different path in search of solutions.

Notice that there is nothing transparent or fixed about the nature of the problem, nor is there any final best answer to the question, "What is the problem?" How you answer the question will shape your response, but if your efforts do not seem to work, you can always step back and reframe your answer. In other words, develop the habit of continuing to ask the question, "What is the problem here?"

The Solution, or Innovation

I will use *solution* and *innovation* interchangeably, although they imply different levels of scale and importance.

"Problem" and "solution" are a matched pair in our culture. In modern technologically advanced societies it is generally assumed that all problems have solutions. And that, in itself, is a problem. The assumption that there are solutions out there allows us to persist in the notion that our way of doing things is essentially correct or natural and that once the solution to the problem has been found, we will be able to return to "normal." It makes us impatient. We tend to want quick fixes, and we fail to see how we ourselves have contributed to the problem over a period of time. It increases the likelihood that blaming others will be seen as a reasonable reaction when innovations fail. It leads us to seek single, simple, direct approaches to problems, when very often what is most required is tolerance for ambiguity and multiple approaches.

Problem/solution thinking is essentially cause/effect thinking, which works fine in billiards but is far less helpful in attempting to understand the human condition.

For those of us caught up in a cycle of New Year's resolutions—declaring them, organizing them, failing to keep them—this might mean that we pause to consider the possibility that we have mislabeled the problem and mishandled the solution. It might be better to think of the situation, and our approach to the situation, in less dramatic and less simplistic terms.

In fact, it is possible to think of my "solution" to recurrent chubbiness as merely a natural part of the rhythms of life; like the seasons, my waistline comes and goes. Crash diets and cookbook fads then become predictable markers of the stages of the year. It is my way of contributing to the GNP and to the inconsequential conversation of faculty meetings and locker rooms.

Similarly, bully-proofing programs constitute one approach to crafting solutions to the increase in violence. Another approach might be more long-range—prenatal support for young mothers, especially single mothers, and federally subsidized child-care programs that include opportunities for parents to further their education and learn strategies for dealing with stress and conflict.

As we learn to think creatively about problems, we begin to see how problems and solutions are interrelated. All the big issues are being worked on by someone, and all problems provoke the search for solutions. When solutions take on economic, political, or institutional importance, they acquire the status of "innovations" and become the basis for policy-making and strategizing. They acquire a life of their own. They in turn spawn other problems. We increase our flexibility in dealing with problems if we remember that both "problem" and "solution" are constructions that emerge from situations and interactions. However "real" they may seem, they are also matters of perception, which means that we exercise a measure of control as we approach them.

The Players

We talk abstractly about change. We discuss new programs for implementing curricula and/or discipline, and we talk about schools and communities adjusting to improved standards and standardized tests, but the fact is that if institutions change, it is because individuals have changed. If we adopt new teaching methods and materials, we will have to change and so will our students. If the change is significant, it may impact our colleagues and require adjustments by parents. As with all of life's conundrums, it is the people who matter, who require our attention.

Effective change agents know this, and they organize their efforts with specific, real people in mind. They ask themselves questions as they develop their approach. Who is involved in the change effort? What are their names, roles, biographical data? What are their concerns? How would you categorize their attitude toward this new way of doing things? Are they a change agent, early adopter, cautious adopter, skeptic, resistor (E. M. Rogers 1995)? How are they involved? What habits and routines contribute to the problem? How will you deal with them?

I may want to think of myself as the only player in my annual weight-loss campaign, but even cursory reflection reveals that if I don't have support from my friends and family, I will not have much success. This is one of the important insights of personal change organizations such as Weight Watchers. They know that people need a supportive peer group, and they provide the structure for that to occur.

Similarly, it may be that my primary attention is focused on the two boys involved in the hallway altercation, but if I do not find a way to involve their parents, older siblings, and peers, I will not have much luck in reducing the tensions.

Evidence of Change

We tend to be so focused on our goals that we overlook the progress we are making. We need to pay attention to how far we have come as well as how far we have to go. As our understanding of the problem deepens, and as we explore ways of working on the problem, we need to be flexible in our assessment of our progress.

The human condition is not susceptible to direct management. People do not conform to managerial blueprints and five-year plans. Therefore, we need to understand the values implicit in and the direction of change efforts, and we need to learn to see movement when it occurs. This is a skill that requires nurturing, because our tendency is to become fixed on particular outcomes, or committed to particular approaches, and we often overlook evidence that things are moving in the desired direction.

It is possible to be so focused on losing 10 pounds that I fail to appreciate the fact that I have lost five. Or I work so hard on sticking with a particular program that I do not appreciate the increase in energy that has resulted from a more balanced diet.

With middle-school students, it is easy to overlook progress toward good citizenship when we have models of perfection in mind. Very often, we continue to demand changes in their behavior rather than acknowledging the progress they are making.

We need to understand the larger issues at stake, and we need to see where we started and in what ways we are making progress. We need to be clear about the core values we are working toward, and we must learn to recognize movement toward those values.

Activity Cycles

It is often the case that we are so caught up in the details of a change project, or in attempting to cope with the demands of an innovation, that we forget that life is a recurring pattern of events and situations. The cliché, "What goes around, comes around," is accurate. And very often, the success of a change effort depends more on selecting the right time for action than it does on selecting the right action. It is important to learn to see where you are in the process you are trying to change.

We need to become relentlessly empirical, to observe and take note of the normal functioning of the systems within which we work.

What are the normal cycles of events that contribute to the problem? What is the typical pattern that characterizes the situation? What are the routines and rituals that constitute "normal" functioning for individuals and groups? We need to learn to see activity cycles on different levels of scale so that we see how local events are influenced by larger societal and institutional forces.

Economic cycles correlate with the buildup of armaments and the occurrence of war—war tends to produce jobs and solve unemployment unrest. Summer brings more people out of doors and increases neighborhood violence. Christmas brings on depression for people whose family-friend network does not match the media version of the season. All of these phenomena reverberate in the details of daily life. It is important to understand where we are in the cycle of a particular issue so that we can judge the efficacy of our response.

Personal resolutions for self-improvement can occur at any time, of course, but January 1 brings with it a whole culture of support for the idea of implementing change. The same thing is true of autumn for most teachers. It is a time of renewal, a chance to try something new, to take advantage of the energy of new students, of new colleagues, methods, materials.

With school violence, we are forced to act at times of crisis, to step in and stop a fight, for example, but it is almost certainly true that the cycle began earlier and functions broadly in other spheres of children's lives. Working with family members on long-term projects of education and employment may seem like a very indirect approach to solving a hallway dispute, but it may be the most effective.

We are dealing with life in all of its minute particulars as well as in its broadest manifestations, and our success will vary according to how well we understand the natural cycles that bring problems around to us on a rhythmic basis.

Constraints and Strategies

We walk into situations where the problems and the players seem fully engaged. We can see what is wrong with the way things are, and we can craft a solution that moves people toward reasonable goals. But it is not always easy to see all the factors that contributed to the reality we have encountered.

In a causal universe, that of bowling balls and billiard tables, we can speak of cause and effect with confidence. If we understand the causes, we can fashion responses to problems that lead directly to solutions. With people, it is far more complicated. People arrive at particular places in their lives, even places they do not desire, through a complex process of making decisions in contexts where foolish choices seemed reasonable at the time. It is often the case, as well, that we do things we do not like because we perceive that we have no choice or that the decision we have made constitutes the best of a sad collection of choices.

The word *constraints* typically has negative connotations, but I use it in a more neutral sense. It is just a word to indicate factors that contribute to an observable situation or a particular event. Understanding constraints permits us to choose strategies that have a chance of success.

The relevant constraints in my annual diet saga range all the way from the genetic disposition of Clarke males to whether my knees will hold out for another year of jogging around the park. Also important are the weekly rounds of lunch meetings with colleagues and the holiday-feast routines of a large family. If I am serious about getting in shape, I will need to pursue strategies that appeal to my personal routines and that comply with my professional responsibilities. They will also have to take into account family obligations and rhythms.

It is the same with school violence. The boys in the scuffle will respond to the teacher's intervention in ways that vary according to their personal temperaments, their histories of family problem solving, and their relationships to the teacher. School rules on fighting will shape the teacher's and students' responses, as will their understanding of the climate in the community toward violence.

We need to think strategically. What are the points in activity cycles that offer the most potential for action? What are the most promising leverage points for change? How might we create disturbances at different levels of scale to increase the positive feedback and amplify change? What are the constraints that contribute to the maintenance of the status quo? What options for action present themselves as opportunities for change? As we decide what responses are available, we assess the relative merits of options. I may decide that there is no sense in trying to convert a particular individual on issues of gay rights, but he might be an ally on affordable housing, for example. In the legislative process, if a bill is already in committee, there is no need to send off blanket messages to Congress; the people to focus on are the ones with seats on the relevant committee.

Let us now turn to some examples and use these lenses to examine elements of the change process in particular situations.

On Seeing Choices

A Zen master was conducting a lesson with a neophyte, coaxing him toward enlightenment. He held a stick above the cowering pupil's head and said through clenched teeth, "If you say this stick is real, I will strike you with it. If you say this stick is not real, I will strike you with it. If you say nothing, I will strike you with it." The miserable youth braced himself for the blow, beads of sweat shivering on his brow. Then, suddenly, he straightened up and removed the stick from the master's hand. (G. Bateson 1999, 208)

A young colleague returned to work after taking a week to be with his wife and first-born child. He positively glowed, strewing pictures in his wake that testified to his full involvement in the birthing process and left the bachelors demanding a "need-to-know" status in the conversation.

A few weeks later, he was struggling with the realities that would soon face them as his wife neared the end of her maternity leave. They had no other choice, he reported. She had to return to work, but they were having difficulty finding appropriate childcare. He made this last statement with a grimace that conveyed a hint of contempt for parents who left their children with strangers and revealed, perhaps, that he and his wife might be having difficulties framing the issue in ways that implicated them both equally in the solution.

From a distance, the problem didn't seem that complex. "Let her quit her job, or take a lower-paying one that permits her to spend more time with the baby." "Move closer to your work, in a house with a more manageable mortgage, so that you can be more available and money is not such a problem." "Take her mom up on the offer to move in with you." These were some of the suggestions, offered with the philosophical detachment that we reserve for other people's problems. He dismissed these and other, equally plausible solutions with a wave of his hand that indicated that they were ravings of the deranged.

All of these solutions to his problem would have appeared reasonable to him if they had been offered to someone else. However, in his case, there were many reasons why they were not acceptable. This is the way it is with innovation; it is easier to see how others should change than to make changes ourselves.

But, in fact, all successful change efforts require individuals to change themselves, and if the problem being addressed is a serious one, one that goes to the heart of important relationships or that threatens foundations of faith or visions of the future, merely *seeing* that there are choices is usually part of the problem. It is very difficult for most of us to see our options because they are obscured by our assumptions.

You may be familiar with the nine-dot problem on the next page. The task is simple. Place your pen on one of the dots and then, without lifting it from the paper, join all nine dots with four straight lines. Try it.

Most people have difficulty with the task because of their assumption that they cannot go outside the box. This may, in fact, be the origin of the phrase, "thinking outside the box." Check the solution on page 93.

•   •   •

•   •   •

•   •   •

Momentous events often provide the opportunity for individuals to think outside the box, to see options that we hadn't seen before. The birth of a baby, the death of a loved one, natural calamities like flood and fire, terrorist attacks–these throw new light on established ways of thinking and comfortable routines that we may not have been aware were shaping our daily activity. Suddenly we see the world and our place in it differently. *Is* the world different, or is it just us? It doesn't matter; if we conduct our lives differently, then the world is different for us.

Thoreau said, "Things don't change; people do." And Maya Angelou said, "If you can't change something, change the way you think about it."

For my young friend, the arrival of the newborn prompted such a shift in perception. Before that day, the big house and its heavy mortgage, and the long commute, which dictated so many other aspects of the day, both seemed important. Now, the requirements of the baby have changed his priorities, and he and his wife are beginning to consider options that were not visible before. Of course, the choices were always there, but they had not seen them because of assumptions that shaped their decision making.

It is not easy to apply this lesson without the benefit of drama or trauma, but if we can get in the habit of attempting to see all the possibilities, we can at least begin to see what assumptions are shaping our decision making.

Here is the drill.

➤ Name the problem.
  ○ List all possible solutions.
    ▪ Identify the constraints that shape your selection of solutions.
      • Reexamine your priorities and change the name of the problem.

Applied to the *10-Pounds-Every-January 1-Problem:*
➤ The problem: too fat
  ○ Solutions: join a gym; exercise regularly
    ▪ Constraints: schedule tightly booked; hard to change without disrupting everything else
      • Reexamination: take stock of priorities
➤ The problem: unhealthy lifestyle
  ○ Solutions: join Weight Watchers; stop attending lunch meetings; eat apples and oranges at desk; inform family and friends of need for support (public disclosure, like AA)
    ▪ Constraints: no slack in the family routine, so fast food and snacks the best way to cope with the schedule; not in control of meetings, so cannot avoid lunch settings
      • Reexamination: pay attention to what matters, prioritize
➤ The problem: too much mental and material clutter; need to simplify, organize!
  ○ Solution: seriously assess career options, opportunities for a serious move
    ▪ etc.
      • etc.

Applied to *middle-school violence:*
➤ The problem: interpersonal disputes
  ○ Solutions: detention, referral, expulsion; anger management for the boys
    ▪ Constraints: time required to work with individual kids; number of kids with problems; number of kids in school, classes
      • Reexamination: focus on resources and reassess problem

➤ The problem: gang violence
  ○ Solutions: home visits to discuss situation with parents;
    "It takes a village" program of multiple mentoring
    ▪ Constraints: schedules of parents don't jibe with school
      schedules; single-parent homes or two parents working;
      lack of money for districtwide program
      · Reexamination: focus on spheres of influence

Math Attack

The chair of the math department at a new high school gets a grant
to implement an innovative math program. The funding pays for him
to attend conferences and visit sites where the new curriculum is in
place. He reads all the research, receives training from master teachers, and becomes a skilled practitioner in the approach. The grant
permits him to purchase sets of materials for the school. He proudly
and enthusiastically presents the new curriculum to the math faculty
at the first meeting of the school year, along with a plan for phasing
the program into all their classes. He is amazed that they are not cap-
tivated by the new materials and innovative approach. A few are cau-
tiously curious. Others are downright suspicious. One or two express
open resistance to the whole idea. He perseveres with a modified plan
for implementation, beginning with the less resistant faculty. He organizes workshops to present the program and give people a chance
to learn more about it. Attendance is mandatory, but engagement is
low, and the veteran teachers don't even make a pretense of interest.
The semester wears on, and events unfold very differently from the
way he had imagined. The department splits into two camps—those
using the new program and those continuing with their tried and true
methods. He continues to push for adoption of the program, but the
grumbling grows into defiance. He has a rebellion on his hands. The
administration of the school threatens to step in and take control of
the department. The chair calls in a team of facilitators from a nearby
university, and over a period of weeks they work with the faculty to
reduce tensions. A workable peace is developed, and they finish out

the year. Some of the teachers have become skilled practitioners in the new method. Others have become interested and promise to explore the possibility of using it next year. A few teachers are transferring to other schools. And a few remain unfazed by the whole thing; they will continue with methods they have used for years. The chair remains in his position, teaching with the new method but not working too hard at recruiting faculty to the approach; as far as his administrative responsibilities are concerned, he is basically marking time until retirement. The university consulting team publishes an article on the experience.

The story, a parable of curriculum adoption in public schools, is based on consulting work by May Lowry (2000). Let's examine the situation using the seven elements of change. Respond to each of the following items and discuss your answers with a colleague.

---

1. Whose fault is it that the math innovation has failed?
   a. The chair of the department
   b. The faculty
   c. The administration
   d. The university consultants
   e. All of the above

2. What is the issue here?
   a. Contemporary approaches to education—the tendency to swing from one fad to another
   b. Theory-practice tensions and the pace of innovation adoption
   c. The hierarchical structure of educational institutions
   d. The conservative impulse of human nature

3. What is the problem?
   a. Authoritarian leadership style of the chair
   b. Unsupportive school administration
   c. Ineffectual consultants—too little too late
   d. Uncooperative, unimaginative faculty

4. What constraints account for the outcome of the innovation?
   a. The history of interaction between the chair and the faculty
   b. The pace of the attempted change
   c. The rhythms of the school year
   d. The differing ages, career trajectories, and personal interests and concerns of the faculty
   e. The demands on the teachers—standardized tests, committee assignments, extracurricular responsibilities, etc.—and their comfort with their own routines
   f. All of the above

The important thing with this exercise is to get to the point where you can see different perspectives on a situation, where you can explore events and circumstances with different lenses. But this does not mean abdicating your own point of view, arriving at the point where you lose your ability to act because you understand everything all too well. In fact, just the opposite. I want to arrive at an understanding of others' points of view so that I can work more effectively with them to accomplish the changes I think are important.

So, in the analysis that follows, I do not attempt objectivity, which is in any case impossible. Rather, I approach the analysis as a partisan of the new math curriculum, as if I were the chair or, more likely, the university consultant, working to move the math department toward a new way of teaching their subject. I am less interested in abstract analysis of this sort of situation than I am in creating a foundation for continuing the change effort. I have therefore responded as if I were a player in this drama committed to long-term solutions.

What follows, then, are my answers and my rationale. Your answers and rationale will vary depending on your own experience in these kinds of situations. But the important thing is to have a coherent rationale for your responses. What is the systemic argument you would provide in each case to support your answer?

1. Whose fault is it that the math innovation has failed?
   a. The chair of the department
   b. The faculty
   c. The administration
   d. The university consultants
   e. All of the above

My answer is *a. The chair of the department,* but with two qualifications. First, I would not say the innovation has failed. Innovations and reforms may be labeled failures by newspaper reporters, critics, or proponents who decide to throw in the towel—people with an "all or nothing" approach to change. But the kind of movement reported in the vignette would be counted as a respectable effort by most seasoned change agents. After all, several teachers have adopted the new curriculum, and several others are reported to be curious about it.

And second, I am very careful in my choice of words when I discuss these sorts of activities. *Fault,* like *blame,* invokes a causal universe, and in any human endeavor there are too many complexities to assign single causes for events. It is a rare and dirty situation when blame must be lodged, and it is done then for political reasons. The negative reverberations from the event last forever; don't work to assign blame to anyone with whom you may want to work in the future.

But, given the limited view we have, I would say that the chair was in the best position to make the math innovation work, and he made several crucial errors. Among them, two stand out. First, he made serious miscalculations about the activity cycles operating here. Most veteran teachers are well organized for fall by midsummer, or they at least know the broad outlines of how they are going to approach the year. The newer teachers or individuals looking for some new ideas would probably be the only ones interested in trying a new curriculum on such short notice. His most significant error, however, was his failure to gauge the players' responses to the proposed innovation. Fundamentally, this is his primary job—to learn the faculty. Theirs is to learn the program. He didn't do his job, so they did not do theirs.

2. What is the issue here?
   a. Contemporary approaches to education—the tendency to swing from one fad to another
   b. Theory-practice tensions and the pace of innovation adoption
   c. The hierarchical structure of educational institutions
   d. The conservative impulse of human nature

All these answers have merit, but based on the information available, and assuming that I would use this as part of my continuing efforts to work with the department, my answer is *d. The conservative impulse of human nature*. It is natural to avoid change, and all efforts at instructional innovation carry with them the implicit criticism of what teachers are doing now (Evans 1996). My approach would be to work on this person-to-person, trying to heal the wounds, and to see if I could get people talking to each other in professional and thoughtful ways. The other choices require some attention. It is true that new math methods come along on a regular basis and that theorists tend to propose changes long before they are adopted by classroom teachers. It is also true that many decisions in schools are tinged with more hierarchical hubris than most of us would prefer, and so I would keep these issues in mind as I worked. But, primarily, I would attempt to respect everyone's reasons for wanting to continue teaching the way they were used to teaching, while trying to open a dialogue so that thoughtful discussion of alternatives might ensue. And, of course, I would keep reminding myself that *I* am the one who will have to do most of the changing.

3. What is the problem?
   a. Authoritarian leadership style of the chair
   b. Unsupportive school administration
   c. Ineffectual consultants—too little too late
   d. Uncooperative, unimaginative faculty

I see glimpses of truth in all these choices, but I refuse to answer on the grounds that they involve me in name calling and blame mongering. In professional discourse—that is, exchanges between professionals that are conducted professionally—we do better if we stick with descriptive phrases that focus on making clear what happened and that give people credit for what they were trying to do, even if the outcomes were less than they desired.

And, as a player in the process, I want to create opportunities for such conversation. In the event, I would step out first, attempting to articulate how I have contributed to the problem and identifying options that I didn't see or failed to select. I would speculate on changes I might pursue in the future.

Easier said than done, I'm afraid, and not without risk, depending on who the players are and what is at stake politically. If I am not in a position to orchestrate such a discussion, I nevertheless attempt to frame events and players using the same lenses and to conduct myself with my values and long-term goals in mind.

4. What constraints account for the outcome of the innovation?
   a. The history of interaction between the chair and the faculty
   b. The pace of the attempted change
   c. The rhythms of the school year
   d. The differing ages, career trajectories, and personal interests and concerns of the faculty
   e. The demands on the teachers—standardized tests, committee assignments, extracurricular responsibilities, etc.—and their comfort with their own routines
   f. All of the above

My answer is *f. All of the above.* Constraints, by their very nature, are partial answers to the question of "Why did this happen?" All of these factors undoubtedly played a role in the observed events. We would need more information to speak authoritatively about this specific situation, but as we work for change in our classrooms and schools these are the sorts of constraints we need to pay attention to as we work for change.

Conclusions and Continuations: Metalogue

There cannot really be a conclusion to this essay, because the topic is life, and life goes on. There are no bottom lines, ultimate solutions, final acts–merely life, punctuated differently by different narrators and observers. Gregory Bateson recognized this and dealt with the indeterminacy of things by developing the metalogue (1999, 3–58). His metalogues are always conversations between a father and daughter, prompted by the daughter's attempts to understand some inconsistency in the world. They were written to illuminate problematic issues without proposing solutions; in the best ones, the structure of the conversation mirrors the problem being discussed. That is, they are examples of themselves.

The metalogue that follows does not measure up to Bateson's criteria in several ways, and the fact that I follow it with an explanation violates the whole premise. But it provides a change of pace from the foregoing argument and therefore might appeal to the reader who is struggling to make connections between systems theory and that most challenging of all teaching jobs, raising children.

Allowances

Son: Dad, why does everything cost so much?

Father: What's the problem?

S: No money.

F: Ah, yes. Your allowance ran out sooner than expected. Been there myself. Got a plan?

S: I was thinking of mowing lawns maybe.

F: Hmmm . . . Do you have a lawn mower?

S: Well, I was thinking I could use ours.

F: I'm not sure it would hold up for very long. You'll need a new one.

S: No money.

F: I see what you mean. Well, you could save up your allowance.

S: Yeah, but by the time I had enough for a new mower, it would be winter. Besides, what I need right now is a new baseball mitt.

F: Ah. What's wrong with the one you've got?

S: It doesn't work so good. I keep missing grounders.

F: Know the feeling. Been there myself.

S: Really? What did you do about it?

F: Well, not much. Decided I wasn't cut out to be a baseball player after all.

S: You wanted to be a baseball player, too?

F: Yes, of course. But I never could find anyone to practice with.

S: I know. The big kids won't let me play with them, and all my friends are into skateboarding. But I really, *really* want to be a baseball player.

F: Well, you've got to practice.

S: Yeah. What are you doing right now?

F: Nothing important. Want to catch a few?

What is your interpretation of this conversation? How would you analyze it using the seven elements? Would you say the boy's problem is money—lack of money, unfair distribution of money, learning how to use money? Or is the problem peer pressure? Or immaturity? And the issue? Father-son relationships? Sports as a defining element in the cultural psyche? The materialism and self-centeredness of the male of the species?

In a systems view of the world, all understandings are emergent. Your views on allowances and child rearing, your experiences growing up, and your attitude toward organized sports—all these topics and more will shape your opinion about the exchange. There are no right answers, and answers that seem right at the time will be questioned later. Just as we will continue to second-guess ourselves after making mistakes.

But then, that's life.

Solution to the Nine-Dot Problem

The key is to think "outside the box"—to go beyond the box formed by dots as you connect them. Most people assume that you have to stay within the box; their attempts at solving the problem are thwarted by their assumptions, not by any factor inherent in the problem itself.

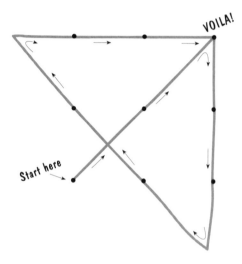

4 Changing Things: The Rhythms of Reform and Resistance

This essay explores the dynamics of change, especially grass-roots change initiated by individuals. It is intended to provide insight and guidance, not prescription for reform. I use systems theory as the lens for examining change efforts and as a framework for action, but I recognize that every situation is unique and that generalized guide-lines are of limited usefulness. On the other hand, reform begins with the reformer, a variation on the old saying, "If you want something done right, do it yourself." So the success of this essay depends on your being able to put yourself in the role of change agent. To help you get started I provide the following questionnaire for you to re-spond to.

Have you ever been totally energized and focused on a school project or a community cause, only to discover that others do not share your enthusiasm for the endeavor? In the space provided give a title to your project, and then assess the effort by scoring the state-ments according to the extent to which they represent your experi-ence. Give each item a score of 1 to 5; the higher the score, the more you see yourself in the statement. It is useful to add specific notes, with names, dates, etc., that describe your particular experience.

Title: _____

1. _____ Black hole! The more time and energy I put into it, the more it takes to keep it running.
2. _____ Herding cats! Lots of good people wanting to help out, but everyone has a different idea of what should be done.
3. _____ Stubborn, suspicious, or just plain lazy! Some people just won't take the time to try new ways of thinking and acting.
4. _____ Tender toes and thin skin! Seems like I am forever stepping on toes and treading on private turf.
5. _____ Officious bureaucrats and meddling administrators! Everyone thinks they have authority over some aspect of my life or of the project. Everything seems to involve a negotiation of who is in charge.
6. _____ Mysterious rules and regulations! I keep bumping up against rules and regulations that serve no discernible purpose. Even the individuals enforcing them do not seem to remember why they were put in place.
7. _____ Ruts, routines, and rituals! People seem to be locked into habits of body and mind that prevent flexible reactions to problems.
8. _____ Jealous backsliders! Family and friends complain that I devote more time to the project than I do to them. And even my closest allies seem to lack the salt and vinegar and attention spans required to get the job done. I have become the enforcer of participation; when they see me coming, they duck into restrooms and phone booths.
9. _____ Ingrates and opportunists! I am amazed at the number of people who would benefit directly from this effort who seem totally uninterested in pitching in.
10. _____ Scarcity of resources! A good cause and yet no one seems to have time or money to make it happen.

The tone may seem exaggerated and melodramatic, but I suspect that some of these will strike a nerve, especially if you tend toward the passionate approach to life. The list is not intended to be exhaustive; I merely want to evoke some reactions that will permit you to connect the analysis that follows with your own personal change efforts.

If we are outraged by an injustice, if we care deeply about a cause, or if we are merely working doggedly for something we believe in, we cannot help but get crosswise of others, and the reason is simple: Things are the way they are *not* by accident, and someone is benefiting directly or indirectly from the status quo. Any attempt to change things, no matter how obvious the benefits, will chafe someone. For some, it will be because our cause and their cause are in direct conflict or competition for resources. For others, it will be because our efforts disrupt their daily routine and comfortable habits.

Whatever the reason, we will discover that people are not sitting idly by, like extras on a Hollywood set, waiting for us to cast them in our personal drama. The world just does not function that way. So if we are determined to change things, we need a framework for understanding change and a set of strategies for stimulating change efforts.

My goal here is to provide such a framework and to suggest some strategies; to provide context I will tell two stories that illustrate the sorts of situations I have in mind. The first is a fictionalized account of a teacher who is attempting to implement an experiential approach to literacy instruction in an elementary school, and the second is a description of my efforts to get a church to live up to its activist ideals.

Story 1: School Reform

The field of language and literacy education has long been a hotbed of debate, with advocates of direct instruction versus advocates of experiential learning. The former tend to line up behind phonics and basal readers and the latter behind whole language. In the late 1980s and early 1990s Nancy Commins and I were involved in a number of projects in the greater Denver area in which this debate energized the discussion, for both language-arts teachers and bilingual teachers. We developed an analysis of the situation using a systems perspective of the debate (Clarke and Commins 1993). The following is based on that work. Commins continues to work for school/community reform in multilingual contexts (Miramontes, Nadeau, and Commins 1997).

The debate has cooled off considerably, although the issues remain central to discussions of curriculum and assessment. How should learning be organized—around predetermined goals and structured activities or oriented toward learner choice and autonomy? The details of the debate are not of central interest here; what is important to understand is the dynamic that develops when a teacher attempts to do things differently than his or her colleagues. What follows is a fictionalized account by one teacher, whom I refer to as Scott, a pseudonym.

> I am a fifth-grade whole language teacher. Today I am prepared for the students to arrive with drafts of an essay they have been working on as part of a class study of family and community. The students will do peer editing in small groups, giving each other feedback on the essays in preparation for publication and dissemination to families, friends, and school officials. This is just one stage in a rather lengthy process that developed out of a class discussion of the nature of culture following a class visit by an anthropologist, the parent of one of the children. The students had been intrigued by the assertion that their own way of life was just one of an infinite number of possibilities, and I suggested that they do some anthropological fieldwork. They wanted to study an exotic culture in the Amazon jungle, but I persuaded them to start closer to home, so we developed a plan for fieldwork in the community surrounding the school and with their own families. The class is composed of African American, Anglo, Latino, and Asian children, and this is just one example of my efforts to draw on students' personal knowledge, build solidarity among them, and use an examination of cultural differences to make explicit the difficulties they have in adjusting to school.

With my help, the students constructed interview schedules and questions to guide them in their work and developed rules of "triangulation" and protocols for the acceptability of data. I used *Ways with Words* (Heath 1983), especially chapter 9, for suggestions on how to orchestrate this sort of activity with students. They completed several drafts of the essays over a period of two weeks, and today's version is to be a near-final draft of their description of their own culture and their connections to the community. The students had wanted to continue their research into the next week, but I decided we needed to get on with other tasks. Also, other teachers on my team were growing impatient for them to continue working on a series of grammar and mechanics worksheets to prepare them for the district tests that were fast approaching. So I asked them to finish up the draft they were working on and bring the essays to class.

On this particular day a number of events occur that illustrates the difficulties I have in implementing whole language instruction; I will describe four that show the range of problems that I deal with regularly.

First are the disruptions of some of the students. Jantar, usually a conscientious student, is struggling with the lack of structure of this work and with my insistence that the students develop their own rules and procedures. Today, she does not bring her essay to school. Several other students are slow to settle down to work in their peer-editing groups. If I had fewer students in the class I might be able to work more sensitively with each one, but basically I see these behaviors as evidence of students' reluctance to take responsibility for their own learning. By fifth grade they are comfortable with the customary roles of controlling teacher and compliant students; the way I have organized this class requires them to assume more responsibility and to take the initiative in areas where before they have only had to follow directions.

Second, the PE teacher appears in the doorway to announce a special assembly on physical fitness; apparently, a mix-up in scheduling resulted in the assembly being moved to this particular day and time, rather than the one we had agreed on. This is no one's fault, really, but it illustrates the lack of autonomy that I have in organizing class time. Depending on the season, there are always special programs and schoolwide events that have to be juggled with the schedules of PE, music, art, gifted and talented programs, etc. I am not alone in my dislike of the fragmented school day, but I do believe that there are requirements of a whole language classroom that are particularly antithetical to the syncopated teaching schedule of the school. I admit to being a bit sensitive on this topic, but I cannot help thinking that my colleagues could work a bit harder on helping me find ways of opening up the day for longer periods of discretionary time. I get the feeling that they view my requests for more time and autonomy as implicit criticism of the way they are used to teaching.

Third, the principal calls me into her office to express skepticism that the students will be ready for the district tests if I do not begin to bear down on the skills worksheets. She is under pressure from central administration to improve the building's test scores, and she passes this pressure along to the teachers. To give her credit, she has been supportive of my efforts to move away from basal readers and workbooks, but the bottom line for all administrators is the school's test scores, and now, rather than take a stand against test-driven curricula, she is leaning on me a bit to conform to the accepted practice of teaching to the test.

And fourth, a person from transportation services calls to confirm the bus to the museum but mentions that we will have to return before 1:30 in order to accommodate the regular bus schedules. This phone call from an anonymous clerk in the transportation office symbolizes the way that the tail wags the dog in our district; the primary purpose of schools, the education of children, often gets subordinated to the requirements of the motor pool or custodial services. I don't want to appear to demand that district bus schedules revolve around my needs, but even in large urban districts there ought to be ways to see that academic considerations mandate organizational functioning, instead of the other way around. The excursion to the museum should have come earlier in the project, when the children were still collecting data for their reports, but another schedule change required us to postpone the trip. Now it looks as if we will have an hour less than I had planned, and this will really put us in a bind. The children have generated questions they wanted to answer concerning culture in general and lifestyles of certain groups in particular. The museum trip was to have afforded them the opportunity to organize their own ways of finding answers to questions, but now I will either have to structure the trip in much more detail to make sure they get the answers they need or permit them to experience the frustration of running out of time.

Schools are complex organizations in which the routines and rhythms of many people have to be accommodated. Typically, this is accomplished without everyone realizing the extent to which all teachers have to conform to school norms in their daily teaching behavior. It is not an exaggeration to say that any teaching method that depends on teacher autonomy and student choice will ultimately challenge every aspect of the system—curriculum and materials decisions; the organization of the school day; the allocation of such basic resources as people, time, space, materials, and money—and in so doing provide implicit criticism of the system itself and the typical practices of most teachers.

This observation may at first glance seem startling; however, it is the nature of change to challenge the status quo. Teachers may not be accustomed to seeing themselves as educational reformers because they believe that they need only focus on the pedagogical merits of their proposals in order to win acceptance for their points of view. Or they may assume that by working from their classrooms they can cause ripples in the system that will gradually and naturally lead to wider changes. This assumption is evident in a review of an earlier draft of this essay by Kenneth Goodman. Taking exception to the characterization of whole language as a reform movement, he wrote:

The "advice" to whole language teachers implies that their main concern is changing the system—which really can't be changed anyway—

what it misses is that they are in fact participating in a grass roots movement which starts change in the classroom and moves out from there—a movement rooted in knowledge and dedicated to kids.

It is true that most teachers have as their main concern the effective instruction of their students, but it is precisely because whole language is a grassroots movement that teachers need to understand how their behavior will require changes in systems beyond the classroom. The same is true for other pedagogical innovations such as bilingual education and experiential teaching.

Story 2: Church Reform

Story 2 relates a similar situation, but this time a church is the focus of attention. As in the whole language example, the changes called for in the church by the activists seemed to be merely ones that would bring the practices of the institution in line with its avowed philosophy—no big deal, or so it seemed. This is a brief summary of my efforts to create a more inclusive environment for gays and lesbians in a large urban church.

We moved to Park Hill in 1977 and began attending Park Hill United Methodist Church shortly thereafter. We have been involved in the church in a variety of ways over the years—in the youth group, social-action committees, Habitat for Humanity, etc.—and my wife has been active in the Park Hill Art Club, which meets at the church. Our three children participated in the youth group during their adolescent years, and our son continued to play basketball there during open gym nights when he was home from college. My mother moved into the neighborhood a number of years ago and is now a member of the church also.

The church has about 900 members and averages 350 in attendance at the two services on Sundays. The staff consists of three ministers, a youth director, a business manager, two secretaries, and numerous volunteers. Located on Montview Boulevard at Glencoe in east Denver, the church is racially mixed and has been active in civil rights since the 1950s. It distinguished itself in the neighborhood efforts at fighting segregation in the early 1960s, and many members of the congregation are counted among the national civil-rights leadership. Martin Luther King Jr. preached here, for example, and whenever national leaders come to town they pay homage to the church's history. The head minister offered the invocation during President Clinton's visit to Denver, and Andrew Young spoke from the pulpit during a tour to promote his book *An Easy Burden* (1996). Oprah Winfrey invited one of our members onto her show to talk about her experiences as one of the seven children in Little Rock who walked through venomous crowds to integrate the schools in Arkansas. Another member of the congregation was a baseball star in the Negro Leagues and has been the subject of book and television histories.

The church is the center of activity throughout the week. The Children's Center provides preschool and after-school day care and education programming for about 80 children. On Wednesday and Friday evenings the gym is full of neighborhood youth, mostly African American males between the ages of 14 and 25, who come to play pick-up basketball under the loose supervision of a volunteer. Saturdays a minority-youth counseling program meets, and the Boy Scouts use the Balcony Parlor one night a week. The church has an active youth program, with some 40 young people involved in a mid-high group and a high-school group. They meet every Sunday evening; work on neighborhood projects; and every summer travel to distant parts to hammer, scrape, and paint in service projects. The choir, a particular source of pride in the church (and a potent force in any debate that might affect the worship service), rehearses every Thursday night and produces numerous special programs in addition to their weekly duties on Sunday.

This is a liberal, activist church, proud of its leadership in social-justice issues. It was clear to me, however, that our support of civil rights and our stance of inclusion did not extend to sexual orientation. As cochair of the social-concerns work area, I mounted an effort to get the church to become a Reconciling Congregation, the United Methodist designation for churches that are officially and actively supportive of gays and lesbians. We held a number of forums during the Sunday-school hour between services that were very well attended. We invited nationally recognized experts as guest speakers, and we heard personal testimonies during church services from members of the congregation whose children were gay or lesbian.

It was all very invigorating and positive. At the end of a four-month process, I sent in a piece for the church newsletter, summarizing the process and identifying the date on which we would bring the matter to a vote of the congregation. Several days later, I received it back in the mail, along with a scribbled note from the pastor explaining that he had pulled the piece and asking to talk to me. By that time, the deadline for the newsletter had passed. When we did manage to meet he explained his view, which was that the congregation wasn't ready for the sort of program I envisioned and that it would be too divisive. Thus ended what had appeared to be a promising chance for change. I was stunned. As I contemplated this frustrating turn of events, Mary (a pseudonym), a diminutive elderly church activist, put her arm around me and said, "Don't be discouraged. It just wasn't the right time. We'll have to wait for a few more members of the congregation to die."

I was appalled by her words, especially given the contrast between the beatific image she projected and the brutality of her assessment. Could this be the same gentle human being who had responded so understandingly and persuasively to those elderly members when they revealed ignorance bordering on bigotry?

In retrospect I understand that she was merely articulating the natural order of change. Each generation carries forth with the unfinished business of the previous generation and in turn leaves work undone for those who follow. She was dedicated to change here and now, but she also understood the issues involved and knew that the older members of the congregation were not ready for so dramatic and public a change. They were content with the level of tolerance in the church, and because they constituted a majority of the congregation, *now* was not the time for change. What was a problem for me was an acceptable state of affairs for them—and for the majority of the congregation.

Systems and System Change

These two stories capture for me the sorts of frustrations I have experienced or observed others experiencing over the years, and they illustrate important aspects of systems functioning that activists need to understand if we are to achieve reasonable success in our efforts *and* maintain some level of sanity and faith in our fellow human beings.

An important decision we need to make early on is what kind of change we require. Will small changes be sufficient, or do we require systemic changes? Do we want the system to do what it does better, or do we want it to do different things? It is like the work we require of the thermostat in the home. There are times when what we want is for the heating system to work more effectively to keep the house at a particular temperature, and there are other times when we want the temperature changed. These are referred to as first-order and second-order changes, respectively (Watzlawick, Weakland, and Fisch 1974). Ronald Heifetz discusses the same distinction but focuses on the work required. When we believe that what is required is more efficient implementation of existing procedures, we need "technical" work. But there are times when we need to change our whole attitude and approach, and this he refers to as "adaptive" work (Heifetz 1994, 69–100).

The most important problems require adaptive work on the part of the participants—second-order change. Because of the profound nature of the change required, conventional approaches—convening meetings, setting goals, putting procedures and policies in place, and getting to work—are likely to be counterproductive. The assumption that people merely need to be informed of the changes and they will adjust their activities to conform to the new regimen is unrealistic.

What would seem to be merely a matter of effective communication turns out to be far more complicated.

Even small changes require some adaptive work by participants, because change always carries with it a criticism of the way things were being done before. And in the event of major change, it is not unreasonable for people to feel that their fundamental values, perhaps even their identities as members of the organization, are being challenged. Awareness of this reaction, and of systemic responses in general, permits change agents to adjust their strategies appropriately.

The perspective presented here is based on systems theory, especially as developed by Gregory Bateson (1999). A system may be defined as a self-governing organism that functions with feedback from the environment. In other words, all living organisms (including, of course, humans) and aggregates of living organisms (such as families, classrooms, and schools) are considered systems and are viewed as sharing certain fundamental characteristics. Let me summarize these characteristics briefly.

Systems are self-governing.

Systems use feedback from the environment to maintain equilibrium. This means that they naturally self-correct, with the result that they resist change. In the case of people, this tendency can be seen in the efforts to resist external pressures to change even minute details of "normal" ways of doing things. This is a natural response, but it is often cast as "resistance" by change agents.

In the school vignette, Jantar's failure to complete her assignment might be a natural reaction to a task that lacked a comfortable amount of structure. She may feel threatened by the prospect of conferencing with peers, choosing to avoid the whole issue by not bringing in her paper. Similarly, the difficulties encountered by the teacher in efforts to gain more control over the school day represent the natural tendency of individuals to do things in customary ways; whether one is a janitor, transportation employee, teacher, or principal, one develops habitual ways of getting through the day, and requests for deviations from routine meet with at least initial resistance. From a systems perspective, these events represent the natural tendency of systems to function toward stability.

The same could be said about individuals in the church story; church was not a place where most of them expected to have to confront the issue of sexual orientation, and they preferred to keep it that way. Or perhaps they believed that the church had achieved an appropriate level of explicit discussion and recognition of these sorts of matters. They would view proposals for becoming a "Reconciling Congregation" as excessive.

Notice that whether we are discussing individuals or institutions, the perspective is the same. This is because the same principles operate at many levels of scale. Schools and churches are, of course, among the most conservative organizations in society, but if you observe any institution over a period of time, you will discover patterns of activity that function to maintain the status quo.

Systems exhibit immanent mind.

That is, there is no locus of unilateral control. Rather, mechanisms of control are distributed throughout the system. This contrasts with the popular belief that someone is in charge. All parts of the system operate within discernible limits, and therefore each part contributes to the overall stability of the system. Systems function the way they do because of a subtle, ubiquitous adherence to what we might think of as a "thermostatic setting" for behavior. Power is always negotiated.

Principals are not in control of their schools, or they would never have difficulty with teachers who choose to teach in ways that do not conform to district guidelines. Similarly, teachers do not exercise unilateral control over their classes; if they did, there would be no need for discussion of classroom management or student discipline.

Ministers are not in control of their congregations, and the existence of scripture or church doctrine that asserts the universal acceptability of all human beings does not translate into a mandate for inclusion. As in any organization, there are formal lines of authority and decision making, and there are informal codes of conduct and established ways of doing things.

This is an important insight, and it helps us understand a lot about the way society and institutions function. We talk about the culture of institutions, for example, and the unwritten rules that members seem to follow. It also helps explain why change does not occur just because the individual "in charge" desires it. Recently, this aspect of complex functioning has been studied under the label of "emergence" (Johnson 2001). People go about their business every day, doing what they believe to be normal and reasonable. Viewed from a distance, however, the patterns that emerge for the organization of which they are a part would seem to reveal hierarchically organized behavior, a top-down order, when, in fact, there is no single source of unilateral control. The control is immanent and emergent, a natural functioning of people attending to what they think is important.

Systems function to continue functioning.

In the goal-oriented world of our modern technological society, we are accustomed to thinking of institutions as having a purpose. However, systems have no purpose, in the usual sense of the term; they function to maintain themselves, to survive. This is not to say that we cannot ascribe purpose to systems; in fact, it is accurate to say that systems have as many purposes as there are individuals to perceive them.

For example, the teacher in our narrative was frustrated by the bureaucratic roadblocks to attempts to integrate authentic experiences into the school day, asserting that the "true purpose" of schools, to educate children, has been subordinated to the mundane concerns of mere functionaries in the system. The principal and the person in the transportation office might take exception to his characterization of the situation, however. From their point of view, their actions constitute appropriate efforts at furthering the goals of the system.

Careful observation of people's priorities as revealed by their behaviors on a day-to-day basis reveals that everyone in the school—children, janitors, teachers, bus drivers, parents, administrators, etc.—has a different perception of the purpose of schools. For some their purpose may be to provide an education, but for others the primary purpose of schools is to supply a paycheck or an avenue to retirement, or to provide day care, or to prepare workers for the needs of business. And each individual believes not only that his or her behavior is consistent with this purpose but also that this is an important purpose of schools.

The same is true for churches. They provide income for a large number of people whose daily activities are focused as much on the mundane matters of keeping a business running as on spiritual fidelity. The majority of the congregation participate in the life of the church only on Sundays, but this does not diminish their sense of ownership and investment in its daily functioning. It is reasonable to expect that there will be differences of engagement and participation for people depending on whether they are clergy, staff, volunteers, or regular Sunday attendees. Each category will see the purpose of church differently.

The importance of this assertion is that it underscores the need for sensitive interactions with others and the potential for miscommunication. Most of us prefer to proceed directly to focal issues without first clarifying the assumptions that govern people's behavior. Primary among these are fundamental beliefs about the nature and purposes of school and church. There are no ultimate, universally valid purposes for systems, only people's perceptions of purposes. This is not to deny that certain groups of people have more power and enjoy more privileges than others and that the system can therefore be said to reflect their purposes more than it does other people's purposes. However, "the system," as this phrase is commonly used, is but one manifestation of systems functioning in general, and everyone contributes in different ways to the maintenance of the status quo.

Events in systems have multiple causes.

Actually, it is more accurate to speak of constraints, rather than causes. We may be able to identify one event that occurred immediately before another, but because of the complex interaction of elements, to understand why something happened we must understand the confluence of events and the pressures of constraints that preceded the event we are interested in. Scott, the whole language teacher, focused in on a single day in his attempt to understand difficulties in implementing his approach to literacy, and this permitted him to identify specific people who contributed to problems he was having. But there was no single cause for any one of the events, merely a pattern of obstacles to his attempts at reform. The principal may be responding to pressure for higher test scores, but a number of other factors contribute to the difficulties he was experiencing—for example, the history of the district with regard to teaching methods, curriculum decisions, and general decision making.

In the case of the church story, it would be easy to indict the senior minister, both for defeating the initiative and for not openly engaging us in the debate. Immediately after the event I did, in fact, harbor such feelings. However, in retrospect, I can see many causes for the outcome, and the minister's actions are merely the most visible. I now see that I was familiar only with a portion of the congregation and particularly out of touch with the older members, especially the benefactors of the church, individuals whose generosity funded many of the programs I supported. I suspect that they were not in favor of the initiative, but I cannot be certain. It is also the case that the large turnout we enjoyed during the information sessions cannot be interpreted as unambiguous support for the church becoming a Reconciling Congregation. Perhaps the minister was getting a lot of information about the initiative that I was not hearing.

In summary, a systems perspective of people and organizations emphasizes the complex interaction of systems within systems. Change is a function of communication. There are no unilateral sources of control or single causes for events. It follows that efforts to achieve reform will not come quickly or easily, nor will efforts to simply change thinking "at the top" be successful. This also means that whether we are the agents or the objects of change efforts, we need a framework for organizing our thinking and our behavior, a way of seeing that the particular situation or project we are engaged in at the moment is merely a variation on all other change efforts that are afoot.

Elements of the Change Process

It is important to understand that what follows is merely one way of conceptualizing change and of organizing efforts to accomplish it (if we are the change agents) or to cope with it (if we are being swept along by someone else's agenda). A systems view of the world underscores the organic unity of all life experiences, so even attempting to construct a list of features of change moves us away from the holistic perspective advocated by systems thinkers. But in the hurly burly of the workaday world, we need to have a way of organizing our thinking, of staying on top of events, and I have found it helpful to have a framework that permits me to step back from what is going on at the moment and think calmly about my next move.

I have become accustomed to thinking about change as composed of seven elements, each related to the others in complex, overlapping ways, but each amenable to independent analysis and strategizing. As I work on projects in the home, school, or community, I systematically shift my attention from one element to another in a methodical process of analysis and action. The perspective is always personal: What can *I* do? What does this situation/event mean to *me?* How should *I* react?

Problems. I try to remember that problems are just my way of naming events that have caught my attention, things that are bothering me. To name a problem is a step toward organizing action. In the normal flow of life, events and situations stream by; if I don't like something, I call it a problem and try to solve it. But the same situation may be beneath the radar screen or even an acceptable state of affairs for others.

Issues. In any case, problems are merely the local manifestation of larger systemic functioning. Understanding the issues helps me position myself for the fray. It also provides a helpful reminder that there are forces at work in the world at large that contribute to the problems I am having and that there is a limit to the changes I am likely to accomplish.

Innovation. Sustained change efforts require some organization and tend to become identified as an object or activity in and of themselves. This has both positive and negative implications. On the one hand, having a name for an innovation permits easy communication with others. Teachers line up behind "whole language" or "phonemic awareness" as debates develop to shape school policy and public opinion. In other, more modest cases, it is helpful just to organize my efforts under a label such as "getting organized" or "personal health campaign." On the other hand, commitment to a particular approach to solving a problem may result in a myopic focus on doing things a particular way, even when a better way presents itself.

Players. All change efforts impinge on people, so I need to understand who the players are and attempt to gauge how they will react. Change initiatives are always negotiated with others and will be successful in direct proportion to the accuracy of my insight into their interests and commitments.

Evidence. As I work for change, I need to decide what I will take as evidence of improvement and take heart from the progress I am making, even if it seems to come slow and hard. This approach requires an appreciation of the emergent nature of goals. Rather than fixing my sights on a distant and ideal goal, I learn to see progress in small, realistic movements in the right direction.

Activity cycles. All events and situations—from the mundane to the magnificent—are variations on the cyclical pattern of beginning, middle, end, start again. Morning, noon, night, spring, summer, fall, winter, etc. Recognizing that change efforts require adjustments in people's comfortable cycles permits me to be strategic in my efforts.

Constraints and strategies. The complex world of human interaction is not susceptible to a simple cause-effect analysis. Therefore, I attempt to understand the most salient factors or constraints that make a particular outcome more likely than others. This process reveals leverage points in the system where particular options are likely to have some success.

I recognize that there are no easy solutions and certainly no prescriptions for success, but by focusing on different elements of the change process at different times, and by adjusting my efforts according to what appears to be the most promising avenue for action, I have developed a number of guidelines that help me remain focused.

Guidelines for Agitators

The world portrayed by systems theory is not susceptible to simple prescriptions for reform, much less agendas for unilateral restructuring of institutions and organizations to suit our perceptions of the way things should be. The status quo can best be understood as the ongoing result of people going about their lives in ways that make sense to them. Change initiatives, therefore, develop as concerted efforts at shaping opinions, creating opportunities for insight and understanding, influencing perception and action. There are no guarantees, and so the approach is different from the familiar "plan-implement-assess" effort often seen in education, business, and government innovations—different at least in the sense that systems thinkers do not assume the linear trajectory implied by that sequence. The best we can hope for is to create disturbances that cause wobbles in the system—hence, the choice of the word *agitators*. As I discuss the guidelines, I will indicate how they relate to the different elements of the change process.

Change yourself.

Gandhi is reported to have said, "In order to transform others, first you must transform yourself." Whatever the spiritual justification for such an admonition, there are systemic reasons that make this true. When faced with the daunting task of reforming the system to match your ideological or philosophical preferences, you need to remember that there is one player over whom you have considerable control: yourself. We know that we cannot force others to change, nor are we in unilateral control of the systems in which we operate. We can, however, examine our own behavior and align it with the values we are working toward.

Changes in my own thinking and behavior will impact others. All of us are in a position to cause "local disturbances" in the system, merely by changing aspects of our daily behavior. While we do not exercise total control over our lives, we can create disturbances that will upset the equilibrium of the system. The key to success with this tactic is to focus on changes we can make without being hypocritical or without fear of "backsliding." The object is not to manipulate others through apparent changes in behavior but to impact the system through genuine changes in our own daily activities. While it is true that we will not be able to control the exact nature of these changes, we will accomplish one goal in the reformer's agenda: movement away from the status quo.

As I worked to bring about a different stance in the church toward gays and lesbians, I had to become more involved in church activities. I found myself being drawn into mundane aspects of church business in ways that affected my daily schedule and commitments. I gradually realized that if I wanted to have an impact on the church, I first had to change my own priorities.

A variation on this procedure is to examine our own behaviors to attempt to discover ways in which we contribute to our own problems. This requires practice, but it follows naturally from the insight that the system maintains functioning through the virtually infinite number of habitual acts performed by everyone in the system on a day-by-day basis. For example, R. P. McDermott and Kenneth Gospodinoff (1979) report on a conscientious, hard-working teacher who contributed to the reading difficulties of some of her students by being interruptable when she was working with the low-level group, but not when she was working with the good readers. The result was that she never made the progress she wanted to make with the low-level readers. A first step in effecting change in this classroom would require the teacher to understand the ways she was contributing to the lack of achievement of her low-level readers.

In the whole language story Scott might need to consider ways that his attitude toward students, colleagues, the principal, and the curriculum contributed to difficulties he was having at school. Perhaps small changes in the way the class project was organized or in the way he talked with students about their work would result in less resistance. For example, he mentions that the children wanted to continue working on the project but says that he told them they would have to wrap it up. This may have communicated the impression that this was just an assignment, rather than an authentic effort at discovering information about the students' cultures. This could account for their lack of cooperation during the peer-editing session; the project was no longer theirs, so they began to lose interest in it. In addition, it is possible that he communicated a feeling of animosity or disrespect toward colleagues, making negotiation difficult. He needs to make honest attempts to see others' points of view and to understand the basis for their actions. Scott may consider an administrator a coward for not championing his cause against the system, but he needs to ask himself if he would behave differently if he were the administrator. Subtle as it may seem, merely making an effort to understand another's point of view can have the effect of changing the climate of interaction, contributing to opportunities for change.

Learn the players.

Organizational change comes about as the result of change in individuals; it stands to reason then that if you are going to be effective you have to make a concerted effort to understand the other people who are involved.

When people are asked to change the way they think or work, they naturally want to know why. The question is, "What was wrong with the way I was doing things?" Robert Evans asserts that a natural part of any change is a sense of loss or mourning (1996, 58–63). Shirley Hord and her colleagues have identified a number of concerns that people have when confronted with the need to change (Hord et al. 1987). Among the questions most on people's minds are: How will this affect me? What is in it for me? How will it help me reach my goals? Am I doing it right? And May Lowry uses the acronym STORCC to remind her of Everett M. Rogers's perceived characteristics of an innovation. The letters of the acronym stand for *support* (will resources be provided to make the innovation work?); *trialability* (will we be given a chance to try things out on a limited basis?); *observability* (are the results of the innovation visible?); *relative advantage* (is the innovation better than what I am doing?); *compatibility* (is the innovation compatible with my values?); and *complexity* (is it simple to understand and maintain?) (E. M. Rogers 1995; Lowry 2000).

As you work for change, you assess the commitments of each of the participants with questions such as these to have an idea of the likelihood of success. Teachers are used to doing this sort of thing with their students, of course. We call it individualized instruction. Scott understood Jantar's reluctance to participate in the writers workshop as anxiety over the lack of structure in the assignment. What Scott failed to do, apparently, was spend the same amount of time thinking about how to instruct his principal and colleagues. Because he considered what he was doing an instructional concern, he failed to appreciate the demands that whole language instruction placed on others in the school.

In my church and community activism I have learned to slow down, to spend more time listening rather that talking to people. Part of this is curiosity—I am interested in learning what my friends and neighbors think about issues—but it is also strategic. If I am working on a change project, I want to assess each individual's attitude toward it and determine the likelihood of his or her participation or resistance. Everett M. Rogers has amassed a mountain of research on responses to change, and he has categorized people according to their stance toward innovation. He believes that people range along a continuum: change agent, early adopter, early majority, late majority, laggard (1995, 252–80). I am not entirely convinced about the categories, but my own experience with change efforts has taught me that in each situation there will be a range of responses to the effort. Knowing people's stance toward an innovation permits me to know how to approach them.

Don't preach.

Another important implication of paying attention to the players in a change effort is recognizing the limitations of sustained explanations and exhortations—behavior that earns the derogatory label of preaching. If we are going to be effective change agents we must avoid being labeled as tiresome zealots.

It is not unreasonable to want to convey our passions to others and to work to convince them of the merits of our position, but we need to limit our desire to give our opinion on an issue until someone asks for it. Do not give advice unless someone specifically requests it.

And teachers need to be cautious about appearing to brag about successes they are having. Do not offer to share materials and ideas unless you are asked to do so. The opposite, in fact, is recommended. Ask for information from others, seek their advice, ask for copies of materials they are using, and encourage them to talk about successes they are having. And, most important, pay attention to the responses. Learn the players.

People will resist knowledge and insight that they do not actively seek. Veteran teachers have survived a number of educational innovations, and they have probably developed a healthy skepticism for claims that the right way has at last been found. They teach the way they do for a variety of reasons—formal training, personal preference, habit, availability of resources, student characteristics, etc.—and merely being told by someone else about a new and different way of doing things is not likely to change their minds. If, however, they seek the information, the likelihood increases that they will use that information to modify what they do.

Similarly, it is impossible to become involved in gay rights issues and not see the extent to which sexual orientation pervades all aspects of society and its institutions. The issue is fundamental to human rights. I see the injustices of everyday life, but I also see that pointing them out is the most effective way of driving people away.

Don't lay blame for problems, and don't take credit for solutions.

This piece of advice concerns the relationship between "issues" and "problems," and it proceeds directly from an understanding of the importance of knowing the players in an institutional change effort.

Given the complexity of the world, and of the motivations of the people who inhabit it, it is rare that we can point to one individual and say, "She or he is the reason we're in this mess." Nor can we unequivocally say that a particular triumph is the sole responsibility of an individual.

Even more to the point, it is rarely productive to blame someone for problems or take credit for successes. The former merely sours relationships and creates an unpleasant atmosphere, and the latter oversimplifies processes while putting you in the position to suffer from others' envy.

An additional possibility to consider is that the act of blaming others often has the unanticipated effect of reducing the amount of time and energy we expend in finding solutions to problems; it takes us off the hook, psychologically. That is, if we have identified someone else who is to blame for our difficulties, then we do not have to work so hard on ourselves to improve.

Form support groups without becoming isolated.

As you work to alter your own understanding of and approach to change, you will discover that people tend to sort themselves out as either allies or opponents to a particular project. The value, both psychological and interpersonal, of talking regularly with like-minded individuals cannot be exaggerated. However, it is also true that perceptions of elitism and isolationism are also possible in situations where adherents of a particular point of view appear to converse only with fellow enthusiasts. This would be of little concern if all we wanted to do were declare victory, but when the goal is to contribute to the greater good, we need to think more broadly. We want to have more contact with individuals from other camps. Efforts to seek common ground with these people will allow us to increase our understanding of their point of view. This, in turn, will increase the likelihood that in an exchange of ideas our perspective can be heard. It might even lead to unexpected coalitions and to modified positions all around.

Create disturbances and force wobbles in the system.

This item comes from an understanding of human nature and of the cyclical reality of life. People cannot be made to do something they do not want to do. The best we can hope for is to create conditions that increase the likelihood of change in the direction we desire. This means that we need to understand the rhythms and routines of the people we are working with and that we need to learn when to nudge them toward our goals.

Open systems function toward stability, utilizing communication along feedback loops. Negative feedback dampens change; positive feedback amplifies change. All systems function within a range of limits, often called "wobbles"–the basic pattern of behaviors that characterize "normal" functioning. Pushing for change is most strategically thought of as creating a disturbance at one point in a cycle and then paying attention as the system adjusts to the information. Draper Kauffman puts it this way:

> Reaction time is important. If it is too slow, change can occur so fast that the system is damaged before it has a chance to respond. In addition, the reaction time is usually the same as the basic tempo or "beat" of a system–the minimum interval between the "wobbles" of the feedback cycle. So, by watching these wobbles and estimating that interval, you can frequently find out the minimum time period (and the fastest change) which a particular system can cope with. (1980, 15)

Teachers are in a position to manipulate variables in the learning environment and to observe the consequences of these manipulations. The changes can be small, and they do not have to be narrowly purposeful; that is, we do not need to know exactly what the effect will be. It is enough to disturb the habitual functioning of the system. Some examples: move the furniture; change the order of events in an activity; walk around; sit down; have the students do tasks that you normally do; use titles and last names instead of first names, or vice versa; sit in rows; sit on the floor; stand up.

Similar changes in our behavior with superiors and colleagues and parents will have an impact on the smooth functioning of systems we would like to change. A colleague of mine, an elementary teacher accustomed to arriving early, leaving late, and grabbing a sandwich while working on the afternoon's activities, discovered that dramatic changes began to occur in her school when she altered her routine. She sat in a different place in faculty meetings and altered her customary route to and from her room. She varied her daily routines and made a point of talking to people she normally only greeted in the hall. And, although she initially chafed at the amount of time she was "wasting" in the teachers' lounge, she made a point of having coffee and eating her lunch with her colleagues, contributing doughnuts and fruit to the common pool along with everyone else, and taking part in the football pools and Friday raffles. She soon discovered that previously distant colleagues warmed to her, and it wasn't long before conversation led to collaboration on a number of projects. An interesting and somewhat unexpected result of these changes was that she developed some productive variations on materials and techniques as a result of discussing classroom activities with teachers with whom she had assumed she had little in common.

The rationale for this approach to change lies in the realization that we cannot possibly comprehend all the factors that contribute to the difficulties we encounter as we attempt to change the systems in which we live and work. This means that we are undoubtedly overlooking opportunities for change that would further our cause. Changing aspects of our classroom, modifying our behavior in faculty meetings, or doing things around the school that we don't normally do may reveal unexpected connections among events and situations and lead to productive changes.

Work for effects.

What will you take as evidence of progress? How will you know if you are moving in the right direction or if you are moving at all? It is possible to be so focused on the ultimate goal that you lose sight of how far you have come.

We need to be flexible in how we work to achieve our goals, and we need to avoid becoming committed more to the method than to the outcomes. If we seek instruction that produces curious and internally motivated students, and we have a program for achieving it, fine. But if we discover that the obstacles to the program are so great that we spend more of our time in political battles than in teaching, we may want to assess alternative means to accomplishing our goals. There is always a middle ground between two extremes; if we let go of our doctrinaire preferences for how we do things, we may still be able to move people in the appropriate direction.

A colleague of mine reports that she has made good use of the mandated basal series that she is philosophically opposed to but required to use. She treats it like an anthology in which the children are allowed to select the stories that are interesting to them personally. The kids do mini-book reports in which they attempt to get their friends to read the stories they like, with an informal competition arising to see who can get the most people to read their favorite selections. In other words, she has discovered a way around the assumptions of the publishers of basal readers—lock-step schedules and controlled reading. She is getting the effects she wants even though she has had to adjust her approach.

In the case of my church story, it is clear to me now that I was initially too committed to the church becoming a Reconciling Congregation as a way of providing a welcoming environment for gays and lesbians. If I had more accurately assessed the congregation, I would have adopted a less public way of accomplishing the goal. As it happens, in the intervening years, the church has attracted a number of gay couples and their children; gays have moved into leadership positions in the church; and we have become the site of a significant number of gay rights organizational meetings, choir rehearsals, etc. In other words, the effects I worked for have been gradually accomplished, *and* the sensitivities of the more conservative members of the congregation have been observed.

Working for effects also has another meaning. We must be content with the right behaviors for the wrong reasons. Perfection is not often possible, nor is complete conversion to a particular point of view a prerequisite for change. In fact, it is a fallacy of our modern, technologically advanced society to assume that rationality lies at the basis of all behavior (Berger and Luckmann 1967; Berger, Berger, and Kellner 1974). There are multiple constraints on people and institutions that account for what happens and how it happens. It is not expectable, therefore, that behavior will always be based on cogitation or that individuals will always have the same reasons we do for their behavior. Consider the grade-conscious students mentioned in Scott's story, for example: it may be necessary to "bribe" them into a process-oriented frame of mind by offering grades for the student who produces the most drafts or by grading material that we would normally prefer not to grade. We must take the view that writing multiple drafts of a composition is a step in the right direction, regardless of motivation. It is unfortunate that students do it because of extrinsic rewards rather than internal motivation, but perhaps a greater understanding of the merits of revision will follow at some later date.

Or consider the bandwagon status of change efforts and the fact that many people begin using catchphrases and jargon indiscriminately. It is far more important to take advantage of the positive bias indicated by this tide of groupie-ism than it is to dispute others' use of a term or to attempt to educate everyone on what the innovation "really means." If a teacher succeeds in acquiring a collection of literary classics because of the principal's enthusiasm for a movement only imperfectly understood, at least she has the books; one would prefer the benefactor to have the correct ideology, but one must take what one can get.

Work for policy reform.

As the preceding discussion demonstrates, it is unlikely that a single individual will be able to implement wholesale organizational change without encountering difficulties caused by structures and procedures already in place. The most obvious target for reform, therefore, is the system itself. This usually comes as unwelcome news to teachers, who got into the profession because of a love of learning and a desire to define their work by the walls of their classrooms. It also comes as a surprise to community activists, who usually embark on their efforts with modest goals, only to discover that they are required to increase the range of their efforts if they want to be successful. Systems within systems within systems—we discover that the solution to a problem lies at a higher level than where it was encountered, and so we decide to serve on a committee or run for office, much to our own surprise. Kauffman discusses this strategy as seeking the highest leverage point possible in the system and investing our time and energy there (1980). For teachers, this may mean getting involved in school and district curriculum and assessment committee work.

Be content with small changes; be patient.

Systems—whether we are discussing individuals or organizations—change slowly. We must work to create disturbances and then be patient. Individuals may come to agree with many of our points of view, but this will not happen overnight, and it will not occur in such a way as to conform exactly to our opinion of how things should be. We must work to see how far we have come, not just how far we have to go. One technique that is helpful in this regard is to make two lists of specific behaviors, one that represents the ideal and another that represents the actual. We then chart even minute changes that indicate movement in the desired direction. This helps us see progress that otherwise would not be readily apparent.

This admonition rests on an understanding of activity cycles in change efforts. It is natural to want change to occur rapidly, but in fact we know that all growth occurs according to its season and that to push the system invites only misery and pain—mostly your own. Many institutions in our society—certainly schools and churches—run on the same rhythmic cycle, beginning in the fall with a lot of energy, building to a crescendo around mid-November, subsiding in December, rising in January, subsiding in spring, and idling through summer. There is likewise a rhythm of the week and the day that is easily charted. The savvy change agent assesses the openness of individuals to change based on where they are in the cycle and puts forward proposals that are likely to meet with a sympathetic hearing.

Work quietly.

Another admonition based on an understanding of cycles of change and persistence. Reformers speak often and insistently about the defects of the system and the advantages of their own point of view, and it is therefore not surprising that they acquire the reputation of enthusiasts who are blinded by the zealot's lack of perspective. The admonition to work quietly is based on the view that it will be easier for skeptics to accept a new perspective if they do not feel others are proselytizing.

For teachers, this means you must close your doors and do your work. If you are using a radically different approach you will attract enough attention as it is; people will want to see what is going on in the classroom, and by the time they ask for information, they will be ready to understand it and apply it to their own situations. If people ask to observe your classroom, you should prepare them for what they will see and tell them what it means. This is especially important if you suspect the visitors are familiar with a different approach than the one you use. You need to help others see the structure and order of events and activities and how these build upon each other toward a coherent experience for the learners.

Conclusions and Contemplations

How did you score on the questionnaire? Here is my score for the church story.

Title: Church Reform

1. __5__ Black hole!

2. __5__ Herding cats!

3. __4__ Stubborn, suspicious, or just plain lazy!

4. __5__ Tender toes and thin skin!

5. __5__ Officious bureaucrats and meddling administrators!

6. __5__ Mysterious rules and regulations!

7. __5__ Ruts, routines, and rituals!

8. __4__ Jealous backsliders!

9. __3__ Ingrates and opportunists!

10. __3__ Scarcity of resources!

Average: 4.4

Now, almost 10 years after the event, I have a different perspective on church and community change initiatives, but summarizing the effort and attempting to account for my behavior and the responses of the congregation using systems theory have confirmed the essential elements of the approach. I think I have acquired a greater appreciation for tradition than I had at the time. It is important to remember that all institutions have histories and established routines that need to be accommodated as we work for change; in the case of the Methodist church, the history stretches back to the Reformation, and although John Wesley founded the order in the eighteenth century as a concerted effort at social activism, the reform agenda of any established organization will conform roughly to the social mores of the larger community. In the east Denver neighborhood of Park Hill, there has been an increase in gay and lesbian households, and the gay membership of the church has also grown. If someone were to raise the issue again, it might pass.

I have also gained an appreciation for structure and procedure. In any organization, the goals and motivations of people involved will vary considerably, and so, therefore, will the chances of getting a critical mass of support for any single change initiative. However, what is required in a democratic organization to launch change is a majority, and the rules and procedures of the church provide the mechanism for change, however slow it may seem to core members of the change effort. I am not surprised by the wide variation of opinions in the congregation, nor am I confounded by the apparent contradictions between principles and action; I have learned to examine events and situations from the perspectives of the participants.

What about your change effort? If your composite score was less than 3, then I would argue that you haven't taken on a very contentious problem or you have yet to be noticed by the people directly affected. I had a professor once who said, "I am uncomfortable when my students are uncomfortable, but I am more uncomfortable when they are comfortable." It's the same with change efforts. You won't get anywhere unless you push, and if you push you are going to cause yourself and others discomfort. And if you push and no one pushes back, you have got to stop and question whether what you are pushing on is important.

It may strike you as an odd theory, one that assesses the value of an effort by the amount of pain it causes to the implementer. Yet this is the logical conclusion with an approach that requires learning in the change agent. Learning is change. Change is painful. If we are going to ask others to change, then we should be prepared to change ourselves.

There is another lesson here, I think, and it has to do with the focus of change efforts. If we take a narrowly purposive view of the work we do, then we tend to have a limited view of what "success" means. In terms of the two stories, "adoption of whole language" and "voting to become a Reconciling Congregation" could be seen as the only acceptable outcomes to the change efforts. But if we take a more systemic view, then we begin to appreciate the natural rhythms of the institutions in which we are working for change, and we work for more general growth and development—in ourselves, our colleagues, our students, and the institutions where we have invested time and energy. This is what I mean by the title of this essay—the natural rhythms of reform and resistance include both movement toward our goals and slippage back toward "business as usual." We need to recognize this and not become discouraged.

Of course, we may decide that our energies would be better invested elsewhere. But even in that case, the systemic view would have shifted from the particular organization to the greater good. I have a friend who decided that the church was too limited an institution for his vision of ministry; he went into work in the state government in the area of childcare reform, where he accomplished many of the goals that had impelled him toward ministry. Same goals, same values, different venue.

There are no easy answers here, but I find comfort in a view of the world that permits me to take what I have learned in one system into another. It seems like an efficient use of time and energy.

⑤ Coherence: Aligning Thought and Action in Teaching

This essay examines the relationship between theory and practice in teaching, an enduring theme in educational circles and a favorite topic among philosophers and teachers. We teachers have to be philosophers to maintain our sanity, and we have no choice about practice–there can be no audience more demanding than classrooms

The stance presented here has developed over many years of studying teaching, my own and others', in a variety of contexts. The intellectual debts are many, and there are undoubtedly a number of arguments that I will present here as my own that came originally from others. I apologize in advance for any such oversights, and I absolve my friends and colleagues from responsibility for any enthusiasms that they do not share. Primary among the individuals most directly implicated in the theses developed in this essay are Alan Davis, Lynn Rhodes, Elaine DeLott Baker (Davis et al. 1994; Clarke et al. 1998), and members of the Lola research lab. Together we pored over tapes of the three teachers discussed here, and together we refined the concept of coherence. More generally, my understanding of teaching and learning is the product of collaboration with Sandra Silberstein and Barbara K. Dobson (Clarke and Silberstein 1977, 1988; Clarke, Dobson, and Silberstein 1996; Silberstein, Clarke, and Dobson 2002).

full of students. So in the constellation of scholarly practitioners, I would nominate teachers as the archetypal practicing philosophers. We read the research and formulate philosophy statements, and we develop lesson plans and materials that we hope will get us through the day with a semblance of grace.

Historically, the conventional mechanism for connecting theory and practice in teaching has been "method," a hotly contested terrain in the profession. The primary purpose of method, and of educational discourse in general, is to improve the learning of students. However, it is not uncommon for the focus to shift from improving learning to improving method, not unlike the gardener who spends an inordinate amount of time building the ideal hothouse and forgets to tend to the tomatoes.

My thesis here will be that we need to consider method to be among the many tools at our disposal and that we need a view of teaching and learning that keeps us focused on the effects of our efforts, rather than on the ways that we accomplish them. In other words, more attention to evidence of learning as we refine our classroom techniques and procedures.

I argue that we need a theory of learning that is broad enough to account for all the contexts in which we work—classroom, school, community—and that we need to include ourselves among the learners. The lens I offer for consideration is constructed by systems theory, in which people and organizations are considered to function according to the same principles—internal norms guiding reactions to external stimuli—and in which phenomena need to be understood in relation to their contexts. Systems within systems within systems, all functioning in a cyclical repetition of primal motifs, presenting opportunities for change that vary according to time and conditions. But, equally important, we need to attend to our instincts in the heat of action. Good teaching is an emergent phenomenon (Johnson 2001). To be successful, we must be in tune with the rhythms and requirements of the systems within which we work. This includes our own sense of equilibrium as well as the activity cycles of the systems we hope to change, whether we are interested in particular learners or in the larger school/community context. Indeed, it is very often the case that we will have only limited success with the former if we do not attend regularly to the latter.

I posit "coherence" as the ideal to strive for, the situation that exists when our actions are perfectly aligned with our intentions. This is a difficult state to achieve. It requires us to be in tune with our own motives and motivations, and it requires us to negotiate with others. It is, in fact, a function of communication, which always depends on our ability to communicate what we believe to be important and on others being able to understand us in the way we want to be understood. This implies that we must constantly examine our own behavior to make certain that we are being true to our ideals, and it requires us to study the individuals for whom the messages are intended so that we can adjust our efforts for better communication. In this conceptualization of teaching, it is the teacher who does most of the changing.

= A RIDDLE =

A two-year-old boy becomes the focus of a toilet-training campaign. The appropriate paraphernalia have been acquired for all the homes he spends time in, and everyone–grandparents, aunts and uncles, and day-care providers–has been briefed about being alert but not distressing themselves or the kid. For their own edification they read books about child development and behavior modification, and to orient the child to the task they read him stories about "big kids" who wear underpants and use the toilet. They lurk surreptitiously in the child's vicinity as he plays, watching for the thoughtful look or pause in activity that indicates swift action is required. In due time, their efforts are rewarded, and the little boy enters the world of the undiapered.

Questions:

   1. Who has learned the most from this adventure?
   2. How do we assess the learning?
   3. Who shall be called "learner" and who "teacher"?

4. When is a lesson?
5. Should we establish schools to ensure universal acquisition of toilet skills?

Discussion

There are times when words get in the way of understanding. *Teacher* and *student* are good examples. By evoking the familiar roles we have all played in our own schooling, they incline us to overlook ways in which we are all teachers and learners every day of our lives. Toilet training provides a good example of the ability of children to teach adults. For the past three years, my grandson has patiently but relentlessly led me from one lesson to another as he has shown me the joy of a dandelion, the wonder of balloons, and how to explore–really explore–the concept "huge." He has taught me some very important lessons in observation and curiosity; in appreciating the world; and in connecting, precisely, the language I use with the reality that surrounds us. Yet, as we play games and hang out together, conventional wisdom would cast me as the teacher and him as the student. And, when is learning most intense–during the moment of interaction or in the reflective time after an encounter, or in the time we spend preparing to be together?

The problem lies in our tendency to force dichotomies on situations and in our desire to neatly categorize people according to role. In the case of teaching and learning, this has placed unnecessary burdens on the participants in classrooms and blinders on the public and politicians.

Consider the earlier question, "Who has learned the most from this adventure?" Did you consider it a fair question? Chances are you are so accustomed to the idea that we can quantify and compare learning that you did not blink at the question. But what do we mean by "the most," and how do we compare the acquisition of social skills, on the one hand, to insights into child development, on the other? The former will confer the basics of societal acceptance on the child, and the latter will contribute to skillful parenting–both important to society and both occurring during the process of child rearing; neither the child nor the parent can avoid learning significant things. And no one, I trust, would suggest that we should establish schools to accomplish this.

What *is* required is an appreciation of the nature of learning and an understanding of the contribution that schools, as one of the most powerful institutions in society, can make to the learning of everyone involved. Also required is an understanding of how the contexts of learning contribute to the experience and constrain our efforts as teachers. Let me focus the discussion with a convention of education—the time-honored quiz.

Assumptions about Teaching and Learning

Respond to each of the following items by giving your answer and by jotting notes to yourself that explain your rationale. Engage at least one other individual in a discussion of the answers, in which each of you uses examples from your own experience, preferably within the past week, to defend your responses.

1. T/F   Actions speak louder than words.

2. T/F   Everyone at a particular age should be able to read and write with similar facility.

3. T/F   Tests and test scores are more valuable as political tools than as indicators of student learning.

4. T/F   A fact is noise until it answers a question in an individual's mind.

5. T/F   All moments are "teachable moments."

6. T/F   Human beings cannot *not* learn.

7.   A teacher is most like . . .
   a. a gardener.
   b. an actor.
   c. a puppeteer.
   d. a warden.

8. Explain how each of the following is an example of teaching.
   a. An adult leads a group of adolescents through a production of *Hamlet*.
   b. A teacher alerts the principal to the fact that noise is considered an important indicator of learning in an upcoming project, so as to avoid alarm or administrative intervention.
   c. A teacher meets with parents to solicit homework support for students.
   d. A citizen votes on election day.
   e. A teenager marches in a gay rights parade.

9. Explain how each of the following might be considered evidence of learning.
   a. An ESL learner puts -*ed* on the end of all verbs to signal past tense.
   b. Students from a particular class sit together at lunch.
   c. Everyone gets quiet and turns expectantly when a student moves to a particular chair in the classroom.
   d. A child raises his forearm to protect his face when an adult makes a quick move toward him.
   e. Adults and children walk down the right side of the hallway during breaks between classes.

10. How would you demonstrate that the following are lessons learned in secondary schools?
    a. Learning is something that occurs in 45-minute blocks.
    b. You haven't learned anything until someone evaluates it.
    c. Facts are more important than attitudes.
    d. In school, it is not what you know but the power you hold that counts.
    e. Reading and writing are something that students do but not something that teachers do.

Discussion

As is the case with all tests, the items reveal more about the writer than the respondent, and they force you to make distinctions that blur variations among real people in real situations. But the device is useful in focusing the discussion. I'll provide a brief summary of my views here; if you want a detailed item analysis, turn to the end of the essay. The intervening text develops elaborations and examples for you to consider.

Learning involves change–typically, in understanding and/or skill. At times this change is dramatic and easily identified, but just as often, it is subtle and difficult to precisely characterize. It is almost always the case that the change involves a much wider and more complex array of factors than conventionally understood. The lessons we learn are acquired every minute of the day as we go about our mundane activities–subtle variations in attitude, insight, understanding; slight wobbles in our routines that indicate we have adjusted our behavior to accommodate information we have encountered, often without even knowing it and most of the time without conscious attention to the effort.

I would assert, for example, that the choices in item 10 are reasonable characterizations about learning in the secondary schools I am familiar with and that they are just as enduring as the academic lessons that the students have mastered. They are offered as descriptions, not condemnations. There are many compelling reasons for the way the school day is organized. It is my point, however, that the attitudes and behaviors identified in 10 a–e are the expectable result if you spend every day of the week moving from classroom to classroom every 45 minutes or so and if the overriding focus of everyone inside and outside school is on grades and test scores. Indeed, it would be startling if this were not the case.

In schools, the focus is on academic knowledge and skills, and evaluation has become a key factor in the process. In fact, it is not an exaggeration to say that if it cannot be measured, it is of little interest. This can be demonstrated in a number of ways. Consider, for example, the question often asked by students, of whether a concept or skill will be on the exam, an indication that they do not want to spend time on anything that won't be evaluated. Or take a broader view. The curricula of schools, and the allocation of educational resources, are very directly influenced by public and political pressure for accountability, in the form of report cards and standardized tests. It is not by accident that art, for example, is not an important part of most curricula. This is the natural result of our attention to learning that can be easily and directly connected to job performance and economic viability.

However, at a time when a wide array of social ills loom for parents, policymakers, and politicians, and the response is increasing the focus on narrowly defined academic skills, the most effective and least likely response would be broadening the effort to systemic solutions. The reasons for this are many, and they are complex, but they relate to a very basic fact of human nature—our inability to see long-term consequences and our tendency to want to directly control immediate details of situations. Both shortcomings are exacerbated by crises.

Schooling can be seen as activity designed to promote desirable change in individuals. The question is, "Desired by whom?" Most children, and adults for that matter, know what they want at a particular moment, and it only rarely coincides with what someone else wants. As is the case with all living organisms, we humans cannot *not* learn, but we are usually deeply engaged in learning what engages us at the moment; we are not waiting around for someone else to organize our efforts. This is undoubtedly the case most of the time in school, especially as emerging adolescent identities confront curricular goals of arcane bits of knowledge selected by adults. The issue is not whether or not to learn; the issue is what learning is going to count, how it is going to be assessed, and how the assessments are going to be used.

Cast in this light, teaching becomes a matter of creating environments where others will learn, and effective teaching is that in which the learners learn what the teacher wants them to learn. It is not an exact science. In fact, it is not science at all, or it is only in fits and starts. Participating in a protest may be considered teaching if it provides an opportunity for the public and policymakers to think differently about an issue, perhaps to change a course of action. Teaching is primarily a matter of communication within relationships, and the nature of the relationship dictates a great deal about how the communication is conducted. Obviously, if you spend most of the day with learners you will have a greater impact on their learning than if you spend only 50 minutes a day with them. But in either case, your chances of being an effective teacher hinge on your noticing what they are ready to learn as you move them in the direction dictated by the curriculum. To accomplish this, you must be a good learner. You learn the students, adjust your approach to accommodate administrators, work with parents and others beyond the school to create the right atmosphere for the lessons you want to teach. Like the adults working to toilet train the two-year-old, you work on the environment to increase the chances that your learners—whether classified as students, administrators, or parents—will notice new ways of thinking and behaving. Methods, materials, tests—these are some of the tools you use, as are tables, desks, time, and political connections. Like gardeners, we teachers have only indirect control over the outcome of our efforts.

As for learners, the most important fact to keep in mind is that they are always learning. All adjustments in thinking or behaving are instances of learning, whether they are noticed by someone else or not. And the most important learnings may be those that are not at the center of consciousness—apperceptive learnings acquired in the conduct of daily life. Such things as how to behave, what constitutes a good use of time, who is important and what is valued, when to speak and how loud, where to stand while waiting to speak to someone else—these are lessons that are rarely the focus of a formal curriculum, but they are essential to survival in school and are variations on the kind of learning that is often referred to as "socialization" or "acculturation." From this perspective, all moments are teachable moments, but only if we are alert to the possibilities. Similarly, if we do not attend to what individuals are disposed to learn, we end up only confusing things, creating noise, rather than messages they can attend to and learn from.

The Systems View

> . . . the experience of nature,
> with its powerful lessons
> in static change
> and
> predictable surprise.
> —Barbara Kingsolver

Our topic here is nature, although putting it that way may strike you as a bit odd—too ambitious, perhaps, or too vague. But learning is just one form of change, the very natural process of life. We are interested in creating opportunities for change at different levels of scale, and our primary task is learning how to see patterns and rhythms and then how to influence the functioning of the natural systems we encounter. The first step, as Kingsolver reminds us, is to submit to the lessons of nature, to pay attention (1995, 170–80).

What we will see, if we pay attention, is that living systems function toward stability. Not on a fixed setting, but within limits that can be determined if we have the patience to observe them. We observe and we establish expectations for probable activity, but we know that it is not possible to predict precisely what is going to happen. So it is, for example, that a particular student tends to be alert in the morning but some days arrives at school very tired and irritable. We adjust our teaching accordingly. The same is true of school; we know that faculty meetings are always on a particular day and time but that things never quite get started precisely at the appointed hour, so we adjust our schedule knowing we have a little slack. Or a community may be predictably calm during the week and somewhat boisterous on weekends but occasionally go through weeks on end when something seems to be happening every night. We learn when it is advisable to venture out and when it is not. Variation is expectable, and if we observe long enough we will understand the range of variation to expect.

The approach to teaching recommended by this view of the world is one in which the teacher seeks an understanding of the rhythms, the cycles of activity in classroom, school, and community, and then organizes opportunities for learning—that is to say, change—and prods things toward his or her goals with focused events, called "lessons" in some circles but in systems terminology referred to as "disturbances." I have arrived at the following points as guidelines in my teaching. I'll summarize them here and then elaborate through an examination of three remarkable teachers I have had the privilege of knowing.

Understanding Life's Cycles

As teachers we enter environments to promote change, and we will be successful to the extent that we can work in synch with the major life cycles we encounter. Perhaps the most important cycle to be aware of is our own, the personal cycle of preferences, metabolism, interests that we would accept as a fair description of who we are. In general, we should work to create opportunities to teach from within the circle of our personal excitements. Enthusiasm is contagious; if we are excited, energy flows from us to the students. We need to make choices that permit us to indulge our inclinations.

Other cycles are also important. The traits and preferences of individual students and the composite personality of the class set rough limits on what is possible; we need to learn what these limits are and to be judicious in our efforts to change their functioning. Similarly, each school and community has a distinctive personality—routines and customs, characteristic pace and use of time. Ethnic, linguistic, and cultural values shape these, as do neighborhood characteristics such as the presence of farms or factories, parks or fairgrounds, winding paths or freeways. There will be curriculum content to be gleaned from the activity cycles of the school or neighborhood, but even more important is that this awareness will shape our decision making as we plan. There is little point, for example, to assigning a large project over a weekend that coincides with an important ethnic art festival or homecoming football game.

Lessons as Organized Disturbances

Learning is prompted by notices of difference. Students are piqued by an idea or event that encourages them to change the way they see or do things. A class becomes silent or noisy in what seems like magical synchronization but is actually merely an example of the group noticing a difference—perhaps the teacher indicating that it is story time or the bell signaling lunch. The notice of difference provides the cognitive or interactional foothold for learning. A successful lesson can be identified by the extent of interest it promotes, the amount of noise it provokes, or the degree of discomfort it engenders. The key is to create just enough tension. Too little and everyone goes to sleep; too much and their anxiety prevents learning.

"Disturbance" may strike you as an odd way to refer to lessons, but if you can get past the negative associations of the word and focus on the effect of disturbances on organizations and organisms, you will see that it conveys an important aspect of systems functioning. Because people cannot be controlled, it is not productive to think of lessons as *planned* change. Rather, lessons become opportunities for individuals and classes to move toward an imperfectly envisioned goal. They nudge learners in the direction desired by the teacher.

Direction as Goal

For the same reasons—because students cannot be controlled and because finely tuned instructional blueprints do not provide a realistic framework for teaching—the best we can do is orchestrate change toward the values we desire. These include, of course, conventional objectives of knowledge and skills, but tempered always by our understanding of the limits of unilateral influence or direct didactic instruction. This may seem frustratingly vague as a goal for teaching, but it is actually very pragmatic. A moment's reflection will remind you that no lesson ever accomplished everything you wanted it to accomplish with all the students and that you often have to console yourself with the partial accomplishments. You might even have considered such lessons as failures. From a systems perspective, however, this sort of movement is all that we have a right to expect. Ours are gradual accomplishments achieved with consideration for the learners and appreciation for the constraints under which they operate.

Activity as End

I think it was Robert Louis Stevenson who said, "To travel expectantly is better than to arrive." He captures an important point that is often overlooked in our goal-oriented culture–that there is value in the mere engagement in worthwhile activity. We learn what we do. Or, perhaps more accurately, we learn a wide range of attitudes, skills, and insights merely by engaging in activity. The tools we use shape us as much as we shape them.

This is a subtle point, because what students are doing in a lesson may not be readily apparent. Two groups of students, one reading work sheets and the other reading novels, may appear to be engaged in the same activity, but it is far more likely that the decision making and the thoughtful reflection required of the novel readers will provide a better foundation for literacy. Apperceptive learning accounts for this. The work sheets provide explicit focus for teaching reading skills, but literate attitudes come from the values implicit in selecting a novel to read, thumbing through the chapters to get a sense of the story, dipping here and there to acquire insight into the characters, even perhaps reading the last chapter to see if the heroine dies. These lessons of personal choice and agency seep in around the edges of consciousness as the reader focuses on the words that constitute the novel.

Messages Sent and Received

A fact is a relatively uninteresting thing until it answers a question for someone, whether the question was explicitly formulated or not. At the point it answers a question, it becomes information; it enters the system and is available for use in future decision making.

This is another slippery point, but crucial to the approach I am taking here. Students are constantly barraged by messages emanating from the world around them, and in school these messages come from teachers, the principal, and other students. The arrangement of chairs in a room, the organization of the school day, the decorations on bulletin boards or the absence of bulletin boards, the messages that come across the school P.A. system—the mere *fact* of the P.A. system—these are all messages that frame the learnings of a particular school.

The messages over which teachers have some control are of primary interest to me as a teacher and teacher educator. There are the explicit messages, of course, those that we articulate—lectures, both academic and disciplinary; the syllabus, classroom rules and regulations, assignments and tests, grades, and comments in the margins of papers. Of at least equal importance are the implicit messages we send in our demeanor, facial expressions, use of time, room arrangement, etc. We convey more to the students about the importance of literacy by having books on our bookshelves and by reading than we do by admonishing them to read. This might be considered the theoretical insight articulated in "Do as I say, not as I do"—an awareness of the fact that our actions convey messages that are just as memorable as our words.

Notice of Difference

All learning begins with a notice of difference, whether we are conscious of it or not. The slight chill on your neck that prompts you to turn up your collar or the diminishing light that signals the end of day—simple notices of difference that signal learnings about the season or the hour. Much learning is prompted by the content of a lesson, of course, but equally important are the learnings gleaned from the way the lesson is organized or conducted and the demeanor of the teacher, the way you treat students, respond to "stupid" questions, etc.

This is not something over which we have total control, because what gets noticed is a function of the individual's history and current state of mind, and our best efforts do not always translate into the messages we hope to convey. Sometimes we can facilitate the process by pointing out facts and relationships for learners, but our best strategy is to create rich environments in which the messages we want learners to receive are repeated over and over.

In summary, a systems view of teaching and learning presents a number of challenges and opportunities for teachers. Because people and all enduring groups of people, such as families, classrooms, schools, communities, etc., are considered to function according to the same sets of principles, the world appears as an infinite horizon of nested systems—systems within systems within systems. Living and teaching become mere variations on a theme.

In particular, a systems view

- challenges the view of the teacher as the primary source of knowledge
- broadens the perspective of what is being learned to include the implicit as well as the explicit curriculum
- changes the footing of teacher/student from roles to relationship and moves us toward more authentic interactions
- broadens the focus of attention and work—from individual students and classroom to colleagues, school, and community
- moves us toward a view of "teacher" as a variation on personal identity, not a role one plays
- encourages us to see how all activity is a variation on the natural order, is all one thing

This may have its philosophical and aesthetic appeal, but it provides little comfort if you are a teacher and it is Sunday evening, the week looming ahead. What you really crave is a file of lesson plans, a box of handouts or other paraphernalia, and the aura of authority that you remember your own teachers having. What we all want is a tried and true method, a set of proven procedures.

If the desire for a straightforward methodological connection between theory and practice strikes a chord with you, you are not alone. For as long as teaching has been a profession, "method" has been a focus in one way or another. Given the external pressures, it is natural to desire an organizing framework that provides both an overarching rationale and a guide for materials production and use, a map of the territory that includes compass and canteen.

The problem is that the terrain is alive and constantly shifting. There are no standard answers, no proven approaches. Earl Stevick captures part of the problem with his riddle.

> In the field of language teaching, Method A is the logical contradiction of Method B: if the assumptions from which A claims to be derived are correct, then B cannot work, and vice versa. Yet one colleague is getting excellent results with A and another is getting comparable results with B. How is this possible? (1996, 193)

A methods view of teaching carries with it the assumptions that make the riddle possible. If we take a causal view of teaching, in which teacher behavior directly and uncomplicatedly causes student learning, then of course different methods will produce different results. If, however, we attend to the results, to the learning that has occurred, and work backward to an examination of the contexts for learning, we will discover patterns of activity that permit us to see how students learned. Among the most important of the factors we will uncover will be the relationships among people in the classroom, an insight that Stevick articulates when he asserts that what matters is what goes on inside and between individuals (1980, 197–212; 1996, 253). Let us now turn to examples of three especially accomplished teachers to see how these principles might look in practice.

Glimpses of Three Good Teachers

Since 1990 I have been engaged in research initially developed as an effort to discover methods that were successful with low-income minority students attending urban schools. The first phase involved an intensive examination of literacy instruction in 40 elementary classrooms. These consisted of fourth- and fifth-grade classrooms from across the Denver metropolitan area, representing a wide diversity of neighborhoods in terms of socioeconomic status, race/ethnicity, and home language. The sample included regular classrooms, bilingual classrooms, and classrooms with ESL learners. An effort was made to select teachers who espoused a wide range of teaching methods. Early in the study we asked teachers to sketch their educational philosophies and followed up throughout the school year with observations and interviews. At the time, the whole language/phonics debate raged at full volume (Edelsky 1990), and most teachers positioned themselves along this continuum.

Difficulties emerged immediately. Teachers who identified themselves as adhering to the same method often used markedly different classroom techniques, and teachers who adhered to opposing methodologies utilized activities that were markedly similar (Davis et al. 1992). Intrigued, we continued the study by focusing on three teachers who emerged as especially successful; they achieved remarkable success under difficult circumstances yet espoused dramatically different philosophies and approached their teaching in strikingly different ways (Clarke et al. 1996). The three teachers are Jackie Arriaga, Mary Fahey, and Barbara Stuckert.

At the time of the study Jackie Arriaga was in her early thirties and bilingual (a native of Ecuador who grew up in Chicago); her classroom was officially designated as a bilingual classroom. Her teaching was marked by a focus on reality; she worked to help her students succeed in the mean streets outside the school. She knew all of the students' family situations, and she called home whenever she thought a child needed encouragement, discipline, or specific help. She emphasized "good choices" and taking responsibility for one's decisions. Her instruction was organized around thematic units, projects, and frequent field trips, all of which were designed to bring the world into the classroom and to take the children into the world. Students were required to organize their own efforts, providing written descriptions of what they intended to do, what they thought they would learn from the experience, and why they should be permitted to proceed. She conferred with individuals and small groups of students as they worked, and she frequently asked them to write in their journals about what they were doing or about problems they were having. She responded in writing to their journal entries. The classroom was a surging mass of energy that undoubtedly appeared chaotic to a casual observer, as students moved freely from computers to art centers to conference tables as they worked on their projects. Indeed, even though we spent considerable time in her classroom, we were not always able to understand exactly what was going on. At one point early in the research we had an extended conversation among ourselves about the inclusion of Jackie's classroom in the study; several members of the research team doubted that her lessons were organized enough to be effective. The memory of those conversations serves as antidote against snap judgments we make about colleagues based on glimpses of instruction seen through open doorways, because she was indeed very successful; it took us a year's worth of data and many hours of analysis to discover the reasons for Jackie's success.

Mary Fahey was in her late forties when we entered her classroom. She had taught for eight years, followed by a 10-year break to raise her family. She had been back in the classroom five years when we met her. Mary's goal was for students to love reading and writing, and all of her instruction was based on literature. She read to the students several times each day and required them to read and write at least two hours of every school day. She is an enthusiastic person who calls students "honey" and "sweetheart" as she talks animatedly with them about their reading and writing. Her interaction with the children resembled that of peers discussing favorite topics. Students had freedom to choose what they worked on, but they were held accountable for pace and productivity. They "published" their writing and spent considerable time reading each other's work and sharing their writing with the group. Mary's classroom was as quiet as the reading room at the Library of Congress, but considerably less formal; students could be seen sprawled on puff chairs and stretched out on the sofa with clipboards and books as she worked on her own reading and writing or circulated to confer with students about theirs. Of the three teachers, Mary came the closest to the "whole language" ideal portrayed in the ideological debates of the day. Her classroom was a book lover's delight. Books were everywhere—crammed into bulging bookcases, stacked on chairs, displayed on window sills. Teen heroes in colorful posters admonished the children to read. A "clothes line" looped under one blackboard was hung with "vocabulary mittens" made of construction paper offering synonyms for the students' use. As children worked on their stories, they would wander over to the clothes line and select a mitten to use in their writing.

Barbara Stuckert was in her midfifties, a few years from retirement when we began the study. She described herself as a traditional teacher who would enjoy teaching in an academy where students were expected to work and where parents signed contracts to assist the students in their schoolwork. She emphasized academic achievement; the classroom was decorated with charts showing the number of books students had read and displaying spelling- and math-test results. The school day was organized around the timely completion of academic assignments. Barbara excelled at whole-class instruction, using a skillful alternation of explanation, drill, and choral work to teach concepts and practice skills. When a lesson had been taught, students worked on their own, knowing what they had to do—spelling words; worksheets in math, science, and social studies; comprehension questions over books they had read; etc.—and when they had to have it done. Barbara's classroom exuded an aura of calm, focused energy, one in which students knew what was expected of them and worked confidently to complete their tasks. As was the case with Jackie, Barbara presented some challenges to the prevailing wisdom about effective literacy instruction. The problem for some of the younger members of the research team was her traditional, almost politically incorrect, teacher-centered, lecture-based approach to teaching, coupled with her formal demeanor. In an era when debates raged between proponents of child-focused, literature-based instruction, on the one hand, and advocates of teacher-orchestrated, grammar-and-phonics-based worksheets, on the other, Barbara seemed blissfully above the fray. Others might debate; she knew what was required and went about her business.

We began the research in 1990 with the assumption that we would be able to identify and describe instructional methods and materials that were effective with inner-city minority children. To a certain extent this assumption was borne out; teachers who used extended texts (i.e., "real" reading and writing, rather than worksheets) with their students tended to get better results than teachers who did not (Davis et al. 1994). Mary, Jackie, and Barbara fit this profile. However, it soon became clear that more than an understanding of method or materials was needed to explain their success. As the earlier descriptions make clear, the three classrooms presented very different pictures to the observer. What might not be so clear is how difficult it was to reconcile the different scenes that greeted us each day with the knowledge that the three teachers were overwhelmingly successful.

It is not possible here to provide a detailed defense of the claim that these are good teachers. Suffice it to say that we consider good teaching to be that resulting in student learning and in which students seem engaged and enthusiastic. We have abundant evidence from two studies that the students in these classrooms made marked gains in literacy skills and that their attitudes toward self, school, and learning were extremely positive. We administered a number of pre– and post–achievement tests—our own, the district measures, and the Iowa Test of Basic Skills; we collected samples of student work throughout the year; we have several hundred hours of video- and audio-tape transcripts of classroom instruction, teacher and student interviews, and home visits. Research method and outcome measures are presented in the final report (Clarke et al. 1996). Anecdotal confirmation of our conclusions comes from our unanimous conviction that we would have been very pleased if our children had had these teachers when they were in school.

The difficulty that a methods analysis of the three teachers faces comes from the fact that the assumptions on which it rests are largely causal and too superficial to account for the successes the teachers experienced. We were able to accomplish much more, because of the extended time we spent in the classrooms and because of the richness of the stories we collected from the teachers, children, and parents. We were able to reach an understanding of the relationships that the teachers forged with the children and of the ways in which they adjusted their behavior to take into account the uniqueness of each student and the variations in activity required by the personalities of the classes.

In the paragraphs that follow, I explore aspects of the activity orchestrated by these teachers that would not be available to an analysis that maintained a methods-level perspective. My argument is based on the assertion that the teachers were able to achieve a level of coherence in their interactions with students that led to student achievement.

Key to the success they enjoyed was the amount of time that students spent reading and writing. All three teachers devoted a considerable amount of the day to extended periods of time for literacy instruction. This is not a surprising discovery, given that they all came to our attention because of their students' gains in reading and writing, but it bears mentioning in an era when class time is increasingly fractionated. In each classroom, students read many books, discussed the meaning of what they read, wrote stories and reports, and revised and edited their writing. However, reading and writing were viewed and approached differently in each classroom. In Mary's classroom reading and writing were ends in themselves—something to be engaged in for the sake of enjoyment and self-expression. In Jackie's classroom reading and writing were more utilitarian, used as tools to learn and to accomplish tasks. In Barbara's classroom reading and writing were ways to demonstrate progress toward and success in academic endeavors. This focused energy should not be confused with formulaic notions of "time on task." Rather, these teachers managed to create environments in which learners sustained focal attention on literacy tasks and activities that fundamentally shaped the students' perceptions of themselves.

These teachers sent clear messages to students that permeated all activity. These are messages in the cyberneticists' sense of the term, the "to-whom-it-may-concern" messages that bombard us from all sides as we go through the day (Wilden 1980, 1987; Harries-Jones 1995; G. Bateson 1999). The messages were evident in language the teachers used to explicitly mediate students' perceptions of situations and events, in their behavior, and in the priorities revealed by how they allocated time and organized activities. This provided students with new ways of thinking about school, themselves, and others and new ways of behaving, often in the face of considerable peer and family pressure. The children learned how to position themselves in a world of complex cultural symbols surrounding school, learning, and literacy. The messages provided a unifying focus in the classroom, around which students rallied early on; by year's end, their behavior and attitude mirrored the teacher's values. In Mary's class the unifying message was love of literature and writing. For Jackie it was personal responsibility. For Barbara the unifying theme was school achievement. Each teacher's message was different, but each message was delivered and enacted so clearly that students were able to articulate it in interviews, often using the teacher's characteristic language to do so. Each theme reflected the central expectations that the teacher had for students, expectations that students began to hold for themselves and for others. This focused attending to central values provided students with the perceptual and procedural learnings that formed the basis for their learning.

The teachers ran their classes with authority, but this was not an authoritarian assertion of power, rooted in societal and institutional convention, but one derived from inner conviction and commitment. Rules and regulations were based on values the teachers held dear, and they regularly and forcefully conveyed the rationale to the students. This was acknowledged by students in their comments that the teachers were "fair." The students were well aware that "being fair" was a complex phenomenon, not merely a matter of treating everyone the same. The teachers responded flexibly to students according to individual temperament, need, and circumstance. As one student said about Mary:

> She treats me with respect and she treats me like I am somebody. I mean, she doesn't treat anybody like nothing. She says we all have a certain talent and she brings that talent out, she shows, and in a way she makes you feel comfortable. I don't know what she does, but she

makes you feel better as a person, and she treats you, not like other teachers, cause other teachers treat everybody the same, and Mrs. Fahey has tried to like be a guide, she tries to make everybody happy, everybody comfortable, and she's like, I don't know, an angel or something, she just wants everybody to be happy.

Because they operated out of conviction, they exuded confidence in everything they did. They had many years experience teaching in urban schools, and they had the courage of their convictions. They took their work seriously. They were confident of their views of teaching and learning, and they had a clear sense of what was important for children. They worked with single-minded intensity to convey clearly to students what was important. Just as we sensed this authority in our interviews and classroom observations, the students also were aware of it. Attendance was consistent, student commitment to the teacher and to the routines of the classroom was high, and students listened to and came to adopt the message the teachers sent.

Michael Fullan and others have referred to this phenomenon as "moral purpose" (Goodlad 1984, 1994; Fullan 1999). They argue that good teachers facilitate critical enculturation, in which students acquire personal understandings of such concepts as truth, beauty, and justice in an atmosphere of openness and honesty, an atmosphere that permits them to see the virtues and imperfections of the world they live in. They emphasize the importance of disciplined encounters with a wide variety of content areas, including evaluative and belief systems, as well as social and political systems. Also key are interpersonal relationships; they stress the importance of viewing teaching as more than the mere technical facility of teaching practices. They argue that good teaching hinges on authentic human relationships, in which individuals are valued for who they are and what they bring to the interaction. This characterization of teachers captures the essence of Mary, Jackie, and Barbara. This is the morality not of zealots seeking to impose their view on others but of individuals who have arrived at an understanding of what works for them and their students.

Because they were so confident in their work, Mary, Jackie, and Barbara created classroom environments where everyone felt comfortable. These were classrooms where individuals felt respected and appreciated, where it was safe to work, to experiment, to try new things. The teachers were always approachable, and virtually every tape had examples of children walking up to them and asking questions, showing them work, expressing opinions. The children experienced the unconditional positive regard that Carl Rogers believed essential for healthy personal growth and that numerous scholars have cited as the foundation of effective classrooms (C. Rogers 1969; Maslow 1970; Stevick 1980, 1998). In Mary's and Barbara's classrooms, much of the predictability came from an established schedule that was rarely, and only with explanation, changed. In Jackie's class, flexibility of schedule and time allotted for tasks provided a safe context for work and development. Students treated each other with respect and expected to be similarly treated by others. Individual rights and group responsibility were values that pervaded class events and individual interactions. All three teachers articulated the rules that established mutual respect and consideration. Jackie constantly asked, "Is that fair? Is that how you would like to be treated?" and Mary admonished the children, on the first day, "No putdowns! When I was a little girl other students made fun of me, and it hurt my feelings." Barbara observed that now that the children were fourth graders, and the best class in the school, certain behaviors just were not heard of. It was common to hear students evoking their teachers' rules in disputes.

The teachers knew a great deal about the students, and they used that knowledge to guide their work. Instruction was individualized, taking into account affective and interactional idiosyncracies of the students. Jackie took a personal interest in her students' families, often having taught their older siblings or cousins in previous years. She was relentless in pursuing a course of action. On one occasion, when she had to run to the office during class, she happened to bump into the older sister of one of her students, and she took the opportunity to tell her that the student, Jaime, was refusing to complete an assignment. The sister, who had stopped by the school to drop something off, immediately went up to the room and pulled Jaime into the hall for a conversation. What she told him never came out, but he stayed in from recess to complete the work. Mary conducted long conferences with students about their work and, when necessary, about problems that may have been affecting their work. When Sheniqua was having a particularly difficult time, Mary worked out a reward system with her involving the assistant principal, a favorite individual among students: for every day Sheniqua managed to control her temper, she was allowed to spend time with the assistant principal after school. Barbara used test scores as the basis for many of her instructional decisions, and she monitored students' achievement closely. When a student was frustrated by an activity, she immediately provided support or changed the demands of the activity; when a student was experiencing success, she quickly urged a greater challenge.

It is important to emphasize that this goes far beyond the approaches implied in "learning styles" or other formulaic models of teacher-student interaction. The attention these teachers paid to each child, the adjusting of tasks and explanations in keeping with each child's ability to participate successfully in an activity, and the sensitivity of the teacher to issues in the child's life outside of school contributed to the building of a significant relationship between teacher and child.

These teachers created classrooms in which learning and work were taken seriously, where high expectations were the norm and the students worked to fulfill those expectations. Tasks and responsibilities were clearly established, deadlines were observed, work was logged in and evaluated, and subsequent efforts were shaped by students' effort and achievement. The teachers required students to improve with every project or task, and they paid close attention to students' progress and efforts. Students participated actively, with focused attention. A key to the success of these classrooms lay in the willing participation of students, in contrast to the passive compliance, boredom, or resistance so often seen in school.

Coherence: Aligning Thought and Action

Depending on where you are in your teaching career, you might find this account either hopelessly confusing or irritatingly obvious. The former reaction is more likely if you are just starting out or if you are deeply committed to a particular method and are suspicious of others. The second reaction is one I hear from some veteran teachers who have seen enough good teaching to know that it does not all look the same. In either case, however, you would be justified in pointing out that I have not yet made it clear how you might be expected to use any of this in your own teaching. In other words, "Nice stories, but so what?" In the space remaining, I would like to address these concerns.

First, let me be clear about the claims I am making here. Remember that in our research we were focused on literacy teaching and learning, so when I say that the three teachers achieved similar results with different methods, that is the focus of my claims. The children in these three classrooms learned a great deal more than what we attended to, and those learnings varied greatly across the classrooms. Just a sampling: Although all three teachers demonstrated a profound respect for and consideration of the children's home life, only Jackie explicitly validated linguistic diversity through her command of Spanish. And while all three teachers clearly valued school achievement, the students in Barbara's class emerged from the school year with a much clearer focus on test scores and grades than did the children in the other two classes. And, in spite of the fact that no child could have spent the year with any of these three women and failed to understand the importance of literacy, I suspect that only Mary's students considered themselves authors who might someday make a living with their writing.

In other words, the children learned a great deal that year that we did not account for. The claim is not that teaching method does not matter. Indeed, the approach I take underscores the fact that how students spend their time with teachers is a primary indicator of what they will learn. However, I *am* arguing that the narrow focus on test scores that drives much of what is happening in schools today, misguided in its own right, is doubly indictable if it leads administrators or policymakers to push for instructional uniformity.

In fact, just the opposite is required. Diversity of instruction is required if we want uniformly high achievement. Leaving aside for the moment a critique of uniform standards and high-stakes testing, both of which are primarily political rather than pedagogical issues, the simple response to the alleged educational crisis facing us today is to recruit intelligent, energetic, and honest people to the profession and create the conditions that permit them to translate their own interests and enthusiasms into pedagogically sound practices.

So, on the assumption that you meet these criteria and you are still wondering how to bring a systems perspective to bear on your own teaching, let me explore this notion of coherence a bit more.

Coherence, in teaching but also in all other aspects of life, is that somewhat rare state that is achieved when our intentions and our actions are in alignment, when we and the people with whom we are interacting perceive a unity of the ideal and the real. It is a dynamic, unstable state, one that we achieve in bursts and that is difficult to maintain.

It is both an outcome and the process by which it is accomplished. Bourdieu refers to it as "practice"—the habitual, routinized, perfected activity that constitutes the day's work and that contains knowledge that is not easily externalized, objectified, or explained (1990). The three teachers bring years of experience to the classroom, and they draw on this experience as they work with children. They monitor several processes at once, anticipate likely responses, and make split-second decisions regarding what direction to take when something unexpected occurs or when an activity is not "working." They devote hours to planning, and at the same time they are masters of improvisation.

One could argue that this account of the teachers is a descriptive statement of outcomes that merely begs the question of how they were accomplished. To a certain extent this is true, because no amount of description of how they teach can translate directly into another classroom or even into another day in the same classroom. The objection, however, reveals the assumption of causality on which conventional views of teaching are based. This is the view that teaching can be reduced to a collection of techniques and activities, the formulaic implementation of specific procedures—follow these steps and students will learn. This would be true if humans were billiard balls, responding to laws of physics in a causal universe. But humans are not billiard balls; they are information-processing organisms whose responses to situations are not *determined*–but merely *constrained*–by external events. Teaching/learning is merely one example of the complex process of human communication and interaction. Learners' behavior cannot be manipulated to produce particular outcomes. As all teachers know, techniques and materials do not come with guarantees; the effectiveness of classroom activities depends on thousands of minute decisions that you make in the course of a lesson.

Teaching is not a narrowly focused didactic event; it is the totality of experiences that learners participate in as a result of who the teacher is and how lessons are conducted. The effectiveness of the three teachers is a function of the environments they have created, including but not limited to the specific methods and materials they have utilized. What is important is not only what teachers do but how they do it. The accomplishment is in the experience as much as in the outcomes–the artful integration of the conscious and unconscious decisions they make continually in the course of the day, glimpses of which are visible when we watch them teach.

Methodological choices can only be understood in the larger context of the practice of a particular classroom–an ongoing nexus of relationships and patterns of activity that make sense and are valued by those participating in them. If we are to get beyond method in our attempts to understand good teaching, we will need to avoid formulaic generalities. What is required is an understanding of teaching as an organic activity, one that can be described in broad outlines, that has recognizable patterns, but that is also unique in each instance of its occurrence. The meanings of a particular lesson emerge as the lesson unfolds, even if it is a variation on a tried and true lesson that you have taught a hundred times before.

What students learn goes far beyond the focused content of the curriculum, as commonly understood; the learnings are apperceptive, implicit in all the minute particulars of the day (G. Bateson 1999, 159–76). Gregory Bateson uses "code" as the cover term for the meanings, implicit in the patterns of activity, that produce particular outcomes. He speaks of art here, where the outcomes are paintings or sculpture, but I believe that teaching must be understood in the same way, when the outcomes are changes in the attitudes and behaviors of learners.

> I am concerned with what important psychic information is in the art object quite apart from what it may "represent." "*Le style es l'homme meme*" ("The style is the man himself") (Buffon). What is implicit in style, materials, composition, rhythm, skill and so on? . . . The *code* whereby perceived objects or persons (or supernatural) are transformed into wood or paint is a source of information about the artist and his culture. It is the very rules of transformation that are of interest to me—not the message, but the code. (1999, 130)

Teaching is multileveled communication, pulsating with messages about the outside world, coded not just in the words of textbooks, curricula, and tests, but in the voice and gesture of the teacher, the tempo of lessons and uses of space, the relationships among people in the classroom, both expected and permitted. This is the process whereby students are transformed into apprentices of the teacher, reflecting her values in ways that are boh conscious and unconscious. This is teaching (and learning) at its most powerful, its most enduring.

When I speak of coherence in the teaching of Mary, Jackie, and Barbara, I am referring not merely to the things they do consciously but to all aspects of their being and doing in classrooms. They each have a distinctive style, one that is only partially captured in descriptions of characteristic methods and materials because, as Buffon says, the style is as much *who* they are as *what* they do. When we turn our attention to the experience of the children in their classrooms we realize that *style* and *coherence* refer to the same phenomenon, but at different levels, the former with regard to the teacher and the latter with regard to the classroom. Or to put it in a slightly different way—we all have our distinctive styles, our characteristic ways of teaching, but only when we manage to get the classroom pulsating to the same rhythms can we use the term *coherence* to refer to our accomplishments. Bateson saw the struggle to achieve this state as the quest for grace, in both a spiritual and an aesthetic sense. It is an effort to reach a level of integration of our various "parts" or "selves"–intellectual, physical, interactional–so that we attain a sense of unity of accomplishment.

The fact that accomplishment and process are one requires us to acknowledge another subtle aspect of effective teaching–that it is not entirely available to conscious understanding. Mary, Jackie, and Barbara make decisions and act with a sixth sense acquired over time with hundreds of children. They know that a particular comment or question or gesture is right, and they can usually give a rationale for it later, but its effectiveness derives from its unconscious application at the moment of maximum usefulness. Bateson continues with his discussion of art criticism; I ask you to read the following paragraph with teaching in mind.

> It is this–the complex layering of consciousness and unconsciousness–
> that creates difficulty when we try to discuss art or ritual or mythol-
> ogy. . . . Samuel Butler's insistence that the better an organism "knows"
> something, the less conscious it becomes of its knowledge, i.e., there is
> a process whereby knowledge (or "habit"–whether of action, percep-
> tion, or thought) sinks to deeper and deeper levels of the mind. This
> phenomenon, which is central to Zen discipline, is also relevant to all
> art and all skill. (1999, 134–35)

There is a validity and authenticity that results from skill exercised at this level of (un)awareness. Lessons are planned, and goals set out, and lessons conducted with a sense of conscious purpose that we expect of professionals. However, once the lesson is under way, the activity becomes totalizing, and they become absorbed in the interacting with students in ways that could not have been foreseen. They make decisions based on knowledge that is lodged very deep in who they are as people. Because their responses to children and situations are unpremeditated, they possess authority that planned activity might not.

> In truth, our life is such that its unconscious components are continuously
> present in all their multiple forms. It follows that in our relationships we
> continuously exchange messages about these unconscious materials, and

it becomes important also to exchange metamessages by which we tell each other what order and species of unconsciousness or (consciousness) attaches to our messages. In a merely pragmatic way, this is important because the orders of truth are different for different sorts of messages. Insofar as a message is conscious and voluntary, it could be deceitful. . . . [W]ith skill, the fact of skill indicates the presence of large unconscious components in the performance. (G. Bateson 1999, 137)

A major shortcoming of "method" as the lens through which to view teaching is that it is too intentional, too narrowly focused on instructional goals and sanctioned activities. It assumes too conscious a level of performance. "Method" forces us to look not at what is happening but at images filtered through established expectations. As when we look at the world through cut crystal, what we see is always in relationship to the biased lens of predetermined values. When one looks at teaching from a methods perspective, one tends to notice what is not being done as much as one notices what is being done. This is analogous to the myopia that Bourdieu attributes to theoretical perspectives of practice in general.

If one fails to recognize any form of action other than rational action or mechanical reaction, it is impossible to understand the logic of all the actions that are reasonable without being the product of a reasoned design, still less of rational calculation; informed by a kind of objective finality without being consciously organized in relation to an explicitly constituted end; intelligible and coherent without springing from an intention of coherence and a deliberate decision; adjusted to the future without being the product of a project or a plan. (Bourdieu 1990, 50–51)

These three teachers achieve coherence in action without consciously working for it, through the exercise of familiar routines coupled with spontaneous responses to the demands of the moment. They see a distant horizon, and they have a sense of how they will get there with the children; everything they do is intended to further the journey, but their efforts exceed the effects of planned actions, because their responses emerge from deeper sources of knowing.

Their knowledge, skill, attitudinal predispositions, socialization, ritual, and routine, when manifested in classroom experience, can best be seen as practice in the most profound sense of the term. We can describe observed events, and we can identify significant features of methods and materials that seem to correlate with success. But these are the mere surface features of communicational exchanges in which teacher and students, engaged in significant relationships, negotiate meanings and achieve learnings together. And because all relationships are unique, however familiar and formulaic they may seem—especially those, like teacher/student, that are reified in socially stereotyped roles—the accomplishment must be viewed with a certain awe. This is remarkable not only in the outcomes that the students achieve, although this is certainly significant, but also in the orchestration of each day's activities. The range of activities is established through years of working in familiar settings, within a comfortable variation of techniques and materials, and anticipating the reactions of students that, while always unique, represent variations from within a repertoire expectable for their age. The day, once rolling, presents familiarity and surprise simultaneously, and the teacher continually finds herself creating something new from something old. As Bourdieu says, "The virtuoso finds in his discourse the triggers for his discourse, which goes along like a train laying down its own rails" (1990, 57).

I realize that the danger of this analysis is that it could not only fail to energize the discourse on good teaching but actively deflate it. By emphasizing the virtuosity of these teachers I may intimidate novice teachers who do not see themselves as aspiring virtuosos and veteran teachers who despair of ever achieving this level of accomplishment. This is not my intent. Indeed, my study of these teachers has convinced me of the impact teachers can have, even in very difficult circumstances. The transformational power of classroom practice lies in its ability to change the individuals who participate in it—to shape the ways in which they think and act, to socialize them into a community of literate individuals. The three classrooms we studied, diverse as they were, shared a coherence that made their transformational power understandable. They were grounded in a clear articulation of values, emanating from the teacher, that gave meaning to individual activities. This meaning, in turn, was given clarity and focus through the efforts of the teachers to add to their teaching repertoire, which inevitably led them back to the search for techniques and materials—teaching as art and science, the teacher improving by discovering and refining new methods. It may be the ultimate irony that "method" provides both the primary source of and the most persistent obstacle to the improvement of teaching.

But to return to the question of, "So, what use do I make of this in my own teaching?" The main thing, I think, is to remain calm. I haven't shown this essay to Mary, Jackie, or Barbara, but I can predict that they would find my analysis overwrought and exaggerated. I doubt that they viewed their accomplishments that year with the admiration that we did, and I know that Mary, for one, believes she has moved beyond what she was doing that year. I bumped into her at the grocery store, and she was incredulous that we were still studying the transcripts from that year. "Oh, I'm doing a lot more with writing now; you should come see what the kids are accomplishing," she told me. My point is this: You have no choice but to be who you are, and how you teach is a constantly evolving process of planning, teaching, and assessing lessons. Attend to the responses of your students and carry on.

Desiderata

I believe I addressed the issues posed in the quiz, but in the event that I did not make myself clear, I will conclude with the following answer key. Like all teachers who devise tests of this sort, I was looking for specific answers. These are the answers I was fishing for.

1. T/F   Actions speak louder than words.

   True. Children and dogs, especially, are adept at sensing your real intentions, because they are not confused by the rationalizations or prevarications that other adults will listen to. So as you examine your motives for assignments, or your rationale for rules in the classroom, examine also your own behaviors. Do you behave the way you ask your students to behave? If someone were to interview your students would they articulate the values you believe you hold?

2. T/F Everyone at a particular age should be able to read and write with similar facility.

False. Human development is vastly more complex than our "grade-level" approach to academic accomplishment would imply. So much depends on the individual's cognitive and family history, and upon the range of experiences she or he has had, and this applies to all skill mastery. We need to approach each learner as an emergent bundle of achievement.

3. T/F Tests and test scores are more valuable as political tools than as indicators of student learning.

True. We need to pay attention to them and take them seriously, because they shape the climate of instruction. They constitute important instruments in focusing public attention and in leveraging change, but they are of limited value in day-to-day pedagogical decision making.

4. T/F A fact is noise until it answers a question in an individual's mind.

True. However important you may consider a fact to be, if your students are paying attention to something else, it will be merely a buzz in their ears. As teachers, we need to help students see how the facts that we consider to be so important relate to their lives.

5. T/F All moments are "teachable moments."

True, although we may not always be prepared to make them work for all the students. The point here is that learners are always learning but that we teachers are not always aware of what they are learning. If we want particular moments to be "teachable" we have to know what students are prepared to learn.

6. T/F   Human beings cannot *not* learn.

True. This puts an imperative spin on the explanation in number 5.
That is, because human beings are always learning, they will always be
learning something from whatever it is we are doing or having them do.
We need to scrutinize our behavior and the activities we have selected
for the day to discern just what our students are likely to learn from
them. This can be chastening.

7. A teacher is most like . . .
   a. a gardener.
   b. an actor.
   c. a puppeteer.
   d. a warden.

My answer: *a. a gardener.* We can create conditions for optimum
growth, but we do not control all of the relevant variables. Also, we
work in seasonal cycles, and each year we have another chance for a
bumper crop. Many of us get into teaching because we enjoy the
limelight, and I do think that there is something to be said for the
energetic teacher who projects effectively, like an actor. But the
difficulty with teacher-as-actor is that it implies a mask, and when
the mask slips, the student will learn what the teacher really values.
I fear that this lesson may be more powerful than the masterful
performances. I doubt if you were tempted to select "puppeteer" or
"warden." I included them as distractors because many of the rules
and regulations under which teachers work today seem to have been
crafted by individuals who think of students as puppets or prisoners.

8. Explain how each of the following is an example of teaching.
   a. An adult leads a group of adolescents through a production of
      Hamlet.
   b. A teacher alerts the principal to the fact that noise is considered an
      important indicator of learning in an upcoming project, so as to
      avoid alarm or administrative intervention.
   c. A teacher meets with parents to solicit homework support for
      students.

    d. A citizen votes on election day.

    e. A teenager marches in a gay rights parade.

Teaching is creating, or working to create, an environment in which others can learn. It is not always associated with a role or a position. All of these behaviors can be seen as individuals' efforts to help someone else learn something and modify their thinking and/or behavior based on that learning.

9. Explain how each of the following might be considered evidence of learning.
   a. An ESL learner puts *-ed* on the end of all verbs to signal past tense.
   b. Students from a particular class sit together at lunch.
   c. Everyone gets quiet and turns expectantly when a student moves to a particular chair in the classroom.
   d. A child raises his forearm to protect his face when an adult makes a quick move toward him.
   e. Adults and children walk down the right side of the hallway during breaks between classes.

Learning is change over time through engagement in activity. If you begin with each of these events and ask yourself, "What is the history of this behavior?" you will discover what aspects of individuals' attitudes and behavior had to change for them to arrive at this point. Because we are so conditioned to the "normal" events of the typical school day, we have difficulty seeing the learning going on around us. In fact, we often see some learning as error—the ESL learner, for example, who says "goed" instead of "went." Barbara Stuckert's students often sat together at lunch, where they continued to talk about the work they were doing in her class, a sure indication of the acquisition of a scholarly attitude. In Mary Fahey's class, the rocking chair signaled story time, and the person sitting there was accorded special deference. The defensive movement of a student is a learned response to an abusive environment, and the gravitation to the right side of the hallway indicates the acquisition of a rule by the inhabitants of a building.

10. How would you demonstrate that the following are lessons learned in secondary schools?
    a. Learning is something that occurs in 45-minute blocks.
    b. You haven't learned anything until someone evaluates it.
    c. Facts are more important than attitudes.
    d. In school, it is not what you know but the power you hold that counts.
    e. Reading and writing are something that students do but not something that teachers do.

See number 9. I actually believe that these are deeply held convictions for most of us in modern, technologically advanced societies, but I happen to be involved right now with middle-school students, so I phrased the item that way. Here are some observations that pertain to each item.

a. We are a society dominated by the clock, whether we talking about bells going off in schools or the rhythms of the TV.
b. Most of us have lost the ability to learn something for the pure enjoyment of learning. Even artists, the archetypical self-involved learners, want ribbons.
c. The fact that we have to argue for "affective" education indicates its second-class rating.
d. "Because I said so" is far more common than reasoned explanation as a basis for decisions, whether we are discussing classrooms or faculty meetings.
e. Teachers in general are too busy and harassed to take time to read when students can see them reading. And how many people do you know who block out time in their day-timers for reading?

The question of how we might demonstrate that these are learnings acquired in secondary school requires us to devise ways of seeing the world differently, of understanding that the way things are is not the way things have to be.

6 Empowerment: Issues, Constraints, and Cautionary Comments

Please respond to the following assertions; use the space provided to edit the wording to your liking or to add variations on the theme of empowerment that reflect your values.

1. T/F One of my goals as a teacher is to empower my students, to help them reach their full academic and personal potential.

2. T/F I believe that schools and classrooms should be places where appreciation of diversity is the norm and where individuals are encouraged to explore and expand their unique abilities.

3. T/F I teach toward a vision of democratic ideals—schools and communities where all individuals enjoy freedom of choice, equality, and justice.

This essay grew out of an article that appeared in *Language Arts* in 1990 (Clarke 1990).

If you have marked these as true for you (or if you are sympathetic with the general sentiment but quibble with the wording), you are among a sizeable portion of the educational community. For some time now there has been a call for empowerment as a foundation for our efforts as educators (Freire 1970, 1985; Giroux and McLaren 1986; Giroux 1988). The desire to liberate learners from the constraints of poverty, discrimination, ignorance, intellectual servitude, or other oppressions has great appeal. This is not merely the position of classroom teachers; it is also at the heart of a great deal of educational research (Heath 1983; Ladson-Billings 1994; Wolcott 1994; Eisenhart 2001).

There is much to admire in the stance: the declarations of learner autonomy; the affirmation of the importance of diversity; the centrality of human dignity and individual importance; the implicit assertion that our work plays a pivotal role in people's lives, that we make a difference in society.

I am attracted to this portrayal of teachers and education, but I want to examine the issues and assumptions behind it, and I want to register some words of caution based on an analysis of the constraints that we face in our roles as change agents and educational reformers. You may find my analysis somewhat chastening to your activist agenda. This is not my intent. Just the opposite, in fact—I believe that an understanding of the way society and its institutions function is an essential condition for the sort of changes we seek. I will use *empowerment, liberation education,* and *critical pedagogy* interchangeably, to designate a cluster of beliefs that affirms the importance of helping individuals gain greater autonomy in their lives. I'll begin with an attempt to define what is intended by the word *empowerment.*

Empowerment

Every wave of educational innovation carries with it a distinctive discourse—an inventory of ideological concepts and phrases that mark the current paradigm. Empowerment is an important part of current educational philosophy and commitment. As is true with all professional discourse, the language of liberation education is used with a wide variety of meanings; a few teachers even assert that the rhetoric accomplishes the opposite of what it intends (Delpit 1988; Ellsworth 1989). And, as is often the case, many people use the language of liberation pedagogy with little understanding of its intellectual roots or its revolutionary imperatives. As in most professions, we in education have to deal with our share of buzzwords, and the catchphrases of empowerment are just one example.

But buzzwords merit consideration, if for no other reason than that they are a consistent phenomenon in our personal and professional lives. An important quality of buzzwords is that they signal public affirmation of who we are and what we are doing. Further, they provide us with the feeling that we are part of something larger, that we are in tune with the times. For new teachers, especially, this is important, but for all of us the sense of community achieved by the discourse should not be minimized. In fact, buzzwords may be more important than commonly realized. They may be the most visible feature of a potential revolution in teaching practice. Sandra Silberstein, for example, develops this theme as she examines the reasons people give for the important decisions in their lives. Echoing Marx and Engels's critique of ideology (Marx and Engels [1848] 1947), she warns that we cannot take at face value the reasons people cite for their actions. Rather, "people articulate as motives the illusions of a particular epoch" (Silberstein 1988, 129).

An illusion of our epoch is that we can help people take some measure of control over their lives. Whether our actions match the rhetoric is only part of the issue. What matters is that now is the time when attempts at liberation are possible, not in spite of the fact that the words are used widely and unthinkingly but precisely because of this. Now is the time when these ideas will find the greatest degree of acceptance, and now is the time to push for action to match the words. Recognizing the "buzziness" of liberation education does not prevent us from using the concept to our advantage.

It is, however, important to have an understanding of what we mean by assertions of empowerment and liberation. For me what is important in the stance is the affirmation of human dignity and individual agency and the possibility of contributing to people's ability to exercise a measure of choice in their lives. In the pages that follow, I will elaborate on what I mean by this, but I want to underscore one point here: When I use the phrase "contribute to people's ability" I am carefully choosing my words. As with all my teaching, I approach the task knowing that the best I can do is create an environment that encourages individuals to grow in a general direction and toward particular values. I can provide choices, but they have to do the choosing. I will proceed with my critique with this assumption in mind, and I urge you to see my analysis as a friendly brief, an attempt at improving the chances for success of empowerment-oriented reformers.

Issues

I want my students to enjoy greater autonomy, more discretion in their lives. The problem implied in that assertion is that they do not currently exercise their fair share of autonomy and discretion. As a teacher and self-styled change agent I need to decide what, exactly, the issue is that I am working on. Identifying the issue helps clarify my thinking and permits me to organize my efforts.

If I decide the issue is racism or sexism, my approach will be different than if I focus on bureaucratic inertia or institutional culture, and different still if I decide that the issue revolves around interpersonal dynamics in the classroom. I may decide that the world in general is unjust and that my institution in particular has policies and procedures that disadvantage certain groups. I will keep this in mind, but I may decide to focus my efforts on my own teaching and my participation on committees and curriculum development. Or, conversely, I may decide to devote all my spare time to the political campaign of a presidential candidate because of my desire to have an impact on the broadest possible scale.

If I decide that the issue is parenting practices and developmental aspects of socialization, I will work with school/community collaborations or Head Start initiatives, in addition to doing what I can in my classroom to increase my students' sense of agency.

In any case, I recognize that my focus is on just one part of a large number of overlapping, dynamically interacting systems within systems within systems. If I find that particular individuals or groups in my school do not enjoy the full range of society's prerogatives and privileges, it is because society as a whole functions to maintain the status quo, in which power is distributed unequally. Things are the way they are *not* by accident.

I imagine that most people would agree that this is a reasonably accurate description of the way the world operates. What you may not have considered is the point I want to make here: *Local examples of unhappiness are manifestations of larger systemic functioning.*

I do not believe that all the injustices I observe are the result of conscious planning by nefarious individuals. It is true that there are evil and angry people out there, and particular instances of injustice can certainly be attributed to them. But an environment of intolerance or ignorance that permits broad-based inequality is not a result of individual initiative but rather of systemic functioning. And in situations where everyone seems to decry a persistent injustice we must stop to ponder why it persists. It is difficult to escape the conclusion that if a situation is considered a problem by enough people, it will be solved. So I approach enduring problems with the assumption that someone must be benefiting to make change more trouble than the problem itself. When I encounter injustice in school or community, I pause to ask, "Who benefits?" For example, when a particular child or ethnic group suffers discrimination or prejudice, who is the direct or indirect beneficiary?

It is important to proceed carefully here, because I do not want to imply that all injustice is the result of conspiracy by evildoers. In fact, it is often the opposite; well-meaning people, working hard for the greater good, contribute unwittingly to the problems they seek to solve. Given this indeterminate view of the universe, it is important to understand why some people seem to enjoy a greater amount of flexibility in matters of personal power and why it is necessary to work for empowerment on the part of others. If we see empowerment as part of our responsibility, we need to develop strategies for action that are based on the way things are out there.

What is required is that we pay attention to effects. That is, we need to be clear on what we will take as evidence of oppression, on the one hand, and of liberation, on the other. And then we need to have a theory that permits us to understand how the situation developed and what we might do about it. An understanding of the function of constraints is important in this regard.

Constraints

I do not subscribe to conspiracy theories, so I do not think that what we are up against is a grand plot to keep people in their place. However, it is fairly obvious to me that the amount of discretion one has in the mundane conduct of life is directly related to a number of easily identified factors, among which I would list the following: gender; money; race; ethnicity; age; education; physical and mental ability; sexual orientation; religion; and "connections," which actually come as a by-product of several of the preceding variables. Different cultures will have different profiles of the "ideal" person. In our society, I have noticed, you generally have an easier time in life if you are a young, white, able-bodied (preferably slim and elegantly muscled) male who, if not rich, is at least in the middle class and who is Christian, heterosexual, and college educated. Of course, none of these factors is determinative. That is, there are no guarantees that fitting this description will put you on easy street; like all social or forensic profiling, this is an inexact science. And, as in all aspects of life, there are notable exceptions. But if you collect the data, you will find that these factors correlate with power. I am not making a startlingly original statement here; this is a widely held view, and a number of authors explore aspects of the social dynamics involved (Rich 1979; McIntosh 1988). My analysis is based on systems theory and the arguments developed by Gregory Bateson and scholars influenced by him (Watzlawick, Beavin, and Jackson 1967; Watzlawick, Weakland and Fisch 1974; M. C. Bateson 1989, 1994, 2000; G. Bateson 1999).

The systems analysis of privilege and power goes something like this. While it is true that inequality is a systemic phenomenon, it is enacted by individual human beings in the minute particulars of everyday life. Human beings are open systems whose day-to-day functioning is constrained by socioeconomic status, interpersonal dynamics, etc. Our reaction to situations, both mundane and extraordinary, is a function of a complex interaction of such factors, including personal history and our perception of the way the world works. In general, we tend to do that which maintains some level of equilibrium in our relationships with others. This means that we generally act in accordance with the (often unspoken and unexamined) norms of our identity group and in accordance with our and others' expectations for particular situations. When this analysis is expanded to include everyone on the planet, then we begin to get a glimpse of the systemic pressures that confer "power" and "privilege" on some and that make life difficult for others. It also helps us understand the persistence of the status quo and the obstacles to reform. I use the word "glimpse" advisedly, because the factors that contribute to the power structure in society are not clear-cut nor amenable to direct action.

The key to understanding a systems perspective of power is to grasp the role of constraints in producing the events and situations we see around us. It may appear as if someone is in control and as if the seemingly inevitable patterns that we see in social and institutional inequality are the result of top-down planning and management. However, it is far more complex than that. The patterns we notice are more accurately understood as "swarm logic"–individuals going about their business making their own individual contributions to the larger problem (Johnson 2001, 73–100). "Constraints" is the concept that permits us to talk about this emergent quality of human events, defined roughly as all those factors that influence the outcomes we notice. Constraints, in other words, are those factors that reduce the randomness of events and contribute to the patterns of power and oppression that we are striving to change.

We use an understanding of constraints as we attempt to organize our understanding of problems and as we work to change things. With regard to the former, Gregory Bateson advocated "cybernetic explanation," which he contrasted with "causal explanation" (1999, 405–15). The latter is appropriate when we are attempting to understand physical phenomena, such as, for example, the trajectory of billiard balls. The former is required when we are attempting to understand human beings, whose behavior is not predictable. The main thing to grasp is that in the systems view of the world, there is no direct control or unilateral power differential. Power is seen as a communicational phenomenon, an indirect exercise of influence, rather than a direct exercise of brute force.

Here is how cybernetic explanation proceeds.

1. The first step is to identify an event that occurred that can serve as a clear example of the process you want to understand, a point in the cyclical pattern of "the way things are."
2. The second step is to account for all the outcomes that could reasonably have occurred but did not.
3. And the third step is to identify the factors or conditions that converged to make the observed outcome statistically more likely to occur than all the others.

This may strike you as unnecessarily arcane and indirect. After all, the observed outcome *did* in fact occur. It would appear to need little explanation. However, that statement merely reveals our tendency to view history as inevitable. This approach encourages us to see the options that were available at specific points in time and to understand the pressures that inclined individuals toward some choices rather than others.

We are interested not only in individuals but also in groups of individuals such as classrooms, communities, and cultures, and we would expect the complexities to multiply as we attempt to understand how they function. So the process we use to explain why things are the way they are will be correspondingly complex. An example will clarify the approach.

First, a bit of background. In my teaching at the University of Colorado at Denver, I work with graduate students who are teachers or studying to become teachers. The majority are women, and there are a significant number of ethnic and racial minorities, as well as many nonnative English speakers. Most of my students would therefore qualify as "marginalized" by the definition of "privilege" I have developed. I have worked with colleagues to create degree programs and graduate courses that empower teachers to act on their beliefs, to improve the lives of their students, to contribute to the greater good. I design my syllabi with these ideas in mind, and I attempt to conduct my courses in ways that explicitly and implicitly convey these values. In particular, I work to create class sessions in which people speak up, express their opinions freely, and participate in vigorous debate without worrying about political correctness or whether their opinions align with mine or with those of the academic establishment. I view this as my attempt to empower students.

Recently I taught a course on methods of teaching English as a second language based on a systems perspective of teaching and learning. I emphasized the importance of creating environments for students to use the language in pursuit of their goals, and I stressed decision points and options, rather than the use of established methods and materials. I wanted students to ask questions of importance to them and to craft their own solutions to those questions. When I attempt to assess the extent to which I achieved my goals in the course, I search for examples that indicate people were exercising their prerogatives or asserting their rights in the class itself and in their planning for the courses they will teach. I take heart, for example, from the times when students suggested changes in the syllabus or amendments to the grading policy; this would indicate that they felt free to offer a critique of the course and, indirectly, of me, a sign of healthy self-interest and assertion. I also am pleased to see creative applications of lessons learned in my class to the contexts in which they live and teach.

I also look for discrepant data, times when individuals misunderstood concepts or appeared "unempowered," disenfranchised, or intimidated by me or the course. Specifically, I look for times when I paused in a class discussion and no one spoke. I am alert for grumblings in the halls that indicated disagreement with me or unhappiness with the course, grumblings that did not get voiced in class. I also attempt to see apparent "tongue-in-cheek" or feigned agreement with me, the practiced compliance of veteran students. These I analyze using the three steps outlined earlier, in an effort to discover ways that I might improve the course as an empowering experience. So, to take one example and work it through:

1. *Identifying an informative outcome.* On the final course evaluation, a student wrote, "I felt a tension between being invited to explore in a very reflective way and producing 'right' answers. I think this subject has a way of revealing itself to each individual and yet I had a sense that some people were rewarded for getting it sooner than others." A good criticism that rings true. I have caught myself gravitating toward students who seem to have "gotten it" rather than toward students who are still struggling, prolonging conversations or examples that are "correct" rather than attempting to work through confusions or questions. The salient feature for this analysis is that the individual made the criticism in the course evaluation, anonymously, and at the end of the semester, indicating reluctance to voice criticism of me, which can be taken as a sign of disempowerment.

2. *Identifying other, possible outcomes that could have occurred but did not.* The person could have spoken up during class discussion, pointing out that I had cut her or him off or moved on before she or he had completely understood. Or she or he might have written the criticism on one of the frequent "scribble sheets" that I used at the end of class sessions to get feedback on the way the class had gone. Another alternative would have been speaking to me after class to voice the same point directly. There are undoubtedly others that could be mentioned, but these will suffice for illustration.

3. *Identifying the constraints that contributed to the observed outcome.* This is a matter of educated guesswork, because it requires me to speculate about who made the comment and then, based on my limited understanding of the individual and the situation she or he was referring to, to generate a list of factors that might have contributed to her or his reticence to speak up earlier. But it is not a total fabrication. The most obvious constraint is the differential power implied by roles; I was the professor, and the writer of the note was the student. Gender and age certainly also must be considered. Most of the students were women, and I was older than most of them. Opportunity for course critique and adjustment is another factor to be considered. When might the student have offered the criticism earlier in the semester?

4. *Creating disturbances that cause wobbles in the system that increase the likelihood of empowerment.* This final step moves me beyond mere understanding toward action. But I understand that my actions will not be direct or causal remedies. I can make adjustments in the syllabus and in my behavior in ways that lessen the chances that such events will recur. There are constraints that offer no chance for change, such as age and gender, but there are adjustments I can make that increase the probability that my behavior in the future will align more closely with my goal of empowerment for my students. Similar analyses could

be conducted at different levels of scale. We might, for example, examine institutional or curricular constraints on empowerment to see if there are ways of increasing students' experience of personal prerogative and power.

An understanding of the role of constraints in system functioning is a powerful tool for educational reformers and teachers seeking to empower their students. It permits you to identify the normal cycles of life that result in inequality and oppression and to identify the constraints that contribute to the pattern. You look to see what you, personally, can do to change those constraints, and you do what you can to move the system toward more equitable functioning.

However, it is important to keep a number of cautions in mind as we work to create empowering conditions for our students. I examine a few of the most obvious ones here.

Cautionary Comments

"Empower" and "liberate" are not transitive verbs.

Grammatically, of course, this is not true; both verbs require objects and therefore are transitive. For example, "I will empower you." Pragmatically, however, the matter is not so straightforward. Empowerment and liberation are not serums that can be administered to others. They are not states of grace that we confer on our students. We do not empower others by declaring them to be liberated, nor can we harass them into becoming empowered, as Woody Allen does when he portrays a psychiatrist who grabs patients by the lapels, shakes them vigorously, and shouts, "Snap out of it!" In other words, liberation education is not a direct-instruction phenomenon. The best we can do is work to create the conditions under which students will begin to take the initiative.

In my ESL methods class, for example, I can state explicitly that I want students to critique the course and offer me direct suggestions for improving both the syllabus and my teaching, but I cannot mandate compliance. It is a matter of trust. Teachers are in the role of authority, and we can only behave in ways that indicate we value empowered students; if students do not take us at our word, there is little we can do but continue on demonstrating our goodwill.

This is a sobering realization, especially for politicians, curriculum specialists, administrators, and textbook promoters. The ennobling goal of liberation becomes disturbingly complex when we cannot list the rules to follow in producing empowered students. There are no prescriptions for empowering learners, no kits, no standardized curricula or textbook series that can be implemented to liberate students. This is not to say that institutional structures and educational materials do not play an important role in empowerment but rather to assert that the process is far too complex to yield to the market mentality of the "latest in empowerment paraphernalia." Jim Cummins, however, has developed an approach based on a thoughtful analysis of the interaction of community, school, and classroom in the empowerment of learners (1986, 1989).

Teachers who seek to empower their students soon discover how complex and difficult the task is. Nina Wallerstein, Thomas Graman, and Patrick Shannon offer thoughtful discussions of classroom techniques based on Paolo Freire's principles of liberation education (Wallerstein 1983; Graman 1988; Shannon 1989, 1990). The impression they convey is one of caring teachers who struggle to avoid the strictures of centralized curricula and test-conscious administrators as they gradually draw from their students' honest evaluations of their lives and their experiences in society. The goal is to help students become "organic intellectuals," individuals whose education is based on an integration of school knowledge and a growing understanding of the historical, political, and economic forces that shape it. Admirable aspiration, but easier said than done. This type of teaching requires time, patience, and flexibility.

Attempts at empowerment have produced mixed results. Elizabeth Ellsworth convened a graduate seminar at the University of Wisconsin aimed at giving voice to students against racism in the wake of racist events on campus and in the community (1989). She encountered obstacles to open dialogue and action in the structure of the university setting and in the opacity of the liberation discourse. With regard to the former, she discovered that she and the students could not escape their roles, and they found themselves pursuing a hierarchically organized, rationalist approach that validated the political structures they were attempting to critique. The university classroom, it seems, remains a tool of the dominant group in society and, as such, an unwieldy instrument for social change. With regard to the second obstacle, the opacity of the liberation discourse, she discovered that arguments for critical pedagogy are typically developed in such vague and abstract terms that they fail to serve as a basis for action. In fact, Ellsworth believes that the rhetoric itself serves to perpetuate the inequalities it purports to change (1989, 307).

Roger Simon encountered similar difficulties with a graduate seminar in Toronto (Lewis and Simon 1986). His intent was to guide the students in an analysis of language and power, thereby illuminating the patriarchal nature of academic discourse. He discovered that the setting itself, and the "natural" ways of student participation in the seminar, silenced the women in the class. Patterns of interaction—including turn taking and ways of nominating topics and indexing participants' contributions—provided the students with a powerful (but frustrating) example of what they were studying: the patriarchy emerging through language use. And, of course, more talk about the problem would not solve the problem because such talk would perforce be merely a continuing example of the problem. And then there was the teacher who worked to give her students voice through writing, only to discover that she was appalled by the topics they chose to write about (Shannon 1987).

In short, we cannot unilaterally liberate learners. We cannot control what students learn nor what they choose to do with the skills they acquire. Liberation education is too complex to be conveyed by lectures on democracy or small-group work on decision making and values clarification. We cannot give others power over their lives; we can only work with them so that they can see how to attain that goal for themselves. Empowerment implies an awakening to the possibilities, and this cannot come as a gift from someone else. Within the classroom, it comes from exercising personal choice in meaningful activities on a daily basis. It develops as a function of experience, as individuals struggle with problems and learn not only how to solve them but that they can solve them.

Empowerment will not come quickly or easily.

Nor, for that matter, is it likely to come to the individuals you are working with while you are working with them. This, of course, follows from the preceding discussion. Marginal individuals–women, the disabled, students from low socioeconomic and stigmatized minority groups–do not exercise full participation in society for a number of complex and interacting reasons, and as teachers we desire to empower them. However, power is an interactional accomplishment; it is emergent in relationships. It is a function of contexts and interpersonal interaction, and it takes time for individuals to develop a strong sense of self in relationship to others. We may sow seeds that blossom long after the fact, but that does not diminish the importance of the accomplishment.

It is true that privileged adults (especially young, white, able, thin, heterosexual, educated, Christian males) carry themselves with an authority that transcends situations, but even here the example illustrates the point, because their behavior is a product of their development. They have learned over the years, from family and society, what is expected of them and what their prerogatives are: "Observe the space men allow themselves, physically and verbally, the male assumption that people will listen" (Rich 1979, 243).

Conversely, individuals are not inherently weak and incompetent; they must learn how to fail. Cummins has documented this through an analysis of minority-group performance in a variety of contexts (1986). Finns, for example, do poorly in schools in Sweden, where they are a low-status group, but they perform well in Australia, where they are a high-status group. Differential distribution of power and prestige, and students' experience of this inequality, contribute over time to a sense of inferiority and incompetence.

It is then just a matter of time and opportunity for the expectation of failure to be fulfilled.

These lessons have been taught by much more powerful individuals than schoolteachers, and in the hard-knocks curriculum of the street. Students, whether children or adults, will be skeptical of claims by teachers that they can change their lives merely by asserting their rights. Experience has taught them otherwise, and the "power curriculum" will be perceived as just one more in a string of gimmicks that one comes to expect in school. This poses problems for teachers, trained as we are to expect to convey lessons relatively efficiently within the customary time and space allotted to us by the academic calendar. However, it is unreasonable to assume that teachers can counteract in the school year what society has so effectively inculcated over generations.

Much less in a four-week intensive summer semester. My ESL methods class must have struck many of the students as strange. They had signed up for a practical teaching class in which they could collect classroom techniques and materials, and they discovered instead that they were being asked to contemplate larger, more complex systemic issues. How they reacted was largely a function of their own experience and their ability to make connections between what I was advocating and their current situations. For the younger teachers, just starting out, this proved too much; it was all they could do to organize basic lesson plans and deal with classroom-management problems. The case was similar for the international students returning to teach in situations very different from the ones that I used in my examples or that they encountered in the field excursions they conducted at our host school, Spring International Language Center.

The course evaluations reflected the ambivalence they felt. Both "instructor" and "course" received positive evaluations, but a number of individuals indicated that they would not take the course again or that they would not recommend it to others. Some said that they would take the course again but that they wouldn't recommend it to others. Clearly, I cannot change the course to accommodate these particular individuals, but I can adjust my teaching in hopes that future students will benefit. However, it is important to emphasize the importance of a philosophical approach to this task; it is highly unlikely that I will ever receive uniformly positive evaluations in a course that requires students to adjust their vision of the world to its greater systemic functioning.

Empowered individuals cause trouble.

If we teach people to act on their beliefs and in their best interests, they will. A number of writers argue that we—teachers, parents, society at large—do not want empowered learners. Freire, for example, says, "It would be extremely naive to expect the dominant classes to develop a type of education that would enable subordinate classes to perceive social injustices critically" (1985, 102). And James Moffett contends that a significant impediment to improvement of English teaching is the fact that teachers and parents want, not critical thinkers, readers, writers, but cooperative learners, what Freire might refer to as domesticated students (Moffett 1985).

Most discussions of liberation education ignore the fact that truly empowered individuals will challenge not only the products of particular situations (grades or promotions, for example) but also the very authority, assumptions, and processes by which people are rewarded in society for the work they do. When we work to create the conditions for empowerment, we help people see that they can act for themselves, but we cannot guarantee that their agendas for action will coincide with ours. A colleague who served as faculty sponsor for the student council at a girls' school in Greece discovered this when the girls emerged under her guidance as articulate critics of the school. Their outspoken efforts at reform (aimed at rules against wearing fashionable clothes and makeup) almost cost the teacher her job. The girls "wanted too much too fast" was her observation. Perhaps. But another interpretation is that she was merely reaping the fruits of her labor; the girls had taken her lessons to heart.

Similarly, when we conduct classes as forums for problem posing and resolution, we must be prepared for the possibility that the students will reject us entirely, either by spurning our attempts at helping them or, perversely, by refusing the independence and responsibility we offer them and demanding that we continue to make decisions for them. We cannot escape the fact that, as teachers, we play an important role in maintaining the status quo. As students acquire a critique of the system, it is only natural that they will also develop a critique of us in our role as teachers. It is at this point that we *will* be faced with the realization that only liberated teachers can foster liberated students. Our next step will be illuminating. Do we back off from our commitments to the empowerment of the students when their actions put us in conflict with colleagues and superiors, or do we challenge the system to deliver on the promises of liberation education?

Our graduate program provides a good illustration of this point. Several years ago, during a group advising session, students who were intending to work abroad with adult ESL learners complained that our course offerings were too narrowly focused on children in public schools and that issues of bilingual education took up too much of the curriculum. The conversation spilled beyond the room and the meeting, and over the period of several semesters, a student group organized to compel us to examine the curriculum. This pressure from students resulted in a radically reorganized program that features collaboration with the Spring International Language Center (Clarke et al. 1998).

Attempts at liberation education must be individually and culturally appropriate.

The desire for liberty may be universal, but it does not mean the same thing to everybody, and learners may have difficulty recognizing the merits of "liberation" as their teachers present it. For example, many teachers reward students who are literate and articulate and who step forward to display their knowledge. This model of self-determination may not fit the cultural values of the learners; liberation then becomes just another version of cultural hegemony.

I developed my ESL methods course with a particular perspective of the educational and political contexts of teachers, one that reflected my values. I had many students in the class for whom that perspective was inappropriate or premature. I had to adjust my expectations to take theirs into account.

Shirley Brice Heath's 10-year study of working-class white and black communities in the Piedmont area of the Carolinas revealed significant differences in the ways that people view reading and writing, differences that led to difficulties in school, where teachers, materials, and curricula were based on mainstream assumptions about literacy (Heath 1983). Teachers, for example, became frustrated with the dogged way that the working-class white children stuck to the literal meaning of texts, rather than permitting themselves to elaborate imaginatively on events and people in their reading. What the teacher viewed as imagination, however, would be labeled as lies in the children's homes. Similarly, the working-class black children encountered difficulties in responding appropriately to the teachers' display questions—questions to which the teachers knew the answers. In the children's homes, a great deal of energetic interaction occurred involving print, but adults never quizzed them on the content of reading. Michaels and Scollon and Scollon report similar clashes between home and school conceptualizations of literacy and school performance (Michaels 1981; Scollon and Scollon 1981). Cultural differences in definitions of success go beyond the classroom. A colleague in Denver discovered that Southeast Asian and Eastern European immigrants and refugees would avoid promotions if they believed that the new status and responsibilities would separate them from their community.

Given that success is culturally defined, our attempts at promoting the success of our students as part of our "empowerment agenda" require us to acknowledge our efforts as "border work." Frederick Erickson contends that points of cultural difference become the scene for struggles between teachers and students as to whose definitions of legitimacy and success are to serve as the standard for evaluating learners' work (Erickson 1987). We are hoisted on our own petard here. We work for the empowerment of our students, defined to some extent as the ability to make their own decisions, to assert their own priorities. What happens if they reject our definitions of success? We then must decide where we stand. What is to change, the learners or the system, and what role do we play?

Skill development is not, by itself, empowering.

Empowerment is not a monovariate phenomenon. People do not become empowered merely by becoming accomplished computer users, literate, or English-speaking, to take examples with which I am most familiar. In the case of my prospective ESL teachers, merely developing classroom-management skills or refining one's command of a particular teaching technique does not guarantee success; the larger context of school and community must be taken into account. It is easy to verify this assertion—merely find individuals who are skilled in these areas and still oppressed. Yet much of what we read and hear, especially in the popular press, leaves us with the impression that if students merely master the curriculum, achieve high scores on standardized tests, they will be empowered.

Let me take as an example the case of literacy in our society. It is not uncommon to find reports of illiteracy linked directly to general societal malaise—high-school drop-out rates, spiraling crime, the sagging economy, homelessness, substance abuse, etc.—as if the inability to read and write were an independent causal variable for a wide variety of social problems. Prescriptions and social-action agendas invariably include programs for erasing illiteracy and (thereby) empowering individuals to improve their lot in life. Brian Street refers to this as an autonomous perspective of literacy, the assumption that reading and writing are no more than technical skills that people can acquire without significantly changing other aspects of their lives (1984).

However, a growing body of scholarship testifies to the inadequacy of this point of view. Literacy is a complex set of discourse practices, acquired over time in particular social and institutional contexts. Because of the diversity of these, we must acknowledge a variety of literacies, each one appropriate to the context in which it occurs. The literacy reform called for by social critics and politicians will require the acquisition of that set of discourse practices found in schools and acquired in mainstream middle-class homes. It may be that acquiring this complex constellation of attitudes and behaviors will empower individuals, but we are not talking about merely learning to read and write. As scholars have shown, becoming literate in this sense requires changing cultures or, at least, improving one's capacity to function effectively in more than one culture. The important point for educators is that "empowerment through literacy" is a far more complicated and time-consuming task than learning one's ABCs (Scollon and Scollon 1981; Heath 1983; Gee 1990).

Recent conceptualizations of literacy stress the importance of individuals actively critiquing society using their newly acquired skills. From this point of view becoming literate is not, by itself, empowering, but it may be an important first step in that direction: "Literacy in these terms is not the equivalent of emancipation. It is in a more limited but essential way the precondition for engaging in struggles around both relations of meaning and relations of power. To be literate is not to be free. It is to be present and active in the struggle for reclaiming one's voice, history, and future" (Giroux 1988, 65).

The societal factors that contribute to a sense of empowerment in individuals are far more complex and dynamically interrelated than usually acknowledged by reformers and politicians. Calling for empowerment may win votes, but it does little to further the cause.

Conclusions: Taking the Heat

I would like to return for a moment to the little quiz with which I started this essay. I answer *True* to all of the items, but with some hesitation. I am aware that by endorsing liberation education I am aligning myself with a large and somewhat cacophonous group of social critics whose values I only partially share. In addition, I recognize that empowerment may be a goal that is beyond my reach as a teacher educator and language teacher, at least as those roles are conventionally defined. The classroom may not be the appropriate venue for liberation tactics; it would seem that institutions are a more likely site for revolution. Similarly, I wonder about the amount of change possible in the semester and the academic year. This seems like too short a re-action time, too small an activity cycle for enduring change of the sort we envision.

I believe that the concept of empowerment is more complex than generally realized and that the task *is* one that merits our attention. Woven throughout this essay is the implication that teachers play an important and largely underdeveloped role as change agents in the empowerment of learners. The dissent in these arguments is meant to be a reminder of the complexity of teaching and learning, not a discouraging presentation on the futility of it all. In step with the il-lusion of the epoch, I want liberty and power for all students and teachers, but I believe that the unexamined endorsement of libera-tion education will produce more heat than light.

Empowerment, as it is commonly discussed in the literature, con-stitutes more than an educational perspective. It requires a radical change in interpersonal relationships; in the allocation of institutional resources, including very fundamental uses of time and space; and, ultimately, in the power structure of society at large.

To become empowered, or to help someone else become em-powered, is to change this equilibrium, to jar the system toward a more equitable distribution of power and privilege. Given the dy-namic interaction between levels of systems—personal and interper-sonal, classroom, school, community, societal, etc.—serious efforts at liberation education constitute much more than mere pedagogy. It is not an exaggeration to say that what we are talking about is radical social change—revolution, if you like. This is not a novel observation, I know, but it is one that needs saying at regular intervals, lest we fall into the easy habit of thinking that these changes will occur without some discomfort.

And this brings us to a critical point. Conspicuously absent from this essay, and from much writing on liberation education, is a response to the question central to any attempt at reform: Empowerment for what? Whose agenda do we follow, and what, specifically, are we work-ing for? What will we take as evidence of movement in the appropri-ate direction? The literature echoes with generic prescriptions—critical democracy, social action, individual freedom, the ability to name the injustice in one's life and to challenge oppressors. And these often ring hollow, as Elizabeth Ellsworth and Lisa Delpit have pointed out (Delpit 1988; Ellsworth 1989). On the other hand, agendas for reform that mold the world in an image acceptable to mainstream critics of the status quo will prove to be just another form of condescension, a yuppie-esque noblesse oblige.

I offer no solution to the dilemma. Indeed we can only facilitate reform; it is up to our students to determine what they value and how they will act. But we will know that we are beginning to have success as empowering educators when we start to feel the heat, from all sides. Teachers may not hold much power in society, but if the seeds of liberation education begin to grow, it will be because we began to take ourselves seriously as agents of change.

⑦ Finding a Place to Stand: Teaching in Dangerous Times

Horrifying events can be the pivot point for a new approach to life. Sometimes, if we are lucky, they jolt us into a new awareness, a heightened sensibility. Life goes on, as they say, but we experience it differently. The world hasn't changed, but we have. Survivors of natural disasters or grave illness, for example, often report that they have returned to their routines with a new determination to live life to the fullest, to make the most of their opportunities. The events of April 20, 1999, and September 11, 2001, had that effect on me.

On April 20, 1999, Dylan Klebold and Eric Harris, after many months of deliberation, planning, and stockpiling, entered Columbine High School and slew 12 fellow students and a teacher before turning their weapons on themselves.

On September 11, 2001, Mohamed Atta led a team of 19 militants in a carefully planned and coordinated attack on the World Trade Center and the Pentagon. The death toll, which continues to be revised as I write this, nears 3,000.

Like most teachers, I entered the profession motivated in part by idealism and youthful confidence in my ability to contribute to a better world. These may be important prerequisites for a career in education, but the daily grind provides ample opportunity to wonder if you are really making a difference in anyone's life. However, whatever feelings of inadequacy and doubt have assailed me on my most frustrating days, the events of these two days rendered them minute and inconsequential.

And they helped me focus. Suddenly, math facts and topic sentences, portfolio rubrics and test scores, curricular scope and sequence, state standards and performance criteria—the minutiae that assail teachers day in and day out—were exposed for what they are: monumental trivialities, the ultimate in deck chairs on the *Titanic,* hobgoblins of little minds that distract us from what really matters. Human tragedy on the scale of April 20, 1999, and September 11, 2001, affirms the importance of teachers in the world, because no other profession is so well positioned to make a difference in the lives of young people, to reduce the violence.

You may be thinking that this is an egocentric assertion of undiluted arrogance and exaggerated self-importance. Or you may be saying to yourself that there is no connection between April 20, 1999, and September 11, 2001, and certainly no connection between violence on that scale and your work. I sympathize with your desire to labor in tranquil obscurity, but the purpose of this essay is to convince you otherwise.

Violence is a natural phenomenon. Literally, it is a reality of nature. You don't have to actually survive an earthquake or tornado or buffalo stampede to see this. A passing acquaintance with natural history and the trajectory of human civilization will make the point. Whether we are talking about the prey/predator balance in an ecosystem, or the succession of brutalities that have marked the growth of nations since humans began congregating in groups, you have to acknowledge the "naturalness" of violence.

This realization has several implications. Most important, I think, is that violence is a systemic problem ("systemic" being another word for "natural" in the way that these events play out). That is, we must address it at all levels of scale—as individuals in families and organizations and as communities and nations and a species. A second implication is that it won't go away; we have to deal with it. And, by the same token, it will not yield to quick-fix solutions; there are no magic wands or secret elixirs and certainly no laws that will eliminate the violence. Related to this is the need to accept the fact that there were no "good old times," eras in which violence was not part of the dynamic of human conduct. When we say that things have gotten out of control, we are merely revealing our sudden awareness of violence close to home. Another implication is that our contributions to the situation must be within the scope of our roles and responsibilities. Both as a matter of practicality and as a matter of mental health, we need to recognize the limitations of our ability to contribute to a peaceful world. This doesn't mean that we can ignore distant carnage. To the extent possible we have to contribute to the cause in all parts of the globe, but on a day-to-day basis we have to find ways to reduce the violence in our own backyards. A systems view requires us to be both philosophers and change agents. As the environmentalists say, "Think globally, act locally."

There are no direct and immediate responses to violence that will prevent future violence. Generations of warfare and human suffering all over the world dramatically demonstrate this; vengeance and retaliation only lead to more violence. The only enduring solutions are those nurtured in caring relationships. And apart from students' friends and family, the individuals most strategically positioned to provide that nurturing are teachers. It may be disconcerting to see yourself in that position, but the conclusion is inescapable. Teachers spend more time with children than any other group of professionals, and time is what is needed to shape alternative alignments to problem solving.

In other words, the most effective response to violence lies in the unremarkable days of the school routine. Farfetched? Just the opposite: this is the only realistic option we have. In what follows I attempt to construct an approach to the mundane that provides a measure of comfort in the face of the cataclysmic.

A Systems View

The first response to news of the magnitude of Columbine and the World Trade Center is to account for our loved ones, to assure ourselves that the important people in our life are safe. Then, it seems, we tend to go through various stages of shock, disbelief, denial, and bewildered coping. As soon as possible, we try to return to normal, whatever that means. This is the way of natural systems—they function toward stability, whether we are talking about individuals, groups, or societies.

For teachers, the response is often to close the door and get on with their work. But—and this is the crux of my argument—what is the nature of teachers' work? My answer: to provide an environment for learning, a safe haven for risk taking and unfettered pursuit of curiosity. I don't intend this statement to provoke a debate about standards and accountability, or curriculum and materials. Each of us has to work out our own approach to our subject areas and our own teaching methods, and all teachers will resist being told what their instructional goals should be. But I want to begin from the assertion that no matter whom or what or where we are teaching, our fundamental responsibility is to create a safe place for learning to occur.

And given the nature of the world—systems within systems within systems—that effort contributes indirectly and cumulatively to a world where Columbine High School and the World Trade Center are statistically less likely to happen. The effects of this work are not satisfyingly direct nor even noticeable most of the time, but they constitute a framework of faith that makes it possible for us to proceed with the work of the day when the news from around the world makes our efforts seem laughably inconsequential.

Throughout these essays I have used systems theory as the framework for my arguments because mine is an academician's stance and I did my scholarly apprenticeship during the time when "systems thinking" was a hot topic. But the perspective has an ancient pedigree. It can be traced back to the selflessness of Eastern philosophies and to Native people's desire to make decisions with the fate of seven generations in mind. Gregory Bateson used the newly coined term *cybernetics* when he discussed these matters, and more recently environmental activists have used *ecology* as a broad label for their efforts. Some writers, like Barbara Kingsolver and Wendell Berry, do not invoke theory at all; they merely move artfully between discussions of farming and foreign policy, of raising kids and raising consciousness (Kingsolver 1995, 2002; Berry 2002).

But the view is this: It's all one thing—life—and whether we are dealing with playground bullying or international terrorism, the issues and approaches are the same. The primary strategy is an unsentimental empiricism guided by a clear eye and an open mind. We face the problems squarely, and we acknowledge our own contributions to the difficulties we face. The view also implies a willingness to change the way we think and act rather than assuming that others must do the changing.

When this perspective is brought to bear by educators on the tragedies of Columbine High School and the World Trade Center a number of points stand out. It is easy to compile a list of differences between the killings in Littleton, Colorado, on April 20, 1999, and those in New York, Washington, D.C., and rural Pennsylvania on September 11, 2001. But it is more important to see the similarities, to understand the patterns that connect these events. Among the most important are the following: violence in response to violence, the sophisticated use of available technology, anger nourished by outrage at a history of feeling victimized, an ideology that rationalizes the death of innocents and makes suicide a reasonable outcome.

And, paramount in my mind, the fact that there is no simple solution, no technical fix. The carnage was the result of problems that were a long time developing, and our response must work within the same rhythms—the rhythms of childcare and respect for your elders, of tolerance for adolescent exuberance and youthful indiscretion in the conduct of patient teaching. In other words, daily attention to the golden rule. Barbara Kingsolver captures this delicate connection between individual behavior and cultural alignment in the following excerpt.

Air travel, like natural disasters, throws strangers together in unnaturally intimate circumstances. (Think how well you can get to know the bald spot of the guy reclining in front of you.) Consequently airplanes can be a splendid cultural magnifying glass. On my family's voyage from New York to Madrid we weren't assigned seats together. I shamelessly begged my neighbor—a forty-something New Yorker traveling alone—if she would take my husband's aisle seat in another row so our air-weary and plainly miserable daughter could stretch out across her parents' laps. My fellow traveler snapped, "No, I have to have the window seat, just like you *had* to have that baby."

As simply as that, a child with needs (and ears) became an inconvenient *thing,* for which I was entirely to blame. The remark left me stunned and, as always happens when someone speaks rudely to me, momentarily guilty; yes, she must be right, conceiving this child was a rash, lunatic moment of selfishness, and now I had better be prepared to pay the price.

In the U.S.A., where it's said that anyone can grow up to be President, we parents are left pretty much on our own when it comes to the Presidents-in-training. Our social programs for children are the hands-down worst in the industrialized world, but apparently that is just what we want as a nation. It took a move to another country to make me realize how thoroughly I had accepted my nation's creed of every family for itself. Whenever my daughter crash-landed in the playground, I was startled at first to see a sanguine, Spanish-speaking stranger pick her up and dust her off. And if a shrieking bundle landed at *my* feet, I'd furtively look around for the next of kin. But I quickly came to see this detachment as perverse when applied to children, and am wondering how it ever caught on in the first place.

My grandfathers on both sides lived in households that were called upon, after tragedy struck close to home, to take in orphaned children and raise them without a thought. In an era of shortage, this was commonplace. But one generation later that kind of semi-permeable household had vanished, at least among the white middle class. It's a horrifying thought, but predictable enough, that the worth of children in America is tied to their dollar value. Children used to be field hands, household help, even miners and factory workers—extensions of a family's productive potential and so, in a sense, the property of an extended family. But *precious* property, valued and coveted. Since the advent of child-labor laws, children have come to hold an increasingly negative position in the economy. They're spoken of as a responsibility, a legal liability, an encumbrance—or, if their unwed mothers are on welfare, a mistake that should not be rewarded. The political shuffle seems to be about making sure they cost us as little as possible, and that their own parents foot the bill. Virtually every program that benefits children in this country, from *Sesame Street* to free school lunches, has been cut back in the last decade—in many cases, cut to nothing. If it takes a village to raise a child, our kids are knocking on a lot of doors where nobody seems to be home.

Taking parental responsibility to extremes, some policymakers in the U.S. have seriously debated the possibility of requiring a license for parenting. I'm dismayed by the notion of licensing an individual adult to raise an individual child, because it implies parenting is a private enterprise, like selling liquor or driving a cab (though less lucrative). I'm also dismayed by what it suggests about innate fitness or non-fitness to rear children. Who would devise such a test? And how could it harbor anything but deep cultural biases? Like driving, parenting is a skill you learn by doing. You keep an eye out for oncoming disasters, and know when to stop and ask for directions. The skills you have going into it are hardly the point. . . .

While there are better and worse circumstances from which to launch offspring onto the planet, it's impossible to anticipate just who will fail. One of the most committed, creative parents I know plunged into her role through the trapdoor of teen pregnancy; she has made her son the center of her life, constructed a large impromptu family of reliable friends and neighbors, and absorbed knowledge like a plant taking sun. Conversely, some of the most strained, inattentive parents I know are well-heeled professionals, self-sufficient but chronically pressed for time. Life takes surprising turns. The one sure thing is that no parent, ever, has turned out to be perfectly wise and exhaustively provident 1,440 minutes a day, for 18 years. It takes help. Children are not commodities but an incipient world. They thrive best when their upbringing is the collective joy and responsibility of families, neighborhoods, communities, and nations.

It's not hard to figure out what's good for kids, but amid the noise of an increasingly anti-child political climate, it can be hard to remember just to go ahead and do it: for example to vote to raise your school district's budget, even though it means you'll pay higher taxes. (If you're earning enough to pay taxes, I promise, the school needs those few bucks more than you do.) To support legislators who care more about after school programs, affordable health care, and libraries than about military budgets and the Dow Jones industrial average. To volunteer time and skills at your neighborhood school and also the school across town. To decide to notice, rather than ignore it, when a neighbor is losing it with her kids, and offer to baby-sit twice a week. This is not interference. Getting between a ball player and a ball is interference. The ball is inanimate.

Presuming children to be their parents' sole property and responsibility is, among other things, a handy way of declaring problem children to be someone else's problem, or fault, or failure. It's a dangerous remedy; it doesn't change the fact that somebody else's kids will ultimately be in your face demanding *now* with interest what they didn't get when they were smaller and had simpler needs. Maybe in-your-face means breaking and entering, or maybe it means a Savings and Loan scam. Children deprived—of love, money, attention, or moral guidance—grow up to have large and powerful needs. . . .

My second afternoon in Spain, standing in a crowded bus, as we ricocheted around a corner and my daughter reached starfish-wise for stability, a man in a black beret stood up and gently helped her into his seat. In his weightless bearing I caught sight of the decades-old child, treasured by the manifold mothers of his neighborhood, growing up the way leavened dough rises surely to the kindness of bread.

I thought then of the woman on the airplane, who was obviously within her rights to put her own comfort first, but whose withheld generosity gave my daughter what amounted to a sleepless, kicking, squirming, miserable journey. As always happens two days after someone has spoken to me rudely, I knew exactly what I should have said: Be careful what you give children, for sooner or later you are sure to get it back. (1995, 99–107)

Every reader will take away something different from this passage, but reading with a systems lens, I see the following points as key.

When Kingsolver comments in the third paragraph that we as a nation must want the worst social programs in the industrialized world, she is invoking an important tenet of systems thinking. What gets done is important; things are the way they are *not* by accident. This is the requirement of an empirical approach—to come to terms with the evidence of your senses, to observe carefully and attempt to understand what you see, rather than explain away inconvenient or discomforting facts. For all our proclamations to the contrary, and in spite of the self-conscious commitment of a whole generation of superparents and doting chauffeurs, the decisions we have made at the polling booths and in legislative assemblies have resulted in a disastrous inattention to the well-being of children.

And as the old saying goes, "As the twig is bent, so grows the tree." Children raised without a sense of nurturing and compassion will have neither as adults, and chances are they will lash out at others without mercy.

Kingsolver's description of our approach to solving problems in the fifth paragraph is an elegant critique of a fatal flaw in our culture—the illusion of top-down, unilateral control of life's events. We are so driven by the Newtonian perspective of a mechanistic world that we consistently fail to understand that people cannot be controlled. Human beings are wonderfully complex and unpredictable, and the best we can do is exercise some influence, create the conditions for particular values and actions to emerge. And, of course, this means an enduring attention to the care of children; the most effective response to Columbine High School, for example, is a gentle and sympathetic understanding of the pain that children are experiencing, not, as was often the case, forceful and punitive attempts at control.

Our ferocious devotion to our own children, coupled with a cultural predisposition to blame people for their problems, inclines us toward a lack of sympathy for others. We attend to the particular needs of a few but ignore the same needs of the whole—myopic generosity in creating pockets of safe havens that contributes, eventually, to a dangerous environment for all.

What is required is not control, but flexibility. Gregory Bateson used the example of the high-wire artist when he spoke of flexibility (1999, 502–13). Tightrope walkers have a very narrow tolerance for error, and their feet do not move very far from the thin path defined by the wire. They appear to be very calmly maintaining steady course. But it is constant motion that helps them maintain their balance. That is, stability of one sort requires flexibility of another. They have to be able to flail their arms in order to stay on the wire. The rules for staying on the wire cannot be summarized and dictated from afar. Each high-wire artist must make his or her own decisions. In fact, providing tightrope walkers with mandated rules will make it possible for them to do only one thing—fall off the wire.

The same is true in all other areas of life and for systems of all sizes. If we define flexibility as "uncommitted resources available for change," then we can see how a class or school needs flexibility in the same way that students, teachers, and administrators require it. The problem is that our tendency is to respond to problems by attempting to increase control, rather than flexibility, and this is precisely the opposite of what is required.

An example might help. In the wake of the events of April 20, 1999, the tendency across the country was to batten the hatches—to increase security, to come down harder on students who dressed and acted like Klebold and Harris, to respond with decisive punishments to unconventional behavior. Some increase in caution was warranted, but most of these responses severely limited adults' ability to respond to particular students or situations with discretion and sensitivity. A more effective mandate might have been one that gave time and resources to counselors and mental-health-care workers so that they could respond to individual students whose behavior warranted attention.

Kingsolver's argument is similar—depend on the discretion of individuals in exercising their freedoms. Identify what you can do at different levels of scale, do it, and get on with the details of your life. Modest contributions to the greater good.

The argument I am building casts a pale light on classroom teaching and on the relationships between teachers and students. The world has come to this, that "the way school is," the normal turn of events, shapes young people is such a way that the quiet child in the back of the room may become the next mass murderer in newspaper headlines. This sobering realization makes it possible to see our daily grind as more directly connected to the greater good than we did before.

A Place to Stand

> Ask not for whom the bell tolls.
> It tolls for thee.
> —John Donne

By "a place to stand" I am talking about the need for educators today to position themselves with regard to the violence. The stance is more abstract and metaphorical when we consider the tragedies of Columbine High School and the World Trade Center; of course we want to work to make such violence less likely to happen in the future, but it is difficult to make realistic connections between our responsibilities and those events. However, when we talk about a place to stand in the social and institutional environments in which we work, the phrase becomes more real and provides us with a principled basis for the daily conduct of our personal and professional lives. It is important to frame these connections in terms of the people we see every day. These are our points of contact with the world, our best chance at effecting change. And although we may not be able to see it, this daily work is our contribution to global peace.

Upon consideration, perhaps I should have said not "more abstract and theoretical" but "on a different scale." Systems theorists have long asserted that the survival of the planet depends on humans being able to see the long-range consequences of their daily behavior (M. C. Bateson 1972; Lovelock 1979; Capra 1990, 1996; Harries-Jones 1995; Fullan 1999; Senge et al. 2000).

But for most of us, the distance between our daily lives and the fate of humanity is too great. Steven Johnson attempts to make the connection more comprehensible through his exploration of "swarm logic," the contribution of local habits and routines to the larger patterns of society (2001, 73–100). He argues that our tendency to impose a mechanistic, causal explanation on natural events has led us to infer that large-scale incidents are always the result of a master-mind, whereas an understanding of natural systems, such as ant and bee colonies, mass migration, and the development of cities, allows us to see that it is the minute particulars of every individual's daily routine that result in the big picture.

Gregory Bateson talked of "immanent mind" in a similar way (1999, 454–73). The universe functions in ways that can be understood if we free ourselves from the notion of hierarchical control and think instead of probabilities that emerge from local instances of general patterns. If we understand, for example, the fundamental animal tendency to protect the self from threats by aggressive action, whether by flight or fight, then we have a basic framework that permits us to understand human violence on both a global and a local scale–the same conceptual framework for understanding international terrorism and playground bullying. Gregory Bateson, for example, approached the issue of dwindling resources on the planet by attempting to be conscious of his participation in even the most remote aspect of environmental functioning. He said that he did this by reminding himself of the limited water supply every time he reached for a glass of water (1999, 486–95).

It is the same principle that puts children in a position of teaching their parents about the importance of ecological thinking in their daily lives. Mary Catherine Bateson talks about the role children play in getting their parents to recycle and to turn off the faucet while brushing their teeth (1995). It may seem like a small thing at the time, but a whole generation of individuals growing up with a keen awareness of the contributions their own behaviors make to the greater good provides the basis for systemic change on a grand scale.

The task is similar for us as educators working in the current environment. Every morning, as we arise to a new day of teaching, we look at ourselves in the mirror and ask, "What am I going to do today to make terrorism of all kinds an historical aberration, to reduce the violence, to increase the health of the system?"

This is a daunting challenge at a time when it seems that merely getting through the day gracefully is often beyond one's reach. And there is the danger of the martyr syndrome—of taking on too much, assuming responsibility for problems that are truly beyond our sphere of influence. So I want to be clear on what I am saying. I do not mean that either you or I, personally, are in charge of assuring the safety of public schools or thwarting international terrorism but that we need to approach our work on a daily basis with the stark images of Columbine and the World Trade Center towers in the back of our minds and an awareness of the contributions we are making, little by little, in very subtle ways, to the attitudes and actions of others. And we need to struggle to make it clear that violence is not a solution to any problem. It is, in fact, always part of the problem.

Simple enough. But how to organize one's life so that this message comes through to others—youngsters, colleagues, parents? And how to help them shape their response to the violence they experience, directly or indirectly, every day of their lives?

My approach is to assume that I am in this for the long haul and that I need a way of thinking and acting that permits me to plan ahead, to work for the greater good at the same time that I am dealing with whatever crisis is facing me at the moment. I use systems theory as the basis for my thinking, and I have developed a list of seven elements of the change process that I monitor as I work. I remind myself to keep all seven in mind even as I work on more immediate aspects of a problem. These are the seven elements.

The problem. What *is* the problem? What, exactly, is bothering me? How does it affect me? How do I frame it in ways that permit deliberate and coherent action? How do I keep it in focus so that the labels I have used to identify it do not obscure it? Naming the problem is an important step toward making progress on developing a solution. It is also very often an impediment to change, because it limits my ability to see all the ways that the situation might be conceptualized. But just being aware of the fact that problems are constructions of my own making is helpful.

The issue. How is this problem a variation on life's natural functioning? All problems are local examples of larger issues. This is just another way of saying that all living systems are nested within other living systems. I need to understand the larger issues so that I am prepared for the variety of ways that they surface in my life. Identifying the larger issue also helps me think about how I will respond to the problems I am dealing with.

Constraints and strategies. Countless details large and small contribute to the habitual functioning of systems. I have to understand what they are and how they function to maintain the status quo. I need to develop strategies that have the greatest likelihood of success, given the constraints. A clear understanding of the constraints that contribute to the problems I am working on permits me to identify points in the activity cycle and individuals within my spheres of influence where my efforts are likely to have the greatest impact.

🙠 **Activity cycles.** All problems are points in a larger pattern, which means that they will cycle around again. I need to learn to see the cycles clearly so that I can identify strategic points for action. Where am I in the process? Is this the beginning, middle, or end of a cycle of change? When will it come around again, and what are the points of the process where I can have the greatest influence?

🙠 **The solution, or innovation.** What will I do to work on the problem? How will I organize my time and energy in the search for solutions? How will I avoid letting the innovation take over my life? How to avoid the "baby-with-the-bathwater" or the "operation-a-success-but-the-patient-died" syndromes? Innovations tend to become problems when commitment to a particular procedure or program takes precedence over attempts to see the problem clearly and to attend to progress being made. Sustained change efforts often take on lives of their own. Remembering that naming the innovation shapes the approach to change helps me keep from getting mired in routines and forgetting what my original goals were.

🙠 **Evidence of change.** How do I know if I am making progress? How do I keep myself psyched up in the face of frustrations? Having a list of visible indicators of progress is helpful. It is as important to see how far I have come as it is to see how far I have to go. Keeping track of progress helps me maintain my energy and enthusiasm in the face of adversity. Having a clear idea of the evidence I am monitoring is also a way of maintaining my focus on change, rather than getting mired in the complexities of a project.

🙠 **The players.** Who is involved, and how? All change requires individuals to change. Who are the primary players, and what are their attitudes toward change? What sorts of influence do I have with others involved? The principal player is always me, and I have to do most of the changing, but I assume that others will have to change as well, and I need to approach them differently depending on their attitudes toward the problem, toward the solution, and toward me.

Think of this list as a set of worry beads on a string, each one a different shape so that, without looking, you can run them through your fingers as you contemplate a problem and ask yourself the questions as you try to think through what to do next.

Or, perhaps, a small pocket set of magnifying glasses, with lenses that rotate out from a little case and that permit you to look at things differently, depending on whether you are thinking about how to define the problem, or what the larger issues are, or how you might adapt someone else's innovation to your situation, for example.

The order in which you work with the elements is not important; that is, you can begin with any one and proceed randomly through the string.

What follows is my attempt at working through this routine with regard to Columbine High School, the World Trade Center, and my daily life. I articulate my understanding of Columbine High School and the World Trade Center and how I see these events connecting to my work, given that I am a fifty-something heterosexual white male tenured professor at an urban school of education doing action research in my own neighborhood, working with colleagues and graduate students on funded projects with middle-school teachers at a school where most of the students are Latino and African American.

Your analysis will be different, reflecting your values and your personal and professional commitments. Each of us has to choose our own paths for action, for engagement.

 The problem.

What is the problem? How is it affecting me?

It is helpful at the outset to attempt to distinguish between "issue" and "problem." In our efforts to create environments that reduce violence, it is important to be clear on what we are doing and why. "Problem" provides the focus for the former and "issue" the focus for the latter. In many ways, the issue provides the context for the problem. Or, to put it the other way around, the problem is a manifestation of the issue.

The best place to begin, however, is very often with the problem, because this is what is most on our minds as we go about our daily business. But the trick is to *problematize* the problem—that is, to put the framing of the problem as the work to be accomplished, rather than assuming that the problem is self-evident. In that way we remind ourselves that "problem" is merely a label for some aspect of life that we would like to change and that it is as much a construction of our imagination and experience as it is a natural phenomenon.

Naming the problem is an important step in identifying potential solutions and focusing efforts for change. It is important to characterize problems in ways that permit us to act, that provide a way of organizing people and resources for action. Viable candidates for the "problem" in these cases are the following, each one with identifiable courses of action.

- Unequal distribution of wealth and resources and the inequality that results
- Lack of tolerance for difference
- Narrowly focused, materialist decision making that leads to individuals being considered commodities. In schools this leads to narrowly defined educational goals and punitive approaches to measurement. In national and global politics this leads to greed, profit, and refugees.
- Disproportionate attention to control and punishment in society in general and in school in particular
- Inadequate funding of prenatal care and early childhood education; lack of attention to children in general. As the twig is bent, so grows the tree.

An important difference between "problem" and "issue" is that the former is stated in ways that permit direct and sustained action, while the latter is articulated so that we are continually reminded of the larger aspects of the problem.

For me, the issue is identity, or perhaps, the perceived threat to one's identity–personal and cultural–and the problem is violence as a response to the threat. As an individual, even as an individual with colleagues and resources, I cannot do much about someone's self-concept (so "identity" does not offer fruitful ground for defining the problem), but I can work to create environments for learning where respect for others and peaceful problem solving are the norm.

This is always a matter of negotiated exploration; it is important to constantly work to refine one's understanding of the issues and to improve one's description of the problems. Both efforts result in more accurate understanding of the work one is doing and its effects on others. You know that your definitions of the problem are improving if you find that you are able to more easily identify the work required and the assessments needed to prove you are making progress. And you know that your understanding of issues is deepening if it leads to better definitions of problems and better development of solutions.

A few caveats are required.

It is important to make certain that definitions of problems are constructed so as to avoid privileging one point of view over another. Beware of building in your own assumptions as you define the problem. For example, definitions of violence should not be distorted by institutional bias or convention. That is, the violence of adults yelling at children, or of schools imposing punitive and humiliating penalties, should be declared as harmful as playground extortions by bullies.

Second, be aware that the innovations themselves can often become problems. You need to continually ask yourself, "What is the problem here?" If you discover that the new homework requirements or the new policy on grades and discipline are causing more difficulty than the problems they were developed to solve, you need to adjust your definition of the problem so that you can take positive steps toward improving the situation. More about this later.

Third, two hints on what should not be called a problem. Particular individuals or groups of individuals, however much they have become a pain in your neck, should not be identified as the problem, at least not in the sense employed here.

Remember, the point of identifying the problem is to provide yourself with a focus for change efforts. You cannot change individuals, and if you live with the delusion that some particular person will decide to retire or be transferred, or that all the special-education students or nonnative English speakers will be sent to another school, you are not only setting yourself up for frustration and disappointment but are misunderstanding the way the world works and how you might productively participate in it.

It may be satisfying to declare an opinionated student, despotic administrator, or meddlesome parent as the problem, but individuals are better considered to be irritating symptoms of a larger problem.

The framing of the problem as a particular individual or group of individuals permits us to place the blame on others and to ignore our own contributions, or the contributions of the institutions within which we work, to the problem. It also results in driving individuals underground and creating the likelihood that they will band together with others who have been identified as the problem, leading to an intensification of their sense of isolation and justifying extreme reactions to the despots in charge.

Another broad category of "nonproblem" is time. Time is not the problem, as in "I don't know why I try to teach anything on Mondays and Fridays (or on the days just before holidays); the kids just are not able to concentrate right before or after the weekend (or holidays)."

I'll say more about this when I discuss activity cycles later, but it is important to point out why time should not be designated as the problem in your change efforts. The reason is simple: time—as in the day, the week, the seasons—is a fact of nature. We can't change time; we can only understand it. Once it is understood, we can adjust our routines to better accommodate nature's rhythms, but the problem needs to be defined in ways that allow us to do something about it.

Given the focus of this essay, the characteristic time pressures of the school year and the evaluation cycle, for example, need to be included in this category of nonproblem as well. You might argue that they are not of the same ilk as the march of the seasons, but for our purposes here–identifying problems so that we can craft change efforts to solve them–they belong in the same category.

 The issue.

How is this problem a variation on life's natural functioning?

There are no local events that are not related in some way to larger systemic patterns. The violence we are discussing here is a variation on what is becoming an increasingly common occurrence around the world. No country is exempt. But we cannot permit this fact to overwhelm us; this is the reality, and we have to find a way to respond to it. The difficulty is to identify the issue in a way that permits us to respond meaningfully to violence at local and global levels. Some possibilities are:

- Democratic processes in political and institutional decision making
- Justice in the minute particulars of daily life and in the larger cycles of society
- Respect for diversity and the inclusion of everyone in the basic benefits of life
- Improvement in prenatal health care and early childhood education
- Improvement in education in general and in cross-generational communication in particular

All of these issues touch in important ways on the lives of children, and all provide opportunities for participating at a broad level in the effort at reducing violence. Merely working on the list was helpful for me. It gave me a focus for my worries, and it provided me with avenues for action. It also permitted me to examine the complexity and range of the problems we face as a species.

If it is true that it takes a village to raise a child, and if we construe "village" to be a metaphor that stretches from the smallest collection of human beings to global dimensions, then it seems obvious that this points us toward innovations that permit us to participate effectively in the lives of other people's children. There are, of course, many constraints on such participation, but it seems clear that sustained effort is what is required.

I believe the issue to be identity—individual, cultural, institutional, national—and the processes by which it is formed and sustained. Threats to identity, which usually are understood as violence or the possibility of violence, are what incline people to take drastic action. I cannot stop thinking about the fact that the perpetrators of violence are increasingly willing to die in the act, and the sheer magnitude of the problem staggers me when I contemplate whole countries of people who are so alienated from themselves and others that they see death as a reasonable solution to the problems they face. Somehow, we have to find responses to individuals and groups that affirm the validity of the identities of individuals and groups both in the minute particulars of the daily routine and in the grand sweep of national and international politics.

From a systems perspective, identity is a dynamic collection of features that characterizes individuals and groups, that permits people to identify "us" and "them." But these features are not an invariable set of traits. Rather, identity is an accomplishment that is relatively stable. But, and this is key, identity is not something fixed at birth or immutable over time. It *is* durable, and historical analyses of countries and longitudinal examinations of individuals and groups will yield a certain amount of consistency of response to events and situations. But identity is forged in activities, through interactions with others over time, and so it provides us with a framework for constructing environments for peaceful decision making and negotiated understandings that directly address the problem of violence.

∽ **Constraints and strategies.**
What are the factors that contribute to the way things are?
What are the approaches that make sense, given the pressures of resistance?

If people were billiard balls, the strategy would be simple—line up the shots and hit them home. Simple cause and effect. The approach is essentially positive and positivist–discover what has to happen and develop rewards and punishments to accomplish your goals.

But with people, irritatingly complex and unpredictable, you need a different approach. Instead of causes, we must understand constraints, and instead of effects, we must learn to think of patterns of observed outcomes. Here is the routine.

1. Identify the outcomes that you believe capture the pattern of events that you would like to address.
2. List the outcomes that you would have preferred and that would have been possible but that did not occur.
3. Identify the constraints that made the observed outcomes the most probable ones.
4. Identify your spheres of influence and the decision points that will provide the greatest amount of leverage for your change efforts.

A word or two about "constraints." A better term might be "factors" or "contributing factors" because the range of things that needs to be considered goes all the way from genetic predisposition and cultural influence to the weather and the time of day. In short, a constraint is any factor that you can see as being relevant to a person's behavior or an event. The list is potentially infinite, but in reality, we soon learn to pay attention to the constraints over which we have some influence. In attempting to reduce the number of fights on the playground, for example, we acknowledge that there is little we can do about the racial tensions in the neighborhood, but we can adjust the recess schedule to change the mix of kids on the playground at the same time and we can develop activities that harness the children's energy in positive ways.

If the process seems unnecessarily opaque and convoluted, contemplate for a moment the last time your carefully organized lesson plan blew up in your face because you had overlooked some detail that in retrospect seemed obvious. The convergence of established habits functions to maintain the patterns that we notice. The multiple constraints of time, place, and routine contribute to the situations that we want to change, and unilateral action will not suffice.

The complexity and scope of these problems can be overwhelming, but they can also be strangely liberating. Once we recognize that we are not in control, that, in fact, the desire for unilateral control and direct solution is part of the problem, then we can afford to be more patient in our efforts. Freed of the burden of total responsibility, we can concentrate on those spheres of influence over which we do have some measure of control.

The phrase "some measure of control" is carefully chosen. We cannot control others, so the best we can do is work toward environments that encourage change in a particular direction and toward particular values. This approach requires you to become an astute observer and to remember that you cannot unilaterally control people or events. Among the most prominent strategies that emerge from this approach are the following.

- *More is different.* If you can increase the number of people with similar values working on a project, you will dynamically increase the effects of your work.
- *Practice your freedoms.* Create situations where everyone—adults and children—is encouraged to explore the things they are interested in. The energy that comes from affirmative commitment, rather than compliance, resonates throughout the system.
- *Identify the highest points of influence with the longest reaction time.* If you can create the conditions for long-term work and sustained effort, you will have fewer problems than if you have to attend to all the details of people's work.
- *Practice humility.* Be aware of the fact that your point of view is just one among many and that everything makes sense to someone. People may not be able to articulate their reasons for particular behavior, but you can count on the fact that what they were doing made sense to them while they were doing it. Work to understand what they were thinking.

- *Create wobbles in the system.* Be content with shaking things up a bit and monitoring the results, rather than expecting that you will be able to accomplish specific changes.

- *Assess distance traveled, rather than distance remaining.* Be alert for movement in the right direction, however small. Change comes in spurts and not always in ways we anticipate, so we have to be careful not to overlook progress made.

- *Remain patient and philosophical.* This proceeds from the approach to assessment just mentioned. There is no failure as long as there is life. "Failure" is a label used by causal thinkers, whose adherence to an "all-or-nothing" stance with regard to change sets them up for discouragement. In life, we commit to the relationships and continue to work.

- *Change systems.* In apparent contradiction to the preceding item, the advice here is to recognize when a particular job is demanding more of you than you can give and to quit and move on. The trick is to recognize that this decision is possible without having to accuse yourself of failure. We define our work by our contribution to the greater good. It may be that your efforts will be more effective when applied to another context.

- *Avoid causal language.* Since Newton, at least, our intellectual heritage has been one of causality. If you are going to think systemically, you need to use language that encourages you to see ecological relationships, rather than causal ones. Among the most common phrases that reveal causal thinking are *in the end, bottom line, beginning, middle, end, like clockwork,* and *in the final analysis.*

Activity cycles.

Where am I in the process?
Seeing the cycle is essential to organizing change strategies.

Part of the difficulty with problems of this magnitude is that they explode into our awareness with terrifying abruptness, belying the length of time it took for them to develop. Klebold, Harris, and Atta–

these individuals were merely agents of a process that had been set in motion long ago. Our response, however, is often forced into tight evaluation cycles in which we are expected to show progress in a brief period of time. This is in synch with election cycles and the school year.

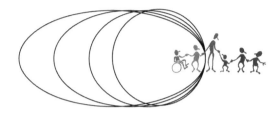

It may be helpful to visualize a set of concentric ovals, all touching at a particular moment in history. The smallest oval represents the here and now, a cycle of a few moments, perhaps, and the other ovals represent larger loops of time. Yes, I am dealing with this group of youngsters at this particular moment, but each of us represents a history and a potential future. There is a natural rhythm in the world of school, one that is punctuated by 45-minute class sessions, lunch, after-school activities, the school week, and the school term. There is also the rhythm associated with the major holidays of the year.

As I make decisions and react to situations, I keep all of the loops in mind. Each cycle comes around, like orbits in a nested solar system of human interaction, and the success of any change effort will hinge in large part on how accurately I have predicted the sequence of events. My success in moving the kids toward goals I have established will depend, in part, on my ability to select appropriate action, timed appropriately.

In my efforts at organizing a response that fits my roles and responsibilities, I have begun conducting action research in a middle school. I have had to make adjustments to accommodate the rhythms of the school—the frenetic pace of middle school and the high energy of adolescents. This is very different from the rhythms of the university; in systems terminology, we say that the reaction time of the feedback loops is shorter (Kauffman 1980; Capra 1996). At the same time, however, I need to adjust to the longer cycles of legislative initiatives and institutional response that have brought standardized testing and mandatory performance review to bear on teachers' lives and, therefore, on my own work.

This combination of middle-school frenzy and political pressure has created a curious riptide of counteracting forces. I often find myself caught between the need to act RIGHT NOW and the desire to step back and reflect on some important insight imperfectly glimpsed through the action. The trick to maintaining some degree of sanity is to recognize that I cannot monitor all of the activity cycles with equal attention and that I need to discipline myself to focus on whatever work I have deemed important at the moment. At the same time I need to remain aware of the reciprocal interaction of activity cycles of different magnitude.

So, for example, if I am committed to providing students with choices in each lesson, I need to arrive at the classroom with all the materials ready to go. This means, obviously, that I will have had to spend time in the past working through in detail what I want to have happen during the lesson, anticipating the tighter decision-making sequences that will confront me when I am with the students.

There is nothing revelatory in this assertion; it is merely a variation on the old saying, "Plan ahead!" But it is no less ambitious for being obvious. I want to work for an organized approach in which I anticipate variety without knowing exactly what is going to happen. I do not want to find myself in the position of telling students that they have to do a particular activity merely because I neglected to create options for them to choose from.

The seeds of Columbine and the terrorist attacks of September 11 were sown early and nurtured through many years of anger and inattention, and our contributions to a peaceful future will seem very indirect and distant. And, of course, we will never hear about our successes, because these students will grow up to lead unreported lives of consequence. It is important, however, to be aware of the contributions of kind words and thoughtful learning environments to the mental health of individuals and the peaceful coexistence of different points of view, even if we have to take this assurance on faith. We work in the moment for the moment, but we have to have confidence that our efforts at this moment contribute to the long-term health of the system.

The innovation
What will I do?
Of the limitless options available, which one to select?

Just as we tend to take a narrow view of problems, we tend to like our solutions neat and simple. In the wake of the Columbine shootings, schools across the country tightened security and clamped down on students dressed in trench coats and Doc Martens. After September 11, the United States declared war on terrorism. But these are not problems that will yield to direct solutions, and they are certainly beyond the scope of reward and punishment. Violence is the problem whether it is called a solution or not.

In general, the search for a solution must be in the development of environments where people have choices and in which those choices lead to healthy decision making. Beware of packaged programs that promise standard results for minimal effort or that require lock-step adherence to formulaic steps. People are too unpredictable and situations too variable for quick-fix approaches to work. The idea is to foster healthy environments for everyone, where a sense of personal identity and value is reinforced in the mundane act of getting through the day.

For me, given my position at the university and my membership in the neighborhood, I have arrived at the conclusion that I need to work for school/university/community partnerships that are focused on providing young people with places to go and things to do. I have been working with a broad coalition of people to establish an after-school club with formal connections to the school district and to the university. The club provides a site for recreational and educational activities for kids between the ages of 10 and 14, and it also serves as a site for community service, research, and teacher training.

We have secured federal funding and financial support from private foundations and community organizations, and we rely heavily on volunteer time and energy. The club, which we call the Tools Club, offers young people a choice of activities around a variety of "tools" associated with bicycles, computers, video, photography, and art. The intent is to create a recreational setting that the kids will be attracted to; that is, the goal is to entice children into play, the pattern of learning that is most natural for them.

The club rests on theory development and research efforts that underscore the importance of systemic change through sustained involvement of individuals in activities in which everyone—not just the children—is expected to learn. We have created a structure and a process based on a network of Fifth Dimension learning sites around the world (Cole 1996, 257–325; Davis and Clarke 2001; Crespo, Palli, and Laluesa 2002; Blanton n.d.), while maintaining an awareness of larger pressures as articulated by systems theorists (G. Bateson 1999; M. C. Bateson 1994, 1995; Heifetz 1994; Senge et al. 2000; Fullan 2001). The club represents an effort to diminish the alienation that often occurs in school and to foster an environment that builds on the innate predisposition to learn that occurs when internal rhythms are validated by authentic relationships with others and activities that resonate with individuals' natural curiosity and interest.

Mary Catherine Bateson discusses this sort of learning as "coming home," the discovery that something new was actually "programmed" in some profound sense when a skill or talent is awakened in the learner and she or he settles into an activity that is truly her or his own (1994, 195–213). The activities that the children view as recreation are scaffolded by coaching from adults and near-peers and by problem solving and literacy development aimed at increasing learner autonomy and technological skill development.

It has started out modestly, on the individual and interpersonal level. But we recognize that effective education is as much a community and institutional accomplishment as an individual achievement or instructional *tour de force* and that a sustained innovation will require changes in the school and the community. We use the club as the platform for collaboration with school personnel and community leaders to improve the experiences of students in the school. And through partnerships with scholars in Scandinavia, Spain, and the United States, we are working to develop an international broad-based program for sustained educational innovation.

But you ask, "Isn't this all just a tad self-serving and pretentious? Where do you get off portraying your pet neighborhood project as a contribution to world peace? Henry Kissinger or Jimmy Carter—maybe. But aren't you stretching it just a bit here?"

Yes . . . well, perhaps it *is* merely hubris.

But it seems to me that it may also be the only way of connecting the details of our lives, as mundane and inconsequential as they may seem, with the broad sweep of the human condition.

Approach it from the other direction and ask yourself, "How many potential Dylan Klebolds (or Mohammed Attas?) have I influenced in positive ways throughout the years to reject violence as a solution to problems?" Of course, you will never know the answer, because individuals who contemplate violence and reject it because of your teaching have more on their minds than calling to thank you for the guidance.

And if thinking of your efforts as a positive contribution to the human race is too much, how should you characterize your work? As just "getting through the day"? "Punching in and punching out"? Of course, it is not necessary to choose between the two extremes; there are many stances between nihilism and egomania. But if the systems view is correct, and all human behavior is a variation on fundamental natural processes, then it is not presumptuous to think of your efforts as a small contribution to the survival of the planet.

Evidence of change.

How do I know if I am making progress?
How do I keep going in spite of frustrations?

The key word is patience. We are dealing with human beings and with life processes, not with automobiles in assembly lines, although increasingly much of the decision making in schools and other institutions is more appropriate for the latter than for the former. We need to identify appropriate benchmarks of learning for the amount of time we have with individuals or programs. Many good ideas get scrapped prematurely because of exaggerated expectations and premature judgment of failure.

It is unreasonable to expect that everyone in a classroom will become respectful of others or that all hallways and classrooms will be perceived as safe places for all kids. However, having these as goals, and then keeping track of the progress made toward them, *is* reasonable. It is important that each of us identifies the markers of progress that we are paying attention to and that we not be discouraged by the lack of progress in other areas. Change comes slowly, and it comes in fits and starts, and it is easy to become discouraged if we attend to the progress we have *not* made.

The important evidence will not be visible to people who are not directly and regularly involved, because we are talking about notices of difference, which is a highly abstract phenomenon (G. Bateson 1999, 454–71). Difference is the change implied by a comparison of events and situations at two points in time, and if we are to be able to see shifts toward nonviolent approaches to interpersonal or international conflict we need to be in a position to collect data that accurately reflect people's learning. This means that we need to adopt a stance of informed activist or active observer—we need the skills of the native and the insights of the anthropologist (Erickson 1992; Wolcott 1994; Eisenhart 2001).

The ability to see change, especially change in a desired direction, hinges on being able to compare different periods in time, being able to remember how things were and how they have changed. Very often the changes are so minute that we miss them, or we miss them because our attention is focused on other things or the ultimate goal. In such situations we cannot appreciate the progress we are making because we are not seeing it. We look around at the injustice and racism today and declare that the civil rights movement did not accomplish anything. But Elaine Baker, who worked as a college student in Mississippi during the 1960s, reports that today she and friends of different races can eat in restaurants together—something that was unheard of 30 years ago (Baker 2000). Comparison between two points in time is the key, and being able to compare requires attention to detail and the ability to understand how perceptions before *and* after an event are both valid (M. C. Bateson 2001).

In our work in the Tools Club we have learned that this requires us to continually remind ourselves of the small things that could easily be lost in the hubbub. In after-school sessions one day seems pretty much like another, with commotion and noise and all the movement that you expect with adolescents. The flare-ups of anger and the hurling of fists and epithets are easier to notice than the comment by a youngster that "I am dealing with my anger" or that of a teacher who says, "I'm calmer these days. I give 'em the evil eye. I'm not yelling as much."

Often, the very frustration and tension we are dealing with are the indicators of movement. Having to adjust my schedule to attend the faculty retreat is one of the benefits (!) of being considered part of the decision-making process at the school. Earlier in the year, I would have been considered an outsider whose work was at best tangential to the workings of the school and at worst an invasion of privileged space.

There are no ultimate indicators of learning, no final determination of success, because we are dealing with life, and life goes on. It is our punctuation of sequences of events that leads us to believe that "all is lost" or "we have finally arrived." In order to keep on in the face of frustrations, we have to remember that we are participating in a small arc of much larger cycles and do what we can to nudge the system toward the values we hold dear.

The players.

Who is involved, and how?

Who are the primary players, and what are their responses to change?

All innovation requires change, and this means, ultimately, that people have to change. We need to be aware of who we are attempting to influence with our change efforts. Our discussion here is prompted by violent events, and we hope that our involvement is always distant and indirect. But it is important to avoid minimizing our contribution to the greater good merely because we seem to be far removed from the fray. How many teachers did Klebold, Harris, and Atta have in their lifetimes? How many scout leaders and soccer coaches? How many of these individuals have paused to think about incidents with the boys where they might have chosen a different direction in their interaction with them?

We'll never know, and in any case, I do not want to give the impression that every single incident in a person's past is equally determinative of their behavior. In fact, just the opposite. No event is totally determinative. It is not the single incidents that I believe are important; rather, it is the pattern of relationships and interactions that matters, and it is the apperceptive learnings that we need to focus on. We cannot know who among our students are future presidents or potential killers, so we have to work to create environments in which everyone—students, colleagues, parents—is treated with respect and understanding.

It is helpful to envision the activity cycles of your life, the people with whom you have sustained contact on a regular basis and therefore with whom you have some measure of influence. I ask myself, "In the course of a typical week, who do I spend time with, and how might I work with them toward common goals?" These are not goals in the sense of a blueprint, a 10-step trajectory toward an articulated vision. Rather, these are emergent goals, implicit in the values and direction of particular efforts (G. Bateson 1999, 159–76)

In the Tools Club, the primary focus is on our own efforts and the learning of the middle-school students, but we also work to foster an atmosphere conducive to change in schools and community, which means developing relationships with individuals in positions of power and influence and pushing for reforms in the way teaching and learning are approached. We also want to have an impact on other scholars and community activists through our research and writing. What we notice, of course, is that we are the individuals doing the most learning. The deeper we become involved in the school and community, the more we have to adjust—everything from our daily schedules to our most cherished beliefs.

Continuations . . .

As I reread what I have written it strikes me as opaque and cumbersome. Let me see if I can render it a bit more transparent and graceful.

As an individual who has enjoyed more than my share of love and support, I would like to do what I can to reduce the chances that some child I know will turn to violence. I recognize that my efforts will be modest and that if I am successful no one will ever know it.

Because I am an educator, I will work within the university and the schools. Because I live in a neighborhood that has a long, proud history of progressive race relations, and recently, of gang- and drug-related violence, I'll focus most of my efforts close to home. I'll work to create partnerships among school, university, and community organizations whose focus will be on creating a safe learning environment for youngsters in the neighborhood. The youth will be the center of attention and the most direct recipients of the effort, but all of us involved—parents, teachers, graduate students, community volunteers—will be beneficiaries because we will all be learning and changing in ways that are invigorating and positive. The by-products of this effort will be improved academic performance among the schoolchildren, creative problem solving among teachers and administrators, scholarly studies by university students and faculty, harmonious race relations among community activists, and a general sense of energy and well-being.

We will work to foster caring relationships and calm resolution of conflict, appreciation for diversity, and democratic decision making. The effort will be aimed at reducing the reasonableness of violence as a response to disputes in an environment in which individual and group identity is affirmed in the process.

By engaging a wide range of participants with multiple goals and commitments, we hope to create a groundswell of activity that will contribute to a shift in local norms of problem solving toward nonviolent and nonpunitive measures.

Evaluations of the effort produced by school and university personnel will lead to increases in private and public funding for a variety of initiatives and to positive media coverage and a general rise in the stature of the neighborhood and the schools. This, in turn, will result in an increasing spiral of positive individual self-esteem and a sense of community among the young people. If we are able to sustain the effort, they will return to the neighborhood as teachers, police officers, and community leaders, working to promote the values that they acquired growing up here.

It will be a quiet revolution characterized by shots not heard.

Appendix

I include here two letters written to teachers who were using early drafts of this book at the time of the attacks at Columbine High School and the World Trade Center. They provide another glimpse at my efforts to make sense of large-scale tragedy using systems theory, to construct a way of keeping my bearings in troubled times.

Columbine High School
April 20, 1999

I wrote the following message two days after the tragedy at Columbine High School. At the time I was teaching IPTE 5080, Principles and Practice of Change, a graduate course for beginning teachers. Most of the students were in their first year of teaching. They were struggling with lesson plans and crowd control, and I was struggling to convince them that insights from systems theory and ecological thinking could contribute to their mental health. Most were skeptical. It all seemed far too abstract and distant from the daily grind to be of much use.

None of the individuals in my class were teaching at Columbine High School, but several had friends who were, and one or two were teaching at the elementary and middle schools that fed into Columbine, so they were working with children whose families were directly affected by the tragedy.

The class met on Tuesday nights, and April 20, 1999, fell on a Tuesday. I arrived at the university at midday unaware of the drama unfolding a few miles to the west in the suburb of Littleton, Colorado, but a cluster of colleagues had gathered around a TV, and I soon was caught up in the horror of the attack. I stumbled through the rest of the day like a sleepwalker. The class began at 5:30 p.m. We talked about what had happened, but at that hour there was very little information and a great deal of speculation. I made an effort to stick with the plan for the evening, but it was a disjointed, unfocused session. I returned home to a dark house to find my wife and my daughter Julia, her month-old son in her arms, watching the TV in appalled silence. Julia said, "I'm not sending him to school."

I brooded and fussed for a day or two and then sent out the following message on email—as an attempt at making sense of the event and as an effort at providing comfort and focus for the young teachers in my class.

From: Mark A. Clarke
To: IPTE 5080
Re: Columbine High School
Date: 4/22/99

Good morning. I am still reeling from Tuesday's events. In fact, I seem to be getting worse, rather than better. Perhaps the first few hours I was in shock. I don't know, but right now what I seem to need is time to think and sort things out, look at it closely from a systems perspective—if a theory can't help you deal with life and death, what good is it?

My first reaction to the shooting was, "Who do I know there? Are any of my students teaching there? Do I know any of the children?" I was trying to situate the horror of the event, to establish the distance between me and this awful thing. I needed to believe that this was an aberration, an anomaly, that the problem was somehow located in the killers, their families, the school, or the community. I wanted to convince myself that this could not be part of my world. I was, like all systems, functioning to maintain stability, to preserve order and predictability in my universe.

Living in Park Hill, I have had to deal with gangs and violence for a long time, and with what I see as media and political indifference to the plight of urban youth, especially minority youth. So I was relieved (!) that the shooters were white, middle-class, suburban. I was anguished by the racism that surfaced in some of the news stories, worried that some of the African American victims were children from my church, and I waited in horrible suspense for the names of the victims. But I have experienced a grim satisfaction in the confirmation of what I have long believed—that we cannot isolate the violence by calling it "an urban problem" or "a matter of Black inner city gangs." Maybe now people will begin to see that gun control is not a neighborhood issue, I thought.

I found myself searching for someone to blame—the parents of the killers, the NRA and the conservative politicians in their pockets, the media and its ghoulish fascination with suffering, Hollywood and the entertainment industry and society's glorification of violence as a solution to problems—the Rambo syndrome. But this list merely reveals my personal and political prejudices, because I talked with others who were equally outraged but whose lists were very different. This is just another example of working toward stability, constructing an understanding of events that will conform to one's perceptions, framing disturbing information, creating pearls from pebbles.

But now, in a forced effort of calm analysis, with a wet snow falling into a gray dawn, I will see if this tragedy yields to my view of the world. Here are some axioms I have lived by, now severely challenged.

* Individual, family, school, community, society—systems within systems within systems. One set of theoretical principles to understand them all. What is true for one is true for the others.
* Things are the way they are *not* by accident. What gets done reveals what is important. What we see happening is, statistically, the most likely thing to happen. What happened at Columbine was not an aberration; it was, if not inevitable, expectable.

* Events have multiple causes. Or, put another way, the daily functionings of many systems converge to produce the events we notice. And, what gets noticed is a complex function of what is happening and what we are conditioned to notice. In other words, this thing was a long time coming, there were many factors that contributed to it, and the danger signals were not being noticed by people around the two boys.

From the moment I learned about the shooting I have been haunted by a question my colleague Kathy Escamilla asked after a particularly difficult day at an inner-city elementary school. A problem had been solved, an altercation dealt with, but, she asked, "What are we doing about these angry little boys? We aren't dealing with the anger."

The enormity of the anger and hatred is staggering. Were Klebold and Harris born monsters? Were they abused as children? What about their lives might explain what they did? What would lead two adolescents to the point that they could take their own lives after cold-bloodedly shooting and maiming their classmates? Is it possible that, in 18 short years, two children could have experienced so much pain and unhappiness that they could commit such a terrifyingly inhuman act? How did others participate in their lives so that this would happen? Why would violence on this level seem to them to be a reasonable response? The complex interaction of systems begins to emerge as I attempt to answer these questions. Here, tentative and incomplete, are my responses to those questions.

They may not have been born monsters, but they were born male, which means that they were genetically predisposed to aggressive, behavior—precisely what a species needs—so we know that fundamental genetic patterns contributed to the situation. As for their upbringing, I haven't read anything about their early years, but I can speculate that they spent time in childcare situations— that they had to deal with separation and anxiety. Harris came from a military family, so he may have moved about as a youngster. They may well have experienced what my counseling colleagues refer to as "attachment disorders," difficulties in the bonding process that contribute to a sense of alienation and disaffection. Things got worse as they entered school. We know that as adolescents they were taunted and teased for being different, and in high school they dealt with their anger by hanging out with other self-described misfits—their motto was "Who says we're different? Insanity is healthy"—and lashing out at others. School was a cruel place for them. They *were* different, and in their school difference is not tolerated. "You wear a black trench coat to school every day of the year, and you're going to hear about it. . . . That's just the way high school is," said Tom Mohr, a classmate of the killers. *The way high school is* . . . . An innocuous statement if it weren't for Tuesday's carnage. Now it rings as a chilling assessment of one of our most important institutions, as damning an indictment of our society as you could make.

So far I have identified genetics, parents, classmates, teachers, and administrators as significant participants in the boys' lives, contributors to their psyches, collaborators in their crime. But as complex as that seems, the story is not complete, because when we attempt to answer the last question—Why is violence considered reasonable?—we enlarge the pool of collaborators dramatically. Why? Because violence and technological mayhem are a time-honored cultural tradition. We pull for the underdog, we glory in bullies getting their just desserts, and we believe in war as a way of making peace. From national politics and international policy to pop culture and media hype, we provided a clear and consistent model for the boys to follow. Klebold and Harris did not invent their strategy for dealing with injustice and humiliation; they merely played a variation on an American theme.

So, systems within systems within systems. Individuals seeking to make sense of the world—growing, learning, adapting to their environments using available models and tools. Learning that it is okay to bully others if you have the power to make it stick. Parents working hard to make ends meet, spending more time on the road or in the office than with their sons, paying off the mortgage, but mortgaging the mental health of their children. Classmates playing the American game of winners and losers, scrambling to be winners, no matter what the cost to the losers. Teachers and administrators coping with too many students, too many laws and regulations, too many tests, going through the motions, punching in, punching out of a job that increasingly looks like penal work. University professors, secure in their tenured positions, writing papers on teaching methods or teen violence and attending conferences to discuss theories of adolescent behavior. Policymakers and politicians responding to public pressure, crafting sound bites to capture the headlines and quick answers to satisfy the critics.

Everyone doing his or her job. Everyone busy. Too busy to notice Klebold and Harris. Until it was too late.

No one person's fault, no one to blame, yet everyone is responsible. Could it have been prevented? How do we act to prevent future massacres? What can I do now, immediately, to help, and how do I contribute, in the long run, to a safer, saner world? These are important questions—one purpose of a theory, after all, is to guide one's thinking and acting both for the long haul and the short run.

The massacre certainly could have been prevented, just as the Vietnam War could have been prevented, but there is no single fork in the road that determines the trajectory of an individual's life—rather, there are countless experiences and decision points, each one contributing slightly to the direction of things. We can't determine outcomes, but we can work to create environments that increase the probability of certain outcomes over others.

Action is required at different levels of scale, and each of us has to act within our own spheres of influence. Here is a partial list of actions that I have compiled for myself.

* Hug my kids; make sure they know that I am available to talk, to work through problems, no matter how large or small.
* Cast my eye about the neighborhood, church, bike club—are there children within my sphere of influence who show signs of being or becoming bullies or of being bullied?
* Act to create an environment in which every individual is valued for his or her individuality. Work for appreciation of diversity.
* Comfort others—listen to how they are coping with the tragedy, respond to their concerns and fears with calm assurance and implicit and explicit valuing of their points of view.
* Work for structures that increase the chances that every individual will experience a sense of belonging and self-worth.
* Participate in committees and other decision-making bodies that work for smaller class size, favorable teacher-student ratios, teacher-support teams, and other measures that increase the chances that students will develop meaningful and positive relationships with adults and each other.

* Break out of the familiar pathological patterns of defensiveness
  and blame, in which I unwittingly construct barriers between me
  and my allies and "others." This is not a competition. There are no
  winners and losers here. We are all in this together.
* Vote for politicians and policies that reflect these values.
* Contribute to organizations that work toward these broad goals.
* Send the occasional letter, sign the occasional petition, march in
  the occasional protest as my other commitments permit.

Small contributions to the greater good, but then what would I expect,
given my roles and responsibilities?

***

The World Trade Center and Pentagon Attack
September 11, 2001

In the fall of 2001 I was on sabbatical, so I was not teaching. I was,
however, working on the final draft of this book, and I was sending
out chapters as I completed them to two seminars taught by colleagues. One seminar was the current cohort of IPTE 5080 graduate students, similar in many ways to the group who had received
the email after the Columbine tragedy. The other seminar was composed of seasoned veterans, teachers at a large suburban high school.
I hadn't met either group, but I felt a strong connection to them
through their professors, and I knew that I could not send along the
next chapter without addressing the terrorist attack directly. This is
the letter I appended to the chapter.

Dear change agents:

As you can see by the date, I am writing this in the aftermath of the
World Trade Center attack, and it is my profound hope that all of you
and yours are safe and sound.

　　Like you, I am trying to make sense of what happened and to
find ways to push on with the mundane tasks of my daily life that un-

til last Tuesday seemed so important. I suspect that your classrooms full of students helped you keep your perspective, that finding yourself being watched by youngsters looking to you for guidance in difficult times provided you with ballast and rudder.

You were probably on your way to school when the attack occurred and only gradually became aware of the scope of the tragedy. I had just returned from my morning jog and was settling into a day of writing when I got a phone call from my daughter. I could hear the TV in the background as she reported what she had heard. It was about 7:15 A.M., and there was still a great deal of confusion about what had happened. I turned on the TV with misgivings, reluctant to let go of my schedule for the day, hoping that this was just some bizarre accident.

I soon discovered, however, that it was far worse than that and very quickly became mesmerized by the macabre events unfolding on TV. By midmorning, all the family had gathered at my mother's house, and we alternated playing games with Evan (at two years old, the individual least aware of what was going on, and the one for whom it matters the most) and attempting to absorb what we were seeing and hearing.

In light of the chapters you have already read you are no doubt struggling to reconcile the very abstract formulations of systems thinking with the all too real events playing out in the life of the country right now. I will try to explain how I am coping, and I invite you to respond if you are interested. I will not try to convince you that my position on the crisis is the one you should adopt; these issues are too complex for prescriptions. But I hope that you will get a better understanding of systems theory and how it might be applied in your work by seeing how I have attempted to apply it in my own. Here goes.

***

Thoughts on the Terrorist Attack

It is said that we can tolerate the unexplained but not the inexplicable. We human beings *must* understand. That is our unique capacity, and it is our curse. In the case of catastrophe, after the initial denial, bewilderment, anger, frustration, and free-floating stress, the most common response is to seek someone or something to blame. Very shortly thereafter comes the urge to act, to do something decisive to make the situation better.

In the case of the World Trade Center attack, I see this pattern clearly in Bush's focus on Osama bin Laden and Afghanistan as the ones to blame, and war as the action required. With very few exceptions, the TV programs I have watched and the phone-in radio I have listened to reflect the same desire for a clear-cut technical solution to the crisis.

I sympathize, and there is an element of the cowboy in me that desires direct action, but I am fearful, and I urge caution. The stakes are too high, the technology for complete destruction too readily available. But more importantly, such an approach ignores the systemic forces at work, and a policy built on hasty response will surely result in long-range disaster. Direct action of this sort turns out to be a bad idea because it increases the problems it was intended to solve. As Barbara Kingsolver has observed (2001), "no bomb ever built will extinguish hatred."

I see two crucial errors in our thinking about the current crisis—cause-and-effect thinking, which leads us, willy-nilly, to piecemeal solutions with unforeseen, more horrific results, and misconceptions about who the "we" is in this "we-versus-them" battle.

Causal thinking leads us to identify the most recent and the most obvious event and to respond directly to it. We are horrified at the attack, and we seek immediate retribution. Clear and simple. This thinking leads us to attack Afghanistan. When we do that, children will die, and Afghans, joined by allies, will point to the death of innocents as evidence of our barbarism. Bin Laden's hatred of the United States will be vindicated. This will justify the next round of attacks, which we will use as rationale for our subsequent attacks. This is the recurring pattern of all escalation.

However, there are two important differences between today's conflict and all previous wars: the technology is readily available to destroy the planet, and this is seen as a reasonable consequence by a significant number of participants. There is no defense against the suicide bomber.

Another related error in our thinking right now concerns our conceptualization of "self"—the "we" in the rapidly escalating verbal battles that provide the necessary political environment for military action. In times of crisis we rush to secure the safety of our families, the primary unit in our lives. Only when this is accomplished do we begin thinking of next steps. This is natural, maybe even genetic. What is open to modification, however, is how we define "family," how we draw a line between "us" and "other." The "other" today is the terrorist, but there are no features that distinguish terrorists apart from their actions—Timothy McVeigh proved this point—and in our rush to lay blame and exact retribution, we include the more easily identified "other"—anyone belonging to the same racial, ethnic, or cultural or religious group as the identified terrorists.

Thus, one terrible simplification is amplified by another, and we generate an out-of-control cycle of blame and retribution that leads, inevitably, to greater atrocity.

As I reread portions of *Steps to an Ecology of Mind* today, in the aftermath of the World Trade Center attack, I am struck by how accurately Bateson saw the tragedy unfolding ahead of us. He discusses "errors in our epistemology" with chilling foreshadowing of the events we have just witnessed and, I am afraid, of tragedies to come. In one essay, "From Versailles to Cybernetics," he argues that Allied treachery in the treaties ending World War I contributed to the rise of nationalism in Germany and to World War II. He describes how expedient behavior—ignoring the gentlemen's agreements around which preliminary drafts of the armistice were built—satisfied the immediate political pressures but led to long-term demoralization of Germany and distrust of the allies, and ultimately to the Second World War (1999, 477–85).

I think it would be unwise to attempt to find single incidents of betrayal in the past that led to the World Trade Center attack, but I believe that it is necessary to work to understand how history grinds people down and makes them desperate. W. H. Auden (1952) captures the argument with the poet's gift for elegant precision.

> I and the public know
> What all schoolchildren learn,
> Those to whom evil is done
> Do evil in return.
>
> . . . .
>
> There is no such thing as the State
> And no one exists alone;
> Hunger allows no choice
> To the citizen or the police;
> We must love one another or die.

The same sentiment is expressed in other ways by scholars. My colleague Sandra Silberstein says that she was horrified by the events of 9/11/01, not as an American, but as a human being. And Mary Catherine Bateson holds out little hope of survival of the species until we learn to define "self" as including all other human beings (1972, 36–54). Gregory Bateson advocated substituting causal thinking with systems thinking, by which he meant examining events and situations for the factors that limit creative solutions, rather than accepting conventional definitions of problems; we need to change the questions, rather than merely seeking answers to the questions as they are customarily posed (1999, 486–95).

Systems thinking requires us to confront reality head-on; the data cannot be ignored, and the theory must account for them. The World Trade Center and thousands of people have perished. How do I understand that? First of all, I stop saying to myself, "I can't believe anyone would do this." It happened, and I must come to grips with it. I force myself to attempt to understand how a fellow human being would consider this to be a reasonable course of behavior. I resist demonizing individuals and groups, and I ask, "What kind of life experiences contributed to the terrorists' values and views of the world?" I look through history to see if I can find patterns of events that might have led to the attack on the World Trade Center.

This is a challenging way of thinking, because it requires me to look, not for causes, but for constraints—factors that make certain outcomes more likely than others. It requires me to identify events and ideas that contributed to the outcome I want to understand. And, in the process, it requires me to acknowledge the expectability of the observed event. That is, I must come to grips with the fact that the World Trade Center attack, while not precisely predictable, and certainly not inevitable, was, in fact, expectable. The following would have to be listed among the factors that contributed to it.

* Poverty and injustice around the world, contributing to envy and easy converts in the war against the United States and its economic prosperity
* The human tendency to group together with people who are like us and to distrust difference, compounded by age-old disputes that fester over the generations
* The increased mechanization of war, with the result of dehumanizing the conduct of battle, making it easier to kill

* Isolationism in the U.S. stance toward the rest of the world. Ignorance of other peoples, customs, histories. Unilateral decision making in dealings with other nations
* Increase of technology. This has made "weapons of mass destruction" more readily available to individuals and groups who answer to no political body. It has also contributed to global communication and rapid flow of information, which increases the speed of errors.
* Increased role of the media in shaping the political climate— linking popular opinion and policy-making in ways that do not permit thoughtful decisions or restraint
* Sound-bite orientation to information, in which media personalities and news stories are shaped by ratings rather than in-depth reporting. It is increasingly difficult to distinguish news from entertainment.
* Fascination with technological approaches to intelligence gathering coupled with relatively little face-to-face interaction with the people we are spying on. We collect more data from a distance than we can possibly analyze. We may discover that profiles of the terrorists were waiting in electronic files for humans to analyze them.
* Disjunct between the rhythms of power and the exercise of judgment—the four-year election cycle requires leaders to make decisions that will get them elected, rather than focusing on issues and making policy based on long-term effects. It also contributes to short-term political memory.

This is not a list that will capture much support in today's climate of retaliation, but I would argue that exploration of points like these, attempts at understanding the cyclical history of attack and counter-attack, would yield important insights into this latest example of terrorism, and it could form the basis for different approaches to decision making in the future.

It is the antithesis of causal thinking. It requires, not technical adjustments to our ways of doing government and international diplomacy, but rather profound change in our orientation to the problems faced by the world. It requires us to learn new ways of thinking.

So how do I, one insignificant individual, use systems thinking to guide my thoughts and actions in these dangerous times? President Bush will not call me for advice, but I will vote in various ways in the future, and I will participate in conversations and meetings where other voters congregate, and so it behooves me to have thought through the issues and options so that I do not get carried away in the heat of the moment. Here is a partial list of reminders I have jotted down to help me maintain a sense of perspective.

* Continue to work on articulating my values, of affirming my faith in my fellow human beings, of aligning my behavior with those values—modeling for students and colleagues the principles that I espouse.
* Work to avoid simplistic formulations of complex problems. Ask better questions.
* Attempt to see the other person's point of view. All human beings behave in ways that make sense to them. Try to see the sense, the rationale, behind others' actions. This applies to neighbors down the block as well as strangers in other countries.
* Enter into conversations with the intent of understanding others, rather than waiting for them to finish talking so that I can change their mind.
* Try to see the big picture. What are the historical antecedents for the current situation? What events count as "the same" as the World Trade Center attack for others? I would identify the bombings of the Chinese embassy and the pharmaceutical factory in the Sudan as recent examples, and the bombings of Hiroshima and Nagasaki as more distant comparisons.
* Identify alternatives to violence of all sorts. Violence begets violence, and what I want is an end to all violence, not merely the violence perpetrated on me and mine. Or, to put it another way, I hope that by reducing all instances of violence, I will reduce the violence to people I love.

I see these as applications of the ideas developed in the essays you have been reading. I suspect that the connections may not be as clear as they could be. I welcome your questions and comments as part of the process of clarifying the connections.

Best wishes,

Mark

Bibliography

Auden, W. H. 1952. September 1, 1939. In *A little treasury of modern poetry,* ed. O. Williams. New York: Charles Scribner's Sons.

Baker, E. DeLott. 2000. They sent us this white girl. In *Deep in our hearts: Nine white women in the freedom movement,* ed. C. Curry, J. C. Browning, D. D. Burlage, P. Patch, T. Del Pozzo, S. Thrasher, E. DeLott Baker, E. S. Adams, and C. Hayden. Athens: University of Georgia Press.

Bateson, G. 1979. *Mind and nature: A necessary unity.* New York, E. P. Dutton.

———. 1999. *Steps to an ecology of mind.* Chicago: University of Chicago Press.

Bateson, M. C. 1972. *Our own metaphor.* New York: Knopf.

———. 1989. *Composing a life.* New York: Penguin.

———. 1994. *Peripheral visions: Learning along the way.* New York: Harper Collins.

———. 1995. Democracy, ecology, and participation. In *Democracy, education, and the schools,* ed. R. Soder. San Francisco: Jossey Bass.

———. 2000. *Full circles, overlapping lives: Culture and generation in transition.* New York: Random House.

———. 2001. Comparison is key. *Whole Earth* 106:4.

Berger, P. L., B. Berger, and H. Kellner. 1974. *The homeless mind: Modernization and consciousness.* New York: Vintage Books.

Berger, P. L., and T. Luckmann, 1967. *The social construction of reality.* New York: Doubleday Anchor Books.

Berry, W. 2002. For love of the land. *Sierra,* May/June, 50–55

Blanton, W. E. N.d. *The virtual Fifth Dimension clearing house and propagation center.* University of Miami. Available at <http://ucerc.edu/fifthd/5dclring.html>.

Bourdieu, P. 1990. *The logic of practice.* Stanford: Stanford University Press.

Bowers, C. A., and D. J. Flinders. 1990. *Responsive teaching: An ecological approach to classroom patterns of language, culture, and thought.* New York: Teachers College Press.

Capra, F. 1990. *Mind walk: A film for passionate thinkers.* Prod. Adrianna AJ Cohen. Dir. Bernt Capra. Hollywood: Atlas Production Company.

———. 1996. *The web of life: A new scientific understanding of living systems.* New York: Anchor Books, Doubleday.

———. 2002. *The hidden connections: Integrating the biological, cognitive, and social dimensions of life into a science of sustainability.* New York: Doubleday.

Clarke, M. A. 1990. Some cautionary observations on liberation education. *Language Arts* 67: 388–98.

Clarke, M. A., and N. L. Commins 1993. Whole language: Reform and resistance. *Language and Education* 7 (2): 79–95.

Clarke, M. A., A. Davis, L. Rhodes, and E. DeLott Baker. 1998. Principles of collaboration in school-university partnerships. *TESOL Quarterly* 32 (3): 592–600.

———. 1996. Creating coherence: High achieving classrooms for minority students. Final report of research conducted under U.S. Department of Education, OERI Field Initiated Studies Program, grant R117 E302 44. University of Colorado at Denver.

Clarke, M. A., B. K. Dobson, and S. Silberstein. 1996. *Choice readings.* Ann Arbor: University of Michigan Press.

Clarke, M. A., and S. Silberstein. 1977. Toward a realization of psycholinguistic principles in the ESL reading class. *Language Learning* 27 (1): 135–54.

———. 1988. Problems, prescriptions, and paradoxes in second language teaching. *TESOL Quarterly* 22 (4): 685–99.

Cole, M. 1996. *Cultural psychology: A once and future discipline.* Cambridge: Harvard University Press.

Crespo, I., C. Palli, and J. L. Laluesa. 2002. Moving communities: A process of negotiation with a Gypsy minority for empowerment. *Community, Work, and Family,* March, 49–66.

Cummins, J. 1986. Empowering minority students: A framework for intervention. *Harvard Educational Review* 56:18–36.

———. 1989. *Empowering minority students.* Sacramento: California Association of Bilingual Education.

Davis, A., and M. A. Clarke. 2001. The Tools Club: The Fifth Dimension in Colorado. University of Colorado at Denver.

Davis, A., M. A. Clarke, and L. K. Rhodes. 1994. Extended text and the writing proficiency of urban elementary students. *Journal of Educational Psychology* 86 (4): 1–11.

Davis, A., M. A. Clarke, L. K. Rhodes, N. Shanklin, S. Nathenson-Mejia, M. Selkirk, N. Commins, R. Galindo, S. Shannon, M. Bookman, and N. Sanders. 1992. Colorado literacy study: Using multiple indicators to identify effective classroom practices for minority students in reading and writing. University of Colorado at Denver.

Delpit, L. 1988. The silenced dialogue: Power and pedagogy in educating other people's children. *Harvard Educational Review* 58:280–98.

Edelsky, C. 1990. Whose agenda is this anyway? A response to McKenna, Robinson, and Miller. *Educational Research* 19 (8): 7–11.

Eisenhart, M. 2001. Educational ethnography, past, present, and future: Ideas to think with. *Educational Researcher* 30 (8): 16–27.

Ellsworth, E. 1989. Why doesn't this feel empowering? Working through the oppressive myths of critical pedagogy. *Harvard Educational Review* 89:297–394.

Erickson, F. 1987. Transformation and school success: The politics and culture of educational achievement. *Anthropology and Education Quarterly* 18:335–56.

———. 1992. Ethnographic microanalysis of interaction. In *The handbook of qualitative research in education,* ed. M. LeCompte, W. L. Millroy, and J. Preissle. San Diego: Academic Press.

Evans, R. 1996. *The human side of school change: Reform, resistance, and the real-life problems of innovation.* San Francisco: Jossey-Bass.

Freire, P. 1970. *Pedagogy of the oppressed.* New York: Seabury Press.

———. 1985. *The politics of education.* Granby, Mass.: Bergin and Garvey.

Frost, R. 1969. *The poetry of Robert Frost.* New York, Holt, Rinehart and Winston.

Fullan, M. 1999. *Change forces: The sequel.* Philadelphia: Falmer Press.

———. 2001. *Leading in a culture of change.* San Francisco: Jossey-Bass.

Gee, J. 1990. *Social linguistics and literacies: Ideology in discourses.* New York: Falmer Press.

Giroux, H. 1988. Literacy and the pedagogy of voice and political empowerment. *Educational Theory* 38:61–75.

Giroux, H., and P. McLaren 1986. Teacher education and the politics of engagement: The case for democratic schooling. *Harvard Educational Review* 56:213–38.

Gleick, J. 1987. *Chaos: Making a new science.* New York: Viking.

goff, k. e. Forthcoming. *You into me into tomorrow.*

Goodlad, J. I. 1984. *A place called school: Prospects for the future.* New York: McGraw-Hill.

———. 1994. *Educational renewal: Better teachers, better schools.* San Francisco: Jossey-Bass.

Graman, T. 1988. Education for humanization: Applying Paulo Freire's pedagogy in learning a second language. *Harvard Educational Review* 58:433–48.

Harries-Jones, P. 1995. *A recursive vision: Ecological understanding and Gregory Bateson.* Toronto: University of Toronto Press.

Heath, S. B. 1983. *Ways with words.* New York: Cambridge University Press.

Heifetz, R. A. 1994. *Leadership without easy answers.* Cambridge: Belknap Press, Harvard University Press.

Hord, S. M., W. L. Rutherford, L. Huling-Austin, and G. E. Hall. 1987. *Taking charge of change.* Alexandria, Va.: Association for Supervision and Curriculum Development.

Johnson, S. 2001. *Emergence: The connected lives of ants, brains, cities, and software.* New York: Scribner.

Kauffman, D. L. 1980. *Systems one: An introduction to systems thinking.* Minneapolis: S. A. Carlton.

Kelly, K. 1994. *Out of control: The new biology of machines, social systems, and the economic world*. Reading, Mass.: Addison-Wesley.

Kingsolver, B. 1995. *High tide in Tucson: Essays from now or never*. New York: Harper Perennial.

———. 2001. A pure high note of anguish: Email message circulated on the Internet after the World Trade Center attack. Opinion, *Los Angeles Times,* Sept. 23, 2001.

———. 2002. *Small wonder*. New York: Harper Collins.

Ladson-Billings, G. 1994. *The dreamkeepers: Successful teachers of African-American children*. San Francisco: Jossey Bass.

Lederach, J. P. 2001. The challenge of terror: A traveling essay. Essay circulated on the Internet after the World Trade Center attack. Sept. 16. Available at <http://emu.edu/ctp/bse-articles.html>.

Lewis, M., and R. Simon. 1986. A discourse not intended for her: Learning and teaching within patriarchy. *Harvard Educational Review* 56:457–72.

Lovelock, J. 1979. *Gaia*. New York: Oxford University Press.

Lowry, M. 2000. Math lessons: A case study in the adoption of an innovative math curriculum. *National Association of Secondary School Principals (U.S.) Bulletin* 84 (615): 61–73.

Marx, K., and F. Engels. [1848] 1947. *The German ideology*. New York: International Publishers.

Maslow, A. H. 1970. *Motivation and personality*. New York: Harper and Row.

McDermott, R. P., and K. Gospodinoff. 1979. Social contexts for ethnic borders and school failure. In *Nonverbal behavior: Applications and cultural implications,* ed. A. Wolfgang. New York: Academic Press.

McIntosh, P. 1988. White privilege, male privilege: A personal account of coming to see correspondences through women's studies. Working paper 189, Wellesley College Center for Research on Women.

Michaels, S. 1981. Sharing time: Children's narrative styles and differential access to literacy. *Language in Society* 10:423–42.

Miramontes, O., A. Nadeau, and N. Commins. 1997. *Restructuring schools for linguistic diversity: Linking decision making to effective programs*. New York: Teachers College Press.

Moffett, J. 1985. Hidden impediments to improving English teaching. *Phi Delta Kappan,* September, 50–56.

Rich, A. 1979. *On lies, secrets, and silence: Selected prose*. New York: W. W. Norton.

Rogers, C. 1969. *Freedom to learn*. Columbus, Ohio: Merrill.

Rogers, E. M. 1995. *Diffusion of innovations*. New York: Free Press.

Scollon, R., and S. Scollon. 1981. *Narrative, literacy, and face in interethnic communication*. Norwood, N.J.: Ablex.

Senge, P. M. 1990. *The fifth discipline: The art and practice of the learning organization*. New York: Doubleday.

———. 1999. *The dance of change: The challenges to sustaining momentum in learning organizations*. New York: Doubleday.

Senge, P. M., N. Cambron-McCabe, T. Lucas, B. Smith, J. Dutton, and A. Kleiner. 2000. *Schools that learn.* New York: Doubleday.

Shannon, P. 1987. Commercial reading materials: Technological ideology and the deskilling of teachers. *Elementary School Journal* 87:307–25.

———. 1989. The struggle for control of literacy lessons. *Language Arts* 66:635–43.

———. 1990. Re-searching the familiar. *Language Arts* 67:379–87.

Silberstein, S. 1988. Ideology as process: Gender ideology in courtship narratives. In *Gender and discourse: The power of talk,* ed. S. Fisher and A. Dundas Todd. Norwood, N.J.: Ablex.

———. 2002. *War of words: Language, politics and 9/11.* New York: Routledge.

Silberstein, S., B. K. Dobson, and M. A. Clarke. 2002. *Reader's choice.* Ann Arbor: University of Michigan Press.

Stevick, E. W. 1980. *Teaching languages: A way and ways.* Rowley, Mass.: Newbury House Publishers.

———. 1996. *Memory, meaning, and method.* New York: Heinle and Heinle.

———. 1998. *Working with teaching methods: What's at stake.* New York: Heinle and Heinle.

Street, B. 1984. *Literacy in theory and practice.* New York: Cambridge University Press.

Waldrop, M. M. 1992. *Complexity: The emerging science at the edge of order and chaos.* New York: Simon and Schuster.

Wallerstein, N. 1983. *Language and culture in conflict.* Reading, Mass.: Addison-Wesley.

Watzlawick, P., J. H. Beavin, and D. D. Jackson. 1967. *Pragmatics of human communication: A study of interactional patterns, pathologies, and paradoxes.* New York: W. W. Norton.

Watzlawick, P., J. Weakland, and R. Fisch. 1974. *Change: Principles of problem formation and problem resolution.* New York, W. W. Norton.

Wheatley, M. 1999. *Leadership and the new science: Learning about organization from an orderly universe.* San Francisco: Berrett-Koehler.

Wiener, N. 1950. *The human use of human beings: Cybernetics and society.* New York: Doubleday Anchor.

Wilden, A. 1980. *System and structure: Essays in communication and exchange.* London: Tavistock.

———. 1987. *The rules are no game: The strategy of communication.* New York: Routledge and Kegan Paul.

Wolcott, H. F. 1994. *Transforming qualitative data: Description, analysis, and interpretation.* Thousand Oaks, Calif.: Sage Publications.

Woods, K. 1998. Park Hill, Denver. *Cityscape: A Journal of Policy Research and Development* 4 (2): 89–103.

Young, A. 1996. *An easy burden: The civil rights movement and the transformation of America.* New York: Harper Collins.

Acknowledgments

This book has been 30 years in the writing, and I owe virtually everyone I know for something—an idea, a conversation, a turn of phrase. It is difficult to adequately acknowledge such a debt, but important that I try. I apologize here for omissions and oversights; they are failings of memory, not of gratitude.

The most consistent contribution to my thinking over the years has been made by Patricia Barr Clarke, artist, community activist, and fellow traveler. Recently, Evan Benjamin Clarke Resendez arrived to teach me important lessons about life and learning. Which merely reminded me of the importance of family in any endeavor worth doing. I have enjoyed more than my share of love and loyalty in this regard. Helen B., Amy, Julia, and Ben—thanks for the time and attention.

The book would have remained a collection of essays and course packs if it hadn't been for Kelly Sippell, who pitched the project at the University of Michigan Press and who read and commented on every chapter as the final version took shape.

My long-time collaborator Alan Davis has provided thoughtful critiques of my attempts to apply systems thinking to teaching, learning, and change projects and has suffered through many an outrageous project with great patience and loyal goodwill. Lynn Rhodes and Elaine DeLott Baker modeled classroom teaching and community activism and provided me with important touchstones as I attempted to see what I thought I was doing. Since 1995 my ideas have been honed within the rambunctious camaraderie of Lola—the Lab of Learning and Activity. Every word in this book has been faithfully debated and doubted by Cathy Bodine, Ruth Brancard, Jim Eck, Jeanne Hind, Dan Jesse, Kathie Goff, Laura Marasco, Joanne McLain, Lee Ann Rawley, Starla Sieveke-Pearson, Maria Thomas Ruzic, and Phillip White.

Since 1973 I have depended on Sandra Silberstein and Barbara K. Dobson for intellectual and emotional support, editorial guidance, and careful reading. They are my models for collaborative writing.

The book is an attempt to translate systems theory into a usable lens for everyday living. I didn't know it at the time, but the seeds were planted when Pete Becker suggested that I read *Steps to an Ecology of Mind* in 1973, a book I have been reading ever since. More recently, Peter Harries-Jones and Mary Catherine Bateson have provided important insights into Gregory Bateson's thinking and thoughtful comments on early drafts of chapters.

A number of individuals gave me important feedback on particular essays as they were being written. Usually this was done under great time pressure and always with great good cheer. Thank you to Karin Chen, Julian Edge, Kathie Goff, Tim Murphy, Viola Moriarty, Karen Myers, Richard Powell, Jennifer Rudkin.

Wonderful teachers took me into their confidence and their classrooms and helped me understand children and dedication: Jackie Arriaga, Mary Fahey, Barbara Stuckert, Andrea Lewis, and Lupe Leece thought they were teaching children during those years I was lurking in their classrooms; little did they know that the oldest person in the room was the greatest beneficiary of their compassionate artistry.

I have been lucky to teach at the University of Colorado at Denver, where students demand both intellectual integrity and pragmatic application. I owe a great debt to the students I have taught over the years who struggled to understand what I was saying even as I was working it out for myself. Several intrepid individuals took on earlier versions of the book at the University of Colorado at Denver and faced skeptical graduate students as they worked to translate Clarke translating Bateson. I want to thank them for their confidence and constancy: Katherine E. Goff, Phillip White, Stan Kyed, Karen Myers, Elaine DeLott Baker, Maria Timmons, May Lowry.

Others exhibited the same confidence in smaller projects without knowing that they were for this book, but then, neither did I: Nancy L. Commins, Ana Maria Villegas, Tom Bellamy, H. Douglas Brown, Tom Scovel, Jean Handscombe, Earl Stevick, Bill Acton, Bill Juraschek, Marie Wirsing, David Sherwood, Julian Edge.

Gill Caldwell and Ginny Chase provided spiritual nurturing and an embodiment of what church might mean in our troubled society if enough people were able to align belief and action as they do. Similarly, I learned a lot about faith and action from Elinor and Tom Lewallen, John Sharp, and Sally Geis.

Last, but certainly not least, thanks to Christina Milton, Managing Editor, and Carol Sickman-Garner for the careful job of editing that saved me from many a misplaced comma and infelicitous phrase.

"Changing Things: The Rhythms of Reform and Resistance" first appeared as "Whole Language: Reform and Resistance" in *Language and Education* 7 (2) (1993): 79–95, coauthored with Nancy L. Commins.

"Empowerment: Issues, Constraints, and Cautionary Comments" first appeared as "Some Cautionary Observations on Liberation Education" in *Language Arts* 67 (4) (1990): 388–98.

Grateful acknowledgment is made to the following authors and publishers for permission to reprint previously published materials.

Curtis Brown Ltd., Faber & Faber, Inc., and The Random House Group for the excerpt from "September 1, 1939," by W. H. Auden. Copyright © 1940 by W. H. Auden. Reprinted by permission of Curtis Brown Ltd.

HarperCollins and Frances Goldin Literary Agency for excerpt from "Somebody's Baby," from *High Tide in Tucson: Essays from Now or Never* by Barbara Kingsolver. Copyright © 1995 by Barbara Kingsolver. Reprinted by permission of Harper-Collins Publishers, Inc., and Frances Goldin Literary Agency, Inc.

Henry Holt and Company, LLC, and The Random House Group Ltd. for excerpt from "Two Tramps in Mud Time" from *The Poetry of Robert Frost* edited by Edward Connery Lathem. Copyright 1936 by Robert Frost, © 1964 by Lesley Frost Ballantine, © 1969 by Henry Holt and Company and Jonathan Cape. Reprinted by permission of Henry Holt and Company, LLC, and The Random House Group Ltd.

Every effort has been made to trace the ownership of all copyrighted material in this book and to obtain permission for its use.

Index